Education, Affect, and Film

New Directions in Comparative and International Education

Series Editors: Stephen Carney, Irving Epstein and Daniel Friedrich

This series aims to extend the traditional discourse within the field of Comparative and International Education by providing a forum for creative experimentation and exploration of alternative perspectives. As such, the series welcomes scholarly work focusing on themes that have been under-researched and under-theorized in the field but whose importance is easily discernible.

It supports works in which theoretical grounding is centered in knowledge traditions that come from the Global South, encouraging those who work from intellectual horizons alternative to the dominant discourse. The series takes an innovative approach to challenging the dominant traditions and orientations of the field, encouraging interdisciplinarity, methodological experimentation, and engagement with relevant leading theorists.

Also available in the series

Affect Theory and Comparative Education Discourse: Essays on Fear and Loathing in Response to Global Educational Policy and Practice, Irving Epstein

Education in Radical Uncertainty: Transgression in Theory and Method, Stephen Carney and Ulla Ambrosius Madsen

Internationalization of Higher Education for Development: Blackness and Postcolonial Solidarity in Africa-Brazil Relations, Susanne Ress

Resonances of El Chavo del Ocho in Latin American Childhood, Schooling, and Societies, edited by Daniel Friedrich and Erica Colmenares

Understanding PISA's Attractiveness: Critical Analyses in Comparative Policy Studies, edited by Florian Waldow and Gita Steiner-Khamsi

Global-National Networks in Education Policy: Primary Education, Social Enterprises and 'Teach for Bangladesh', Rino Wiseman Adhikary, Bob Lingard and Ian Hardy

Education, Affect, and Film

*Visual Imaginings and Global Explorations
Through a Comparative Lens*

Irving Epstein

BLOOMSBURY ACADEMIC
LONDON • NEW YORK • OXFORD • NEW DELHI • SYDNEY

BLOOMSBURY ACADEMIC

Bloomsbury Publishing Plc, 50 Bedford Square, London, WC1B 3DP, UK
Bloomsbury Publishing Inc, 1359 Broadway, New York, NY 10018, USA
Bloomsbury Publishing Ireland, 29 Earlsfort Terrace, Dublin 2, D02 AY28, Ireland

BLOOMSBURY, BLOOMSBURY ACADEMIC and the Diana logo are trademarks of Bloomsbury Publishing Plc

First published in Great Britain 2024
This paperback edition published in 2026

Copyright © Irving Epstein, 2024

Irving Epstein has asserted his right under the Copyright, Designs and Patents Act, 1988, to be identified as Author of this work.

For legal purposes the Acknowledgments on p. x constitute an extension of this copyright page.

All rights reserved. No part of this publication may be: i) reproduced or transmitted in any form, electronic or mechanical, including photocopying, recording or by means of any information storage or retrieval system without prior permission in writing from the publishers; or ii) used or reproduced in any way for the training, development or operation of artificial intelligence (AI) technologies, including generative AI technologies. The rights holders expressly reserve this publication from the text and data mining exception as per Article 4(3) of the Digital Single Market Directive (EU) 2019/790.

Bloomsbury Publishing Plc does not have any control over, or responsibility for, any third-party websites referred to or in this book. All internet addresses given in this book were correct at the time of going to press. The author and publisher regret any inconvenience caused if addresses have changed or sites have ceased to exist, but can accept no responsibility for any such changes.

A catalogue record for this book is available from the British Library.

Library of Congress Cataloging-in-Publication Data

Names: Epstein, Irving, 1951- author.
Title: Education, affect, and film : visual imaginings and global explorations through a comparative lens / Irving Epstein.
Description: First edition. | New York : Bloomsbury Academic, [2024] | Series: New directions in comparative and international education | Includes bibliographical references and index. | Summary: "What can a study of international film contribute to our understanding of education in a globalized context? How can such an exploration further push the boundaries of comparative and international education (CIE) as an academic field? In addressing these questions, Irving Epstein brings together insights from film theory, affect theory and CIE to explore the ways in which educational meanings are mediated through globalization processes. Some of the many films discussed in detail in the book include Parasite, Small Axe, My Octopus Teacher, The Pearl Button, and A Separation. Epstein shows how films can speak broadly to issues involving social class privilege, racism, colonialism and indigeneity, and environmental justice regarding educational concerns"–Provided by publisher.
Identifiers: LCCN 2023051028 (print) | LCCN 2023051029 (ebook) | ISBN 9781350332508 (hardback) | ISBN 9781350332546 (paperback) | ISBN 9781350332522 (epub) | ISBN 9781350332515 (ebook)
Subjects: LCSH: Comparative education. | International education. | Affect (Psychology) in motion pictures. | Education and globalization.
Classification: LCC LB43 .E676 2024 (print) | LCC LB43 (ebook) | DDC 370.9–dc23/eng/20240122
LC record available at https://lccn.loc.gov/2023051028
LC ebook record available at https://lccn.loc.gov/2023051029

ISBN: HB: 978-1-3503-3250-8
PB: 978-1-3503-3254-6
ePDF: 978-1-3503-3251-5
eBook: 978-1-3503-3252-2

Series: New Directions in Comparative and International Education

Typeset by Deanta Global Publishing Services, Chennai, India

For product safety related questions contact productsafety@bloomsbury.com.

To find out more about our authors and books visit www.bloomsbury.com and sign up for our newsletters.

In honor of Ron Mottram (1940–2018), whose kindness, intellectual curiosity, and generosity of spirit lives on in the lives of all of his family members, colleagues, and friends who he so deeply touched.

Contents

Series Editors' Foreword	viii
Acknowledgments	x
Introduction	1

Part I Theoretical Musings

1	Engaging in Comparison: The Power of Affect	23
2	Film, Comparative and International Education, and Affect: Some Theoretical Considerations	41
3	Globalization, Commodification, and Affect	68

Part II Case Studies

4	Social Class: Oppression and Aspiration	97
	Parasite (Gisaenchung)	102
	A Separation (Jodaeiye Nader az Simin)	113
	Still Life (San Xia Hao Ren)	119
5	Racism and the Struggle to Assert Identity	130
	The Underground Railroad	138
	Small Axe	145
	Tsotsi	153
6	Indigeneity/Colonialism: Cultural Elimination and Resistance	160
	Rabbit Proof Fence	165
	We Were Children	168
	The Pearl Button (El botón de nácar)	171
7	Environmental Consciousness: Exploiting, Understanding, Respecting the Natural World	178
	Anthropocene: The Human Epoch	183
	My Octopus Teacher	186
	Heart of Sky, Heart of Earth	189
	Concluding Remarks	196
	References	205
	Index	224

Series Editors' Foreword

The field of comparative and international education requires its researchers, teachers, and students to examine educational issues, policies, and practices in ways that extend beyond the immediate contexts with which they are most accustomed. To do so means that one must constantly embrace engagement with the unfamiliar, a task that can be daunting because authority within academic disciplines and fields of study is often constructed according to convention at the expense of creativity and imagination. Comparative and international education as an academic field is rich and eclectic, with a long tradition of theoretical and methodological diversity as well as an openness to innovation and experimentation. However, as it is not immune to the conformist—especially disciplinary—pressures that give academic scholarship much of its legitimacy, we believe it is important to highlight the importance of research and writing that is creative, thought-provoking, and where necessary, transgressive. This series offers comparative and international educators and scholars the space to extend the boundaries of the field, encouraging them to investigate the ways in which underappreciated social thought and theorists may be applied to comparative work and educational concerns in new and exciting ways. It especially welcomes scholarly work that focuses upon themes that have been under-researched and under-theorized but whose importance is easily discernible. It further supports work whose theoretical grounding is centered in knowledge traditions that come from the Global South and welcomes those perspectives that are associated with post-foundational theorizing, non-Western epistemologies, and performative approaches to working with educational problems and challenges. In these ways, the series provides a space for alternative thinking about the role of comparative research in reimagining the social.

Irv Epstein's *Education, Affect, and Film: Visual Imaginings and Global Explorations Through a Comparative Lens* is the seventh book in the New Directions in Comparative and International Education series, and it truly embraces what the series is all about. To our knowledge, it is the first book to bring together film studies, affect theories, and some of the central concerns within the field of comparative and international education, in a work that transgresses disciplinary boundaries and innovates in its outlook and approach.

While affect theories have had a strong presence in the humanities within American academia for the past two decades and have started to influence some conversations in educational fields such as curriculum studies, very few comparative and international education scholars have engaged with these ideas. Epstein's use of films—ranging from the widely acclaimed *Parasite* and *Small Axe* to the lesser known *Rabbit Proof Fence*—as case studies for exploring how movies can move us to feel differently in relation to issues such as social class relations, racial oppression, and environmental consciousness acknowledges that more traditional, liberal deliberative approaches to contemporary crises have not produced the effects we have sought. It is not enough, then, to produce solid arguments about the ravaging effects of colonialism; we need to be moved in different directions, we need to experience different ways of being in our bodies and relating to one another, we need to let go of the myth of rational individualism, if we are to confront our current moment in solidarity. This book is an invitation to do just that by using the power of film to create new forms of inhabiting the commons beyond disciplinary and geographical boundaries. We hope readers embrace this invitation in their pedagogy and their scholarship, as Epstein helps us open up new possibilities for the field of comparative and international education.

Stephen Carney and Daniel Friedrich

Acknowledgments

Even in the best of times, writing can be a solitary and lonely process. I conceived of this project during the Covid-19 epidemic, acutely aware of the unique challenges such an effort would create under these particularly unique circumstances but still determined to press forward. Unfortunately, as much of my writing attests, cognitive awareness isolated from affect is an insufficient mechanism for coping in the real world. But fortunately, I was able to count on some extraordinary individuals who offered support for this endeavor, and their assistance aided in making the writing process enjoyable and satisfying while strengthening my coping mechanism. My New Directions in Comparative Education series coeditors, Steve Carney and Dani Friedrich, were terrific sources of support when I approached them with my initial ideas for starting this project, and they offered valuable insight after reading an initial draft of the work. My former colleagues at Illinois Wesleyan University, including Abigail Jahiel, Tom Lutze, Chuck Springwood, Carmela Ferradáns, and Carolyn Nadeau, listened patiently as I shared ideas with them and offered the kind of encouragement that is a by-product of true friendship. William Munro, whose alacrity is complemented by his encyclopedic knowledge of political and social theory, offered regular insights as I developed different chapter ideas. Margot Ehrlich, Wes Chapman, and Holly Mottram provided enthusiastic support and demonstrated authentic interest in the project on a consistent basis. Bill and Dannielle Manthey, and Lawry and Susan Finsen, lifelong friends, offered their own insights and provided needed emotional assistance as well. However, the book could never have been written without the help of Cecilia Raquel Delia Sanchez Novoa, whose love, patience, inquisitiveness, and infectious joy for the sharing of new ideas helped me translate a series of disparate thoughts into the words on these pages. Finally, I wish to thank Mark Richardson, Elissa Burns and their staff at Bloomsbury Academic, for their assistance in the publication process as well as reviewers who offered particularly salient insights. I feel truly blessed to have found such a high level of editorial support that has been so professionally competent and accommodating.

Introduction

Two Anecdotes

In 1976, I was teaching English and social studies at Kent Street Senior High School in Perth, Western Australia, finishing a year and a half contract. I was selected to be part of a program that recruited a number of US teachers to work in the country on a short-term basis and was nearing the end of my stay. On one noteworthy day, I found myself substitute teaching for a colleague who was absent from her typing class. Having little proficiency or expertise in business education or typing per se, and feeling the need to keep the class in order, I gave the class a spelling quiz. The day was rainy and cold, and the wooden classrooms within the high school lacked central heating. Instead, small space heaters were placed within each classroom. Having to move from one classroom to the next in a short period of time, I kept my raincoat on while giving the spelling test, uttering a spelling word, using it in a sentence, repeating the word, and then asking students to type the word on their typewriters. In the middle of the test, a student shouted out, "Sir!" I ignored the comment and proceeded with the next word. The student called out again "Sir!" At this point, I stated, "Keep quiet, this is a spelling test. There should be no talking." The student then emphatically stated with utmost sincerity, "Sir, you are on fire sir!" I was completely oblivious to the fact that my raincoat had become caught in the space heater, burning a hole in the back section, with smoke arising as a result. Channeling my best efforts to conduct a form of "stiff upper lip pedagogy," I took off the coat, made sure that all smoke had dissipated by stomping on its burnt portion, and proceeded to force my students to complete their spelling test.

I wish to offer a second anecdote by way of comparison and contrast. Six years after I had finished my Australian teaching venture, I was completing a PhD dissertation, examining the role of reform schools in addressing the needs of delinquent children in China, Taiwan, and Hong Kong. In doing so, I noticed different institutional styles reflective of the political and social differences within these three Chinese societies. Upon visiting sites in the three regions, interviewing officials and administrators, and collecting documentary evidence,

I chronicled and compared the various approaches in question. For example, in Hong Kong, I noted the use of "affectionate discipline" terminology when administrators talked about youth offenders. Their use of therapeutic terms to indicate concern for their youth's welfare was pervasive, even though harsh treatments were employed, including the placement of disruptive youth into lengthy solitary confinement situations where straightjackets were regularly used. In Guangzhou and in other parts of China, I noticed that the consequences of lengthy social exclusion practices toward offenders were much more severe and life-changing than specific institutional treatments that included varying degrees of coercion. These youth had little chance of resurrecting family and neighborhood supportive relationships upon their institutional release because the social stigma of having been labeled delinquent was so strong and the political ramifications of associating with these youth were so serious. And, in Taiwan, I saw how the reform school was thought of as a militarist institution. As a result, eight-year-old boys were forced into wearing leg irons in addition to experiencing additional degrading rituals (Epstein, 1986a, 1986b).

The two anecdotes are illustrative of my own challenges in negotiating teaching and scholarly responsibilities in cultural and social situations with which I was not familiar. However, it is my view that these anecdotes additionally highlight some of the generic considerations with which comparative and international educators, scholars, and practitioners must regularly engage. In both of these cases, I played the role of an outsider, forcibly inserting myself into sensitive social and cultural contexts, arrogantly assuming that my positioning would not compromise my ability to teach or research effectively. Such positioning was not pursued with malicious intent, although self-interest was definitely part of the motivation. With respect to the Australian situation, the allure of securing a paid teaching position in fields where there were few open positions in California in addition to the opportunity to travel to a different part of the world were major factors governing my decision-making. More pernicious than such self-interest, though, was my unexamined assumption that my US-centric teacher training generically qualified me to teach in Perth, without having had any real exposure to local procedures, expectations, or values. The obliviousness in evidence with regard to the raincoat incident was not anomalous. With regard to the dissertation research, a prime motivation in pursuing the juvenile delinquency theme was that of learning more about members of these Chinese societies who had not received, in my view, due attention in the Western literature. I naively assumed that subjects would be willing to share difficult experiences with an outsider they did not know and that this outsider could objectively comprehend the significance of the interpersonal relations that emanated from observed policies.

There also was an element of fear that colored my behavior in both of these instances. Upon entering the typing class, my fear was one of losing control of the classroom with chaos ensuing as a result. The motivation for creating a test was not one of determining students' learning progress since I was in no position to evaluate what appropriate expectations might be for such an assessment. No, my overriding obsession was one of asserting and maintaining instructor authority at all costs. Thinking back to my dissertation project, my overriding fear then was one of being unable to acquire meaningful data, a fear that was not unreasonable given the political sensitivity of the research topic. Such fear involved more than obtaining access to the research sites, a legitimate concern in and of itself. Perhaps more importantly, the fear was embedded in perceptions of what would constitute "meaningfulness," perceptions constructed from Global North perspectives that governed the terms with which the dissertation was formulated. In both cases, a fear of upending prevailing authority shaped my behavior.

Implicit in our understanding of authority is the notion of legitimacy, and I certainly believed that my participation in both of these events was not only legitimate but spoke to moral imperatives as well. In the first instance, I believed that my Australian students needed and deserved to be protected in a safe and controlled environment, ensuring that this occurred was what I viewed as a personal ethical as well as professional responsibility. In the second case, I viewed the treatment of children labeled as delinquent to have been harsh and at times horrific, and believed it to be imperative to report my findings to a broad audience. My embrace of these normative values, applied by rigidly ascribing them onto my students and research subjects, did not include a degree of introspection and self-criticism that the situations demanded. The external gaze that induced such categorization was made possible by the privileges I asserted as an outsider, a status that allowed me to dictate the terms of engagement with my students and research subjects. Those terms were heavily influenced by my ability to enter and leave environmental settings according to my own discretion, and to exert some control over the intensity and timing of the engagement that occurred.

There are codas to the two anecdotes that are worth noting. Upon finishing my teaching contract in Perth, I decided to travel around the world, purchasing a plane ticket from Perth to London with unlimited stopovers, along with Eurail and other train passes. I kept the damaged raincoat, and while traveling in Spain, got a haircut. After reaching the French border, I was stopped by gendarmes who suspected me of being a Basque terrorist, based upon my physical appearance and damaged raincoat. After I was intensively interrogated and strip-searched, I was finally allowed to proceed with my travel plans and entered France. In this case, I personally experienced, albeit in an extreme manner, the negative consequences of the same type of external gaze that I had employed during much of my stay in Australia. Upon returning to the United States, I began teaching in a public alternative school in Los Angeles, humanistic in orientation, where traditional teacher and student roles were less strict and more flexible. I was subsequently forced into dramatically reassessing the nature of classroom dynamics and the influence of power and authority upon their expression as a result.

With regard to my dissertation project, after I returned to the United States, and in the process of writing up my research, I discovered that the California Youth Authority regularly chained young female offenders to their beds in handcuffs for lengthy periods during their incarceration, sometimes for over twenty-four hours at a time. A recognition of the fact that children and youth in my own residential state were being severely abused forced me to reconsider the vehemence of my moral outrage directed toward the officials in Taiwan, Hong Kong, and China with whom I had interacted. A lifelong interest in questioning the nature and meaning of children's rights was one important result of this reflection, and the events depicted in both of these anecdotes contributed to my later development and growth as a teacher and a scholar. Nonetheless, I believe that the issues that arose in lieu of these encounters, as they involved the power of the outsider and the objectification of otherness, remain as salient today as they did over forty years ago.

The Significance of Affect Theory

The experiences represented by these anecdotes have been personally transformative, but the formal academic vocabulary that I have used to make sense of these experiences is quite limiting. Terms such as "authority," "objectification," and "otherness," while useful and important as intellectually derived framing devices, don't do justice to the fullness of the experiences themselves. For example, upon recalling the anecdotes, I remember the small size of the classroom where I gave the spelling test, the diminutive stature of the space heater that was supposed to heat the room, the wooden floors where it was situated, the veranda leading to a courtyard where students would pass from class to class, the smells of the damp classroom and of the burnt raincoat. I recall my students wearing their dark gray compulsory school uniforms in a public school setting, rigidly sitting in their seats, contrasted with the white t-shirt uniforms with badges indicating inmate numbers that eight-year-old children were forced to wear while walking in their leg irons at the Taiwan reformatory. And I remember hair: be it the shaved heads of those Taiwan children and youth or my own haircut in Madrid that later proved to be personally disastrous. The interactions that comprised these experiences are too numerous and complicated to fully identify, many of which I was probably unaware. With the passage of time, even those with which I was aware have faded through the years. Yet, to fully appreciate what those interactions involved, giving greater respect for their complexity, volume, and impact, I have come to realize that additional terms of reference and different conceptual frames need to be explored, and I have looked at the various components of affect theory in pursuit of that aim. Situated within the larger embodied knowledge discourse, theories of affect gained widespread recognition in the 1980s and 1990s but have become even more influential in the early twenty-first century, significantly contributing to post-humanism discourse. There are four concepts prominent within theories of affect that I identify as being particularly insightful: intensities of encounter, assemblage, meaning-making, and contingency, each of which is deserving of further elaboration.

Intensities of Encounter

The notion of intensity was central to Gilles Deleuze's philosophical thinking and is prominent in many of his writings, especially in *A Thousand Plateaus*, which he coauthored with Felix Guattari (1987). Their North American translator, Brian Massumi, in his own work, *The Power and End of Economy* (2015), expands upon the usage of the term and associates it with encounter, especially when applying it to the political realm. As suggested in *A Thousand Plateaus*, such encounters tend to be rhizomatic with the authors offering a critique of the overreliance upon vertical and hierarchical categorization that has dominated conventional Enlightenment thinking. Intensities themselves can be conceived of as being both immanent to and a part of experience. As Massumi notes,

> Although the realm of intensity that Deleuze's philosophy strives to conceptualize is transcendent in the sense that it is not directly accessible to experience, it is not transcendent and is not exactly outside of experience either. It is immanent to it—always in but not of it. Intensity and experience accompany one another,

like two mutually presupposing dimensions, or like two sides of a coin. Intensity is immanent to matter and to events, to mind and to body, and to every level of bifurcation composing them and which they compose. Thus, it also cannot but be experienced, in effect—in the proliferations of levels of organization it ceaselessly gives rise to, generates and regenerates, at every suspended moment. The Kantian imperative to understand the conditions of possible experience as if from outside and above transposes into an invitation to recapitulate, to repeat and complexify, ground level, the real conditions of emergence, the never-yet felt, the felt for less than half a second, again for the first time—the new. (Massumi, 1995, 94)

The Deleuzean notions of intensities and rhizomatic connection have been influential within post-humanist thought on a number of levels. On the one hand, they offer refutation not only of the traditional Western view of the autonomous subject, whose humanity is derived from one's consciousness, but also of the structuralist and even post-structuralist assumptions that assert the existence of universally applicable rules and patterns that govern the relationship between subject and object. In drawing attention to the writings of Benedict Spinoza and Henri Bergson with reference to his focus upon intensities, Deleuze promoted a contemporary reconsideration of their work (Smith, Protevi, and Voss, 2022). Massumi (1995) has also relied upon selective research in neuroscience to argue that intensities can surface when one is preconscious as well as conscious and that they may occur virtually, pre-experientially, while also accompanying recognizable experiences. Scientific studies of the physics of emergence, which analyze the ways in which structures in complex systems become functional, are potentially applicable here as well (Protevi, 2006).

There are a number of implications for the emphasis Deleuze and Massumi give to the notion of intensity. First and foremost, neither scholar views affect as being synonymous with emotion. Emotions contain intensities and can shape them, but as their presence can be identified at a preconscious level, their existence is not dependent upon them. For these scholars, it is thus overly simplistic to equate affect and emotion. As Massumi reiterates,

Affects are virtual *synesthetic perspectives* anchored in (functionally limited by) the actually existing, particular things that embody them. The *autonomy* of affect is its participation in the virtual. *Its autonomy is its openness*. Affect is autonomy to the extent to which it escapes confinement in the particular body whose vitality, or potential for interaction, it is. Formed, qualified, situated perceptions and cognitions fulfilling actual connections or blockage are the *capture* and *closure* of affect. Emotion is the intensest (most contracted) expression of that capture—

and of the fact that something has always and again escaped. Something remains unactualized, inseparable from but unassimilable to any *particular*, functionally anchoring perspective. That is why all emotion is more or less disorienting, and why it is classically described as being outside of oneself, at the very point at which one is most intimately and unshareably in contact with oneself and one's vitality. If there were no escape, no excess or remainder, no fade-out to infinity, the universe would be without potential, pure entropy, death. Actually existing, structured things live in and through that which escapes them. There autonomy is the autonomy of affect. (Massumi, 1995, 96–7)

However, not all scholars agree with such a depiction of intensities and their relationship to emotion. Some affect theory scholars (Sedgwick and Frank, 2003) looking for validation of the contention that affective intensities exist in an a priori form that generate generic emotional states rely upon the research of Sylvan Tompkins and Paul Ekman in support of their assertion (Epstein, 2019, 26–7). Yet, that research has been critiqued by other neuroscientists who argue that the identification of physiological response is inexact and that emotional expression is always context-specific (Barrett, 2018; Epstein, 2019, 28). In my view, it is important to acknowledge the power of affective intensities without reducing our understanding of affect (and/or emotion) as simply a universal physiological response. As Sara Ahmed notes, an overemphasis upon such responses

> risks transforming emotion into a property as something that one has, and can then pass on, as if what passes on is the same thing. . . . Emotions in their intensity involve miscommunication, such that even when we feel we have the same feeling, we don't necessarily have the same relationship to the feeling. Given that shared feelings are not about feeling the same feeling, or feeling-in common, I suggest that it is the objects of emotion that circulate, rather than emotion as such. (Ahmed, 2015, 10–11, as cited in Epstein, 2019, 29)

I thus view the intensities of encounter to which I refer as comprising both the processes of potentiality and emergence that are described by Deleuze and Massumi and the emotions, themselves, contextually formulated, that accompany or result from those processes. Both, in my view, are important to the larger theoretical discussion of affect.

Meaning-Making

A second issue that relates to the ways in which intensity is contained involves its relation to consciousness and intentionality. An overemphasis upon the automaticity through which intensities emerge raises implicit skepticism about the limits to which consciousness and intentionality operate and are functional. This is a basic concern of affect theorist Margaret Wetherell (2012), who emphasizes the importance of meaning-making, which she views as being key to experiencing affect. In her view, affect, in its totality, is not restricted to the preconscious experience of and reaction to sensory stimuli, nor does it only involve the experience of feeling. It does include the uses of all of our faculties as we attempt to make sense of the world. From Wetherell's perspective, overemphasizing the presence of intensities while ignoring the desire to formulate meanings derived from those intensities leads to a fundamental problem, where thought becomes siloed and separate from other forms of experience. As a theorist who has argued vociferously against the proposition that discourse is distinct from praxis, the importance of conceiving of meaning-making as complicit in the experiencing of affect is clear. To assert otherwise, or to hold discourse as being separate from other forms of human activity, is a fundamental error that reinforces the very mind/body dualism that an embodied perspective firmly rejects. I thus view meaning-making as one of the important elements of affect in support of Wetherell's thinking.

Intensities vary with regard to their duration and power of presence. They can build upon or become fragmented from other intensities, but their presence argues in favor of a more expansive understanding of the nature of relationships with other humans and with the nonhuman world around us. Conceiving of experience as a set of fragmentary encounters, at times connected and at times disconnected with one another, encourages us to reject the use of grand meta-narratives to contextualize life events, interactions, and occurrences. It compels us instead to appreciate those that are ordinary and underappreciated. I have found Kathleen Stewart's *Ordinary Affects* (2007) and Lauren Berland and Kathleen Stewart's *The Hundreds* (2019) to be two of the more significant works that are powerfully illustrative of this perspective. What they, and other affect theorists, emphasize is not only the fact that encounter can involve fragmentation as well as interconnection, but that such linkages are always fluid and dynamic, and it is in this vein that the theories of assemblage are also important to the larger discussion of affect.

Assemblage

In *A Thousand Plateaus*, Deleuze and Guattari made reference to the French term "agencement," which has been somewhat inaccurately translated into English as assemblage. A more accurate definition of its meaning would be arrangement, construction, or layout, with the English term "assemblage" conventionally being defined as the joining or union of two things, or a bringing or coming together (Nail, 2017, 21). The difference is significant insofar as for Deleuze and Guattari, assemblage meant an embrace of multiplicity and a rejection of essences. Assemblages, according to Nail's analysis, share a structure that includes a specific condition, various elements, and agents. They are arranged according to different political types and are constantly changing, undergoing processes of "deterritorialization" (Nail, 2017, 36–7). Assemblage is attractive as a conceptual framework insofar as its rejection of essentialism allows for a view of social organizations and their interconnections that emphasizes fragility and fluidity. In building upon Deleuzian perspectives, Manuel DeLanda (2016) argues that because each assemblage is unique, they always contain parts that retain their autonomy, can detach themselves from existing networks, and reattach themselves to new ones. As Andrew Ball summarizes,

> DeLanda's assemblages consist of parts that remain autonomous and independent of their network. Each part is capable of detaching to form new relations and therefore assemblages are characterized by "relations of exteriority. . ." However, while the parts of an assemblage remain independent and are not defined by the whole, the nature of the whole assemblage is a function of the interrelations of its parts. . . . That is, while the parts maintain an autonomous identity independent of their relations, the nature of the whole assemblage is contingent on the emergent properties that arise through the relation of its parts. (Ball, 2018, 241–2)

Bruno Latour, on the other hand, through his vision of Actor Network Theory, conceives of the social as a series of assemblages that are even more relational and fluid than that to which DeLanda would admit. In Latour's writings, assemblage is used as a tool to describe the ways in which ideas become associated and disassociated with one another, sometimes through intentionality, often through happenstance. The key to understanding interconnection, in his view, is to continually track relational elements by breaking down their linkages in an iterative fashion, which will inevitably result in the discovery of new heretofore unexplored connections. As he states,

> the question of the social emerges when the ties to which one is entangled begin to unravel; the social is further detected through the surprising movements from one association to the next; those movements can either be suspended or resumed; when they are prematurely suspended, the social as normally

construed is bound together with already accepted participants called "social actors" who are members of a "society"; when the movement toward collection is resumed, it traces the social as associations through many non-social entities which might become participants later; if pursued systematically, this tracking may end up in a shared definition of a common world, what I have called a collective; but if there are no procedures to render it common, it may fail to be assembled; and lastly, sociology is best defined as a discipline whose participants explicitly engage in the reassembling of the collective. (Latour, 2007, 247)

DeLanda's notion of exteriority has been embraced by those looking at new ways of understanding policy (Savage, 2019); Latour's insights have been extremely influential to scholars examining the interrelationship between science, technology, and politics, as well as social relations more generically. In spite of their notable differences, Deleuze and Guattari, DeLanda, and Latour all view assemblage and dis-assemblage as not only affirming fluidity and contingency but as transgressive, insofar as their presence casts doubt upon the common binaries we have come to rely upon to define and interpret social phenomena, be they individual versus community, autonomy versus circumscription, fact versus belief, or structure versus agency. For these authors, the notion of interconnection is framed within the context of instability, as they illustrate the promise of fostering creative change under conditions of impermanence.

Contingency

Contingency is thus embedded not only within the concept of assemblage but within all aspects of affect. Rather than bemoan its existence, affect theorists applaud its presence, insofar as the uncertainty we live with forces us to continually imagine new possibilities while illustrating the limitations of practices based upon uncritically examined assumptions. Although affect theoreticians embrace perspectives with different degrees of similarity, contingency is a quality whose importance they regularly affirm. This being said, there are contradictory approaches that are articulated under the theoretical umbrella of affect, as one might expect for an interdisciplinary field whose proponents draw from different domains within the humanities, sciences, and social sciences. In this project, I make no attempt to reconcile such contradictions. Instead, I draw upon intensity of encounter, meaning-making, assemblage, and contingency as tenets that holistically communicate what I believe to be the major strengths of the outlook. Those strengths include a refutation of essentialism, a rejection of rigid classification and categorization, a dismissal of stasis, and an embrace of flux and fluidity with regard to understandings of time and space. It is therefore unsurprising that those drawn to affect theory have also participated in post-humanist discourse. Affect theory scholars were at the forefront of critiquing modernist assumptions that conflated consciousness with identity and viewed individual autonomy as a defining characteristic of being human. They set a predicate for reimagining what it means to be human through deconstructing the culture versus nature divide, demanding a reconsideration of what it means to be sentient, animate, inanimate, organic, mechanical, natural, or artificial. And, they have contributed to calls for embracing a new politics of materialism (Bennett, 2009) and planetary consciousness (Chakrabarty, 2021) that speak to the realities of survival amid the climate crisis. Nonetheless, there are critiques of such scholarship that need to be recognized.

Criticisms and a Rejoinder

As is true of much of later twentieth-century French thought, affect theory was borne out of a response to the events of May 1968. Mass student demonstrations culminated in general strikes that eventually captured worker support, and the country, in a state of national paralysis, came to a standstill. However, the student/worker alliance proved temporary as the deGaulle government was able to reassert control over the political system, dismissing the National Assembly and calling for new elections after offering wage concessions to trade union workers. Stability being eventually restored, a calcified, conservative government was able to maintain its power. Nonetheless, the events symbolized an important revolutionary moment, even though the full political aspirations of the student demonstrators were never realized. In 1969, Deleuze obtained his first permanent teaching position at the University of Paris VIII in Vincennes, an experimental institution that was founded in the aftermath of the May protests. It was here that he met activist and psychoanalyst Felix Guattari, commencing their long professional collaboration (Smith, Protevi, and Voss, 2022).

The failure to produce lasting political change spurred a widespread reconsideration of conventionally held assumptions regarding culture, society, and politics, influencing Foucault's analyses of the relationship between knowledge and power, Bourdieu's embrace of post-structuralism, as well as the Deleuzian embrace of affect. For Foucault, an archaeology of knowledge approach unmasked historical patterns involving the exercise of state power affecting even the most intimate aspects of daily life. For Bourdieu, a deconstruction of the supposed binary between the personal and the social resulted in an elaborate explanation of how cultural and social capital was acquired and distributed. And for Deleuze and Guattari, a focus upon the rhizomatic nature of affective interconnection promised an alternative to an acceptance of the determinism implicit in global capitalist practices. In all of these cases, the writers were critically reacting to a European tradition that embraced modernism and Western Enlightenment thinking. But at the same time, they asserted an authority that emanated from the asserted generalizability of their conclusions. With regard to affect theory specifically, critics note the specificity of its Western origins in contradistinction to its universalist claims. Furthermore, they point to an underlying belief in the universality of pluralism as being injurious to those who express their identity on the basis of group affiliation as well as sense of place, not to mention historical conditions of oppression that are specific to the group in question (Karkov, 2016). In *A Thousand Plateaus*, Deleuze and Guattari have additionally been criticized for their stereotypical depictions of women, and of animals, in their mapping of deterritorialization processes (Karkov, 2016; Haraway, 2008).

Criticisms of Latour's Actor Network Theory center around its failure to fully commit to antiessentialist and anti-dualist perspectives regarding the human and nonhuman, its willingness to embrace causality without accounting for resistance to and the failure of interconnection, its employment of a descriptive analysis that can be distant from actors' own perceptions of their lived realities, and its occasional failure to account for when action becomes purposeful and meaningful rather than mundane (Whittle and Spicer, 2008).

Nonetheless, although these critiques should not be minimized, I nonetheless believe that the central tenets of affect theory are compelling and are deserving of further exploration and investigation. It should be noted that among the critics that have been mentioned, there is little appetite for a categorical dismissal of affect theory and/or its particular tenets, and as has been noted, its presence within scientific, social science, and humanities discourses remains robust. Whether notions of assemblage be applied to contemporary social movements (Butler, 2018; Epstein, 2015, 2019), or to comparative and international education as an academic field, (Salajan and jules, 2023), they remain useful tools of analysis for CIE scholars. A recognition and embrace of the power of contingency is also evident in more recent CIE scholarship (Carney and Madsen, 2021; Vavrus, 2021) with affect theory principles more generally having been applied to CIE (Epstein, 2019; Zembylas, 2015), youth studies (Lesko and Talburt, 2012), pedagogy (Albrecht-Crane and Slack, 2003), and teacher education (Colmenares, 2018). I believe that the reason for the popularity of affect theory concepts is due to their embrace of critical reflexivity. Because an intellectual engagement with these ideas allows for a continual reevaluation and reassessment of their applicability in general as well as specific contexts, they include a degree of elasticity that allows such engagement to remain relevant.

The Argument

When theoreticians began writing about affect, they made the case that affect is not limited to certain settings but is discoverable throughout all of our various interactions. One of the reasons that I found their work so personally compelling is that I always viewed educational experiences to be reflective of and broadly connected to encounters of all types. Viewing those experiences through the lens of affect allowed for a deeper and more expansive frame through which more robust comparisons could be formulated. Comparing the application of affect theory concepts to both the comparative and international education literature and to film theory and criticism is one way of pursuing this goal. To be clear, affect theorists have made significant contributions to film theory and criticism for many decades. Indeed, Gilles Deleuze, in his two-volume study of cinema, *Cinema 1* (1986) and *Cinema 2* (1986), has been extremely influential in furthering the discourse in this field. However, one of the purposes here is to use affect theory principles to examine the similarities and differences between the two fields, an effort that has not been previously pursued. A second goal of this project is to determine how images of educational experiences are circulated through films on a global basis, analyze how they are positioned within broader cinematic portrayals of social experience, and examine why they are similar or different from the ways in which they are depicted within the CIE literature. The assumption that we make here is that film should be scrutinized as text, in the same way that we examine scholarship generally and CIE scholarship in particular. Comparisons are insightful not only for purposes of thematic and content analysis but for our broader understanding of how these texts in different fields are constructed and circulated. I attempt to address these goals from both theoretical and empirical perspectives within the book. In Part I, I focus upon theoretical issues and in Part II, I examine the content of twelve films grouped according to four themes. I should note that I use the term "film" loosely in two instances to include moving images that have been depicted as part of television programs.

In Chapter 1, there is a discussion regarding the basic commonalities of educational meanings that are worthy of comparison when depicted in international films and in traditional CIE texts. Both CIE scholars and practitioners, and international filmmakers, engage with audiences that are more diverse and broader than those with whom their peers would normally associate. The acts of comparison that both filmmakers and comparative and international education scholars employ offer the promise that the artistic and scholarly meanings that are conveyed have relevance for such audiences. In addition, there is a notion of generalizability implicit in the comparative act that both domains share. Although subject to legitimate critique, especially with regard to the terms with which one pursues global engagement, the urge to extend oneself beyond the familiar is visible in each arena.

A second area of comparison involves the relationships with audiences that are crafted by comparative and international education scholars, policymakers, and practitioners, and international filmmakers. Audiences engage in meaning-making as they tap into their personal experiences when responding to film. Educational actors also actively shape and interpret educational experiences on a regular basis. The roles of film spectator/viewer and educational participant are never entirely passive, even if there are significant social limitations placed upon their agency. Finally, it is my contention that the social interactions that result from cinematic and educational experiences can create responses that are authentic as they holistically tap into our multiple ways of striving to make sense of human experience through the invocation of intellect, emotion, and spirituality. Cinematic and educational encounters reiterate the ways in which knowledge is embodied, and they call upon us to use all of our faculties to enhance our understandings of our social world. I make the case that by applying the tenets of affect theory to the study of international film and CIE, one can bring in the commonalities shared by these disparate knowledge areas into sharper focus.

In Chapter 2, a more specific focus upon the CIE and film theory literatures is presented, including an examination of comparable trends within each knowledge domain. There are particular epistemological considerations that help explain how the two knowledge areas have evolved, and there are external influences that have shaped the contours of each field. Affect theory clarifies how they have contributed to the insights and inconsistencies within each field. Specifically, the comparative and international education field has historically embraced competing paradigms that have been promoted more broadly within Western social science research. Some have been based upon public policy analysis, and planning and evaluation within international development contexts, where the products of one's subjects' efforts or specific treatments imposed upon the subjects rather than the subjects themselves tend to be scrutinized. Others offer more humanistic orientations focusing upon ethnographic techniques, discourse analysis, personal recollection, and the chronicling of direct forms of interpersonal interaction, where the subjects' voices are more prominently expressed. Within the history of film theory and study, theorists have commented upon the role of filmmakers in creating images that present their own vision of reality as well as the ways in which film spectators actively use their own experiences to interpret and shape the meaning of those messages. Affect theory, with its emphasis upon intensity of encounter as well as contingency, is one venue for addressing criticisms of the pseudo-scientific orientations within CIE. As film theorists turn to an appreciation of the role of movement, time, and the ways in which visual imagery contributes to audience understandings, affect theory has played an increasingly important role in analyzing the nature and evolution of cinematic experience as well.

In Chapter 3, I examine the ways in which CIE scholarship and film are constructed and delivered within globalized settings. Both CIE scholarship and international film are cultural commodities that circulate within neoliberal spaces. There are specific ways in which the creation of both cultural forms reflects neoliberal sensibilities with regard to the relationship with the state, the publisher or media company, and the filmmaker or scholar. One can see comparable patterns by analyzing the nature of scholarly publication and the use of the film festival to enhance cinematic visibility. Norms that are imposed upon these entities shape the quality of the cultural product and influence the nature of the audience that will have access to it. But even within such strictures, there are possibilities for reinterpretation, reinvention, and reimagination, and affect theory can assist in conceiving of such possibilities.

In Part II, I apply the theoretical questions that have been posed to a study of twelve cinematic pieces, grouped according to four categories: social class, race, colonialism and indigeneity, and environmental awareness and climate justice. The films selected for analysis have each received broad acclaim and have been widely circulated on a global basis, having been produced by film industries in the United States, Canada, the United Kingdom, Germany, Iran, Chile, South Korea, South Africa, Australia, and China. Both feature-length films and documentaries have been selected for analysis; many were first shown at prestigious film festivals; most of the selections are now available through online streaming services. In short, their popularity is indicative of what a global audience, primarily situated in the Global North, has accepted as being artistically satisfying within its prescribed boundaries of ideological acceptability.

One could of course identify alternative films to those selected that speak to similar issues with differing perspectives. Many filmmakers examine educationally related issues through focusing exclusively upon institutional practices; only some of the films selected for this volume do so. I view this as a strength, as I contend that a fixation upon education solely according to institutional context can be quite limiting. For me, educational presence can be pervasive even in situations where it is less overtly visible and can only be inferred. Recognizing the range of situations where its presence runs the gamut from being visible to evanescent expands our appreciation for its significance.

Issues involving education and racism and colonialism in particular are complex and multifaceted as they often intersect with important aspects of gender, ableism, and classism. In selecting specific films tied to the discrete themes of social class, racism, colonialism, and environmental awareness and climate justice, one might argue that an appreciation for intersectionality is missing in the presentation of these issues and in the films that have been selected to illustrate their importance. As a rejoinder, I would argue that in spite of their thematic framing, there are elements of intersectionality apparent in these films, even when such elements are not as explicitly emphasized as one might prefer. I would also suggest that as issues involving the nature of racism, colonialism, social justice, and identity are subject to sharp debate, it really is useful to reference film as part of the ongoing conversation as how to inform our analyses of their meanings, acknowledging that there are artistic and conceptual limitations within particular cinematic efforts.

In Chapter 4, I discuss issues of social class by examining *Parasite* (South Korea), *A Separation* (Iran), and *Still Life* (China). In all three films, family relationships play an important role in influencing social class aspiration. Educational concerns are present in the films to varying degrees, at times exacerbating but not mitigating social class oppression. Education is repeatedly used as a social class marker; its effectiveness in bridging social class division is often muted though.

In Chapter 5, race is examined through a miniseries, *The Underground Railroad* (United States), a compendium of five films, *Small Axe* (United Kingdom), and in the full-length feature film *Tsotsi* (South Africa). The three works display differing views of race and identity, veering from the virulence of racism as a mechanism for legitimizing continued oppression and extermination, to a vehicle for subjugating an immigrant group to inferior social status, to a force where its victims commit acts of violence and criminality. Educational institutions are depicted as being complicit in perpetuating racism, at times contributing to deadly outcomes, but in other circumstances, they are viewed as life-affirming, encouraging expressions of resistance and collective self-efficacy.

Chapter 6 examines issues of colonialism and indigeneity as depicted in *Rabbit Proof Fence* (Australia), *We Were Children* (Canada), and *The Pearl Button* (Chile). To varying degrees, the films illustrate how education was used to facilitate physical and cultural genocide. At the same time, the films also illustrate how the consequences of colonial oppression continue to reverberate in contemporary times. *We Were Children* and *The Pearl Button*, in particular, demonstrate in documentary form how the "othering" of Indigenous Peoples has contributed to widespread destructive acts of violence. The three films together illustrate how closely education is linked to identity, history, and memory, and how, whether in formal institutional settings or in informal ways, it has been implicated in ways that perpetuate violence and tragedy. Although these films are crafted within different genres, they touch upon all of the senses to evoke strong audience reactions.

Chapter 7 focuses upon issues of environmental consciousness and climate justice. In *Anthropocene: The Human Epoch*, environmental destruction is chronicled through stunning visual imagery over four continents. The third film of a trilogy, scientists and filmmakers work together here to record the results of human activities that are simultaneously occurring throughout the world. In this documentary, it is not simply the privileging of human interest over that of other species that is repeatedly chronicled but the callousness with which the natural beauty of the earth is being destroyed, which creates a deeply affective set of responses. The negative impact of mining extraction upon the earth's natural beauty is graphically displayed, as is the slaughter of elephants for the ivory trade, along with numerous other examples of environmental exploitation offered.

My Octopus Teacher chronicles the encounters of Craig Foster, an underwater diver who over time bonds with an octopus in a relationship that evolves into a deeply meaningful set of encounters. The film raises interesting issues regarding the nature of learning and mentorship while exploring the boundaries and possibilities of human/species engagement and interaction. Together, the three films present different ways in which human beings view themselves within the natural world, leading to behaviors that include domination, destruction, engagement, and respect. They implicitly raise issues germane to comparative educators, including questions involving the mainstreamed values that are transmitted within formal and informal school curricula, and the assumptions that are made with regard to humans' responsibilities to other living things and the natural world.

Heart of Sky, Heart of Earth chronicles the lives of a number of Maya, living in Guatemala and the Chiapas region of Mexico, who fight to preserve their own cultural beliefs while protesting against gold mine exploration, genetically modified corn hybrids that encroach upon their own native corn farming, and more generally, the consequences of NAFTA (the North American Free Trade Agreement). There is also an embrace of Indigenous belief and custom as a necessary shield against contemporary political violence, with one member drawing a connection between the historical collapse of the Mayan population and the impending ecological catastrophe, brought on by climate change.

Conclusion

I was initially attracted to the study of comparative and international education because embedded within its literature was a kind of soft cosmopolitanism that spoke affirmatively to my own experiences of being an outsider, having been placed in different educational and social settings that demanded interpersonal and intellectual engagement. Through the lens of affect theory, I have decided to examine resonances between comparative and international education inquiry and film study and theory. Those similarities speak to the dynamics of globalization, where both ideas and cultural artifacts are circulated within neoliberal structures, but nonetheless are subject to recreation and reimagination, due to the vibrant cultural and social contexts to which they are exposed. I have pursued this project assuming that although that the terms of global engagement are restricted, often reinforcing Global North hegemony, the results of these interactions can be surprising, creating new possibilities for enhanced understanding within prescribed limitations.

Yet, when we examine the twelve films that have received international recognition, their views of education are inconsistent. Although some filmmakers view traditional educational models as being empowering, others see them as restrictive or oppressive. Still others don't see education as being central in any form to the resolution of the crucial social, political, and interpersonal issues that mark contemporary experiences. And, still other filmmakers rely upon alternatives to educational modernism, highlighting the power of wisdom gained from Indigenous knowledge and spiritual tradition to negotiate these questions. In doing so, they compel us to redefine the meaning of education in the broadest of terms while reassessing its importance.

Why is this the case? The four tenets of affect theory that I identify—intensity of encounter, assemblage, meaning-making, and contingency—speak to the challenges of engaging in both film studies and comparative and international education inquiry. The concept of intensity of encounter obliges us to question the contexts in which we identify with cinematic characters, plotlines, and events, underscoring the fact that our associations can be as powerfully meaningful as they are ephemeral and are often dependent upon what the spectator brings to the viewing experience, apart from the intentions of the filmmaker. Intensity of encounter, when applied to educational concerns, forces us to admit that interpersonal interactions that involve teaching, learning, mentoring, planning, evaluating, in short, all of the polymorphous activities we associate with education can be both powerful and fleeting in their impact and consequence. But they cannot be separated from other interpersonal encounters that shape our identities. The notion of assemblage reinforces the interconnected nature of ideas and cultural products, as well as the natural tendency of human beings to come together for the shared purpose of seeking social change. But assemblage also implies dis-assemblage, and the fragile nature of interconnection is implicitly affirmed in its definition. The processes of assemblage and dis-assemblage are evident in the ways in which films can reorder our conventional senses of time and place; their presence further explains the different filmmaker insights that privilege or ignore contemporary educational experiences when seeking to investigate crucial notions of identity, belonging, respect for the natural world, and social conflict.

Filmmakers and comparative and international education scholars and practitioners regularly engage in meaning-making in pursuit of their respective crafts. Whether it be expressed in a fascination with the supernatural, a focus upon the underrepresented and disrespected, or a depiction of difficult situations and conditions, their efforts go beyond the act of recording or reporting but speak to deeper desires to foster interconnection. And, overriding all aspects of affect is the notion of contingency. The challenges of living in the twenty-first century demand that we approach prescribed solutions to our pressing social problems with skepticism and that we embrace the uncertainty and flux that characterize our daily lives with some degree of accommodation. At the same time, when we do see educational success stories, we acknowledge their presence, placing them in appropriate perspective. The films reviewed here argue for achieving such a balance through embracing contingency. Film study is but one way in which we can broaden our appreciation for the importance of engaging in interconnection, and in so doing, discover new ways in which educational themes present themselves as part of our larger shared experiences.

Part I
Theoretical Musings

1

Engaging in Comparison

The Power of Affect

It is my contention that comparison invites both inclusivity and exclusion, symbolic violence as well as idealistic possibility. The study and practice of both comparative education and (international) filmmaking, in their utilization of comparison, reflect these tendencies, even though they produce different kinds of texts that adhere to distinct protocols. Through employing theoretical constructs related to affect, some of these contradictions are made more visible; others can be resolved. In either case, the possibility of emboldening comparative work with a new degree of dynamism is always present. The four aspects of affect that have been identified in the introductory chapter—intensity of encounter, assemblage, meaning-making, and contingency are particularly salient to this task. Because intensity of encounter, as conceived of by Deleuze and Guattari and Massumi, frames the nature of interconnection as occurring horizontally or rhizomatically, it eschews the tendency to objectify and classify otherness. For a field such as education, where the interactions among and between students, parents, teachers, administrators, and community members, be they positive or negative, can be as powerful as they are intimate, the notion of intensity of encounter makes intuitive sense. When examining modern film in its various inundations, its corporeal appeal derives from its ability to tap into so many of our sensual experiences. Intensity of encounter, as a conceptual tool, appears to be especially relevant to this context as well. Part of its appeal is its dynamism, as encounters vary in their intensities and, as has been noted, sometimes their presence is felt before conscious awareness ensues. The scope of such encounters can even extend beyond human-to-human interaction, including our encounters with nonhuman entities. For those who study educational concerns, this also makes sense, as the material objects that structure those experiences—the classroom walls and furniture, the textbooks and learning materials, the sights, smells, tastes, and touches we associate with formal learning—all contribute to the ways in which education becomes an embodied part of our identities. When observing film, the gaze we project onto the images we see becomes enticing because those images authentically reflect our interactions, drawing our attention to the importance of movement as well as many of the senses that help shape our daily experiences. As was noted in the introductory chapter, because of the variability of their intensities, encounters need not be linear and are often fragmentary, their fragmented nature reflective of the unpredictability of interconnection.

Dynamism and unpredictability are characteristics one also associates with the concept of assemblage, which can be thought of as both an intellectual exercise and a form of practice. As an intellectual exercise, the assembling of ideas requires one to recognize that the impermanence that characterizes intensity of encounter is true of the ways in which we construct and deconstruct concepts. When applied to practice, with specific reference to the ways in which we organize and come together for a common purpose, assemblage reminds us that in the twenty-first century, such gatherings tend to be fluid and evanescent, even when they are incredibly important and significant. In both realms, the classification tendencies that evolve from engaging in comparison are challenged and resisted. Within the educational realm, the concept of assemblage challenges us to reconsider the boundaries we apply to educational pursuits and the ways we distinguish educational endeavors from other forms of social practice. With regard to the study of cinema, assemblage asks us to challenge and then reexamine the differing definitions we ascribe to artistry as opposed to technical proficiency and mastery when examining the nature of filmmaking, as well as the discrete boundaries we pose in describing the roles of filmmaker and audience viewer. Assemblage occurs when we strive to make sense of what is not understood, and in the realm of praxis, when we attempt to change conditions with which we are familiar for the better. It explicitly requires us to engage in meaning-making, another important component of affect.

Because affect is not simply reactive, meaning-making becomes an important factor to consider, complementing the concepts of intensity of encounter and assemblage. Although the results may be ambiguous and even at times destructive, acts of comparison generically involve meaning-making. The initial effort to seek comparison in the first place is grounded in an effort to rectify incomplete understandings of our world as well as ourselves. For affect theorists, meaning-making is corporeal and is not restricted to traditional notions of consciousness and self-reflection that reify the divisions between mind and body and theory and praxis. More importantly, it is through engaging in meaning-making that we break down the classification and categorization impulses that stultify the comparative project. It is not hyperbolic to assert that meaning-making creates the fuel that gives agency to comparative engagement.

Embedded within the notions of intensity of encounter, assemblage, and meaning-making and generic to the overall concept of affect is contingency. The power of affect lies in part in its lack of permanence, a condition that resonates with twenty-first-century lived experiences that can be as intense as they are ephemeral. Embracing contingency with regard to this project compels us to affirm the metaphorical and reject the categorical when invoking comparison. It requires us to dismiss a reflexive embrace of educational exceptionalism that consistently frames educational reform as a guarantor of positive social change, and it forces us to temper our faith in our powers of prediction and futuristic prognostication. Within the context of educational experience, an embrace rather than a pessimistic acceptance of contingency allows for an appreciation of those spontaneous and creative learning situations that we remember as transformative, particularly because they were unanticipated. Within the context of filmmaking, the uncertainty that accompanies the artistic process, extending onto the ability of the filmmaker to realize one's vision and the audience to appreciate that intent, is what makes this form of artistic engagement exciting and the results of the process unpredictable.

Using these aspects of affect as tools for investigating comparison offers a number of advantages. They help us reconcile the ambiguities and contradictions that can mark comparative work. Those contradictions, when not resolved, can create status and inertia, resulting in a reification of existing assumptions rather than the carving out of a space where they can be challenged and critiqued.

The Paradox of Comparison

It is not overly hyperbolic to assert that engaging in acts of comparison can be fundamental to who we are and how we view one another. Intrinsic to the learning process is our ability to compare entities. Indeed, one cannot conceive of using language or employing human communication of any type without also utilizing comparison. On an even deeper level, the variety of social interactions with which we engage could never occur without our participating in numerous comparative actions. Comparison can facilitate self-awareness, it can invite creativity, it can promote curiosity. But engaging in comparison also involves classification and categorization. Comparison involves not only looking for similarities but also enunciating differences. It invokes separation and distinction in spite of an overall embrace of commonality. In so doing, it focuses upon specificity even while it promotes generalization.

As a subset of all social interactions, educational encounters are inherently comparative. Learning, for example, is commonly associated with gaining new knowledge or skills that result in a permanent change in behavior (Gross, 2012). Discerning what constitutes information, how relevant or new such information may be and how such information influences or changes our current understandings or amplifies existing skills, requires the use of comparative tools. Education, broadly conceived, involves efforts to bring about learning. The facilitation of comparative acts is thus essential to what education is supposed to do. But the aims of education can only be realized when comparative acts resist narrow classification and categorization tendencies. As Foucault astutely reminded us within the realm of social relations, the act of classification involves the exercise of power in ways that are as pervasive as they are at times obscurant (Foucault, 1994).

Historically, education has continually been delivered in multiple ways. Graeber and Wengrow note that archaeologists have identified formal classrooms, with students sitting in seats, taught by the individual instructor who was responsible for the delivery of knowledge, as having existed in Sumerian society as early as 3,000 B.C. Private methods of instruction, with scribes serving as tutors to individuals within households, operated in parallel fashion from 2,000 to 1,500 B.C. (Graeber and Wengrow, 2021, 307, 576). Indeed, a comparative lens compels us to acknowledge the historical importance of diverse educational efforts that contributed to contemporary global understandings. By way of specific example, the Chinese shuyuan private academies that were initiated in 725 A.D. in the Tang Dynasty served to buttress the world's first civil service examination system, established during the Sui Dynasty (586–618 A.D.). Our notions linking government service and social mobility to meritorious achievement evolved from these Confucian origins (Lee, 1999). In the Muslim world, the Abbasid caliphate (750–1258 A.D.) not only promoted intellectual and scientific inquiry within the caliphate but also brought scholars from China, Greece, and Europe to Baghdad, Cairo, and Damascus for conversation, discussion, and knowledge exchange. Abbasid caliph Al Ma'mun (813–833 A.D.) created the Bayt-al Hikma or House of Wisdom, a public library and academy, where issues involving science, politics, and religion were freely discussed and major scientific and philosophical works were translated from the original Greek. Even after its demise in 1258, its model was replicated through the creation of institutes and academies throughout the Muslim world. In the eleventh century, for example, Nizam al-Mulk (1018–1092 A.D.) established nizamiyya, or higher learning centers, which later influenced the formation of European and Middle Eastern universities (Hoodfar, 2020).

As Graeber and Wengrow argue, the regular transmission of ideas and practices within and among people of differing backgrounds has been a characteristic of human interaction since our origins; the acceptance of new ideas and practices has transcended cultural, geographic, and linguistic difference. The aforementioned examples from the realm of education offer further evidence for their contention. Graeber and Wengrow's primary finding, though, is that distinctive modes of thought and corresponding social practices have existed throughout history in ways that have been *both* complementary and oppositional, inclusive as well as exclusive, depending upon circumstance. Loosely formed social and political configurations, promoting varying degrees of social and political equality, have repeatedly coexisted with centralized and concentrated power relations throughout history. Graeber and Wengrow thus reject explanations that privilege assertions of inevitability or determinism when explaining why specific social practices, forms of political organization, and modes of thought evolved in certain ways. As they state,

> We can see more clearly now what is going on when, for example, a study that is rigorous in every other respect begins from the unexamined assumption that there was some 'original' form of human society; that its nature was fundamentally good or evil; that a time before inequality and political awareness existed; that something happened to change all this; that 'civilization' and 'complexity' always come at the price of human freedoms; that participatory democracy is natural in small groups but cannot possibly scale up to anything like a city or a nation state. We know, now, that we are in the presence of myths. (Graeber and Wengrow, 2021, pp. 525–526)

Their admonition can certainly be applied to our perceptions of educational practice, which have too often tended to narrowly associate teaching and learning with what singly occurs in formal schools and likeminded institutions, and which assume the veneer of inevitability, when examining the possibilities and consequences of such practice. Such perceptions influence the practices they frame; they define the spaces within which educational practices are affirmed, critiqued, reformed, and reimagined. One of the major conceits of this book is the contention that the study of film represents an important method for expanding that frame. But in order to offer support for the contention, it is important to examine the similarities and differences between conventional comparative educational research and the study of film.

A Tale of Two Texts

Comparative and international educational research and film studies occupy distinctive intellectual spaces within Western knowledge traditions. Comparative and international education, which currently owes much of its orientation to larger social science and international development discourse, is somewhat of an anomaly, in that much of what can be called mainstreamed educational research is closely tied to principles and methods crafted within the discipline of psychology and the subdiscipline of educational psychology. This is not surprising given the importance of understanding learning processes as part of educational pursuits. However, when placed within that disciplinary frame, one adheres to a number of assumptions that reject or at least narrow the possibilities for engaging in comparative inquiry, to the extent that an inherent universal applicability of one's results is assumed and then asserted, to be confirmed through repeated testing of experimental and quasi-experimental designs. The goal is to minimize subjects' distinctiveness without acknowledging or comparing differences from the start, in the hopes of discovering results that are predictive for as general an audience as possible. Mainstreamed educational research has followed suit. As modern psychology evolved into an academic discipline that embraced scientific principles during the nineteenth century, its focus upon methodological rationality underplayed the truism that psychological investigation should always be viewed as a type of social construction rather than as a form of independent research reflecting an objective search for truth in the purest sense. Instead, even in their early inundations, the types of experimental designs that psychologists embraced and the research questions that they entertained reflected prevailing cultural, economic, and social crosscurrents. By way of example, as the field of psychology gained increased acceptance in the United States, there was a conscious shift in focus from a holistic emphasis upon child study to one emphasizing the comparative measurement of individual attributes according to prescribed norms. Such a shift had the effect of supporting North American public school administrators, who felt pressed to create bureaucratic efficiencies within public school systems in response to their rapid expansion at the turn of and in the early beginnings of the twentieth century (Danzinger, 1994).

The comparative education field, on the other hand, by necessity, has traditionally tended to at least acknowledge the existence of cultural, geographic, linguistic, political, and social differences that must be identified if not accommodated, in order for the generalizations that derive from one's findings to be convincingly asserted. Comparative education thus evolved both from existing social science paradigms of the nineteenth century, many of which also applied the positivism associated with scientific method to social issues, and then from broader, humanistic perspectives that viewed the transmission of ideas and social practices in holistic terms, emphasizing the importance of national character in contributing to educational institutional development (Epstein, 2008).

The study of education has traditionally been tied to educational practice, and as education became more professionalized during the nineteenth century, its place within the Western academy as a legitimate, applied, professional field grew, mimicking the trajectory of other professional fields including law and medicine. The characteristics we attribute to the modern professions, including a service ethic situating one's work in support of the greater good, some degree of autonomy with regard to determining the conditions of practice, and peer evaluation that enforces agreed-upon standards of performance, were in various stages of development prior to these disciplines acquiring space within the Western academy. Professional training occurred on site, often in apprentice-like settings. Later, in the United States, independent professional schools arose with varying degrees of academic quality. By the early 1900s, though, a presumed need for students to receive more rigorous scientific training resulted in the decline of independent professional schools, as their curricula became absorbed within the formal university setting (Goldin and Katz, 1999). The education field followed this pattern, as teacher and administrative training, along with broader areas of educational research, eventually became firmly situated within the academy, although the status of the education has traditionally been relatively low in comparison with other applied and pure academic areas. Comparative education's role has been especially precarious, not simply because of its efforts to bridge academic and professional polarities but also because of its struggle to assert its importance as a generalist field while other areas of educational inquiry have become increasingly specialized. At the same time, the audiences with whom comparative educators communicate have been both diverse and fragmented.

As the study of film has evolved, one can see some interesting similarities. The initial production of moving images, during the nineteenth century, focused upon mastery of a new and exciting technology. Such efforts bear a striking resemblance to what we would today label as "home movies," attempts to faithfully (realistically) record common interactions. The "Horse in Motion," a compilation of individual photographs edited and compiled to form a single motion picture in 1878, is often credited as the first film (Prodger, 2003). The first commercial films that were produced were credited to the Lumiere Brothers, manufacturers of photographic equipment, with their initial film, *La Sortie des ouvriers de l'usine Lumière* (*Workers Leaving the Lumière Factory*), having been produced in 1895. For most of their lives, their commercial film distribution efforts were of secondary importance and interest to their primary manufacturing business (Russell, 1995; Hill, n.d.). The first film course taught in the United States was titled "The Photoplay Composition Class" and was sponsored by Columbia University's adult education extension program in 1915. The Moscow film school, founded in 1919, emphasized the teaching of film theory and included noted directors Sergei Eisenstein, Vsevolod Pudovkin, and Andre Tarkovsky among its faculty (Gerasimov Institute of Cinematography, n.d.). The USC School of Cinematic Arts, established in 1929, was more closely tied to the Hollywood studio system and was the first in the United States to offer a bachelor of arts degree in film (USC Cinematic Arts, n.d.). In the United States, film studies, as an academic discipline, gained widespread popularity in the 1960s and 1970s, in response to broader efforts to democratize and reform university curricula and in light of social movement activism (Grieveson and Wasson, 2008).

Comparisons noting the formation and evolution of comparative education and studies of film theory and criticism are striking. Both areas were incorporated into the academy in spite of their "applied origins." Their incorporation has been relatively recent. Both fields include elements of theory and practice. Both fields speak to multiple audiences, be they within or outside of the academy. Both fields from their origins incorporated international influences. And, both fields aim to address elements of human experience that extend beyond the familiar. Yet, there are significant differences that are worth analyzing, differences that center around their disparate uses of text and the ways in which text frames discourse for their multiple audiences.

To engage in comparative education inquiry requires one to commit to a series of conventions reflective of broader educational and social science research. While educational encounters are ubiquitous and are certainly part of our everyday interactions, their depiction is contingent upon the ways in which issues of interest are constructed and then presented according to standards that gird the broader research fields. Thus, the artifacts commonly deployed within comparative education efforts—data collection derived from testing, curricular plans and guidelines, policy proposals and legislation, questionnaires, interviews, participant observation, evaluation mechanisms, examples of student and/or teacher work, diaries, and written and oral recordings of specific encounters—all play a role in supporting the comparative education frame. There is considerable variability within that frame when one examines issues of scale. Although many comparative education researchers use the case study as a template for their analyses, focusing upon policies and practices within a certain country, region, or social group, others pursue cross-cultural inquiries that involve multiple institutions and institutional actors in a variety of settings. Not surprisingly, the constituencies for whom such research is generated—policymakers, practitioners, government officials, representatives of multilateral organizations and NGOs, fellow scholars, and the general public—are similarly diverse. There is no doubt, though, that the texts that are employed to circulate knowledge among these various groups are grounded in the educational, social, scientific, and international development discourse that is produced and reproduced within the academy, even when such discourse seems rarified or arcane to nonelite publics. This chapter began with the assertion that we all have experienced educational encounters throughout our lives. Yet the language that is used among comparative educators to explore the meanings of those encounters can be formalistic when it asserts its legitimacy through adherence to academic convention.

Those who engage in film study base their inquiries according to a different kind of text. In many respects, film study has come to resemble literary criticism, with the types of techniques utilized to produce a unique aesthetic product akin to the tools employed within conventional literary analysis. Although this will be explored in greater depth in Chapter 2, the nature and purpose of film have changed, as technological advances have allowed for enhanced creative exploration in areas including but certainly not limited to the use of sound, color, lighting, editing, screen writing, and so on. What was initially considered to be a faithful objective and realistic recording of daily life, enhanced through the then revolutionary ability to record physical movement, has become its own art form, establishing different conventions for specific genres, be they documentary, melodrama, comedy, horror, or science fiction. The development of editing processes allowed filmmakers to create narratives and tell stories, reflecting their personal artistic visions. Thus, the questions of central importance to those who engage in film analysis are similar questions posed by those who study literary texts. Why do specific images evoke certain meanings? How do specific signs work with one another to create effective images? How does image juxtaposition create new meaning? Can such meanings be understood as being intertwined with what viewers bring with them to the cinema, or are they solely expressions of the vision of the filmmaker? Although an understanding of the relationship between filmmaker and audience is crucial to an appreciation of the artistic nature of film, it is an understanding that continues to evolve and it is important to note the open-ended nature of these questions. Befitting an academic field that is indebted to the humanities, the framing of this academic field is broad and expansive. Filmmakers are thus able, when they choose to do so, to depict plotlines with ambiguous outcomes and subjects with mixed character traits. The creative space that allows for such ambiguity is less operational when restricted to the conventions of mainstreamed educational and social science research.

All of this being said, one would be remiss to avoid noting that the practice and study of filmmaking has its own history of perpetuating racism, violence, and injustice, a history it shares with certain areas of educational practice and research. There is indeed a darker side to the ways in which we have historically interpreted the meanings and purposes of both educational practice and filmmaking which deserves specific comment, a perspective that emphasizes the manipulation of both fields as communicative tools for the rationalization of destructive aims.

Investigating the Dark Side

We began this chapter making reference to the classification and categorization tendencies that tend to be part of comparative work. An examination of the ways in which these tendencies have been applied to the areas of educational practice and research, and filmmaking practice and critique, is illustrative of their potentially harmful effects. In 1916, Stanford educational psychologist Lewis Terman wrote the following words, in support of his effort to adapt French psychologist Alfred Benet's IQ test to a North American setting.

> It is interesting to note that M. P. and C. P. represent the level of intelligence which is very, very common among Spanish-Indian and Mexican families of the Southwest and also among negroes. Their dullness seems to be racial, or at least inherent in the family stocks from which they come. The fact that one meets this type with such extraordinary frequency among Indians, Mexicans, and negroes suggests quite forcibly that the whole question of racial differences in mental traits will have to be taken up anew and by experimental methods. The writer predicts that when this is done there will be discovered enormously significant

racial differences in general intelligence, differences which cannot be wiped out by any scheme of mental culture.

Children of this group should be segregated in special classes and be given instruction which is concrete and practical. They cannot master abstractions, but they can often be made efficient workers, able to look out for themselves. There is no possibility at present of convincing society that they should not be allowed to reproduce, although from a eugenic point of view they constitute a grave problem because of their unusually prolific breeding. (Terman, 1916)

One year earlier, D. W. Griffith directed *The Birth of a Nation*, one of the most influential films in the history of cinema for its then experimental use of close-ups and quick editing, but equally noteworthy for its reverential treatment of the Ku Klux Klan and its virulent depiction of racist stereotypes.

In 1934, Fredrick Schneider, coeditor of the *International Education Review*, the first and at that time the only comparative education journal of its type, was replaced by an avowed Nazi, Alfred Baeumier, who transformed the journal into a Nazi propaganda periodical (Epstein, 2017). In 1935, Leni Riefensthal directed *Triumph of the Will*, the infamous film extolling Hitler's virtues as savior of the German masses. Although these historical moments demonstrate the convergence of racist beliefs and attitudes within the educational and filmmaking spheres, racism didn't begin in the early twentieth century, and its scope extends beyond these particular domains. Nonetheless, its presence within both areas is striking. How is it that modern educational provision, closely tied to the moral imperative to deliver a public good, could encourage intellectual proponents who were so heavily steeped in racist beliefs that served as a justification for exclusionism and dehumanization? How is it that a then newer technology such as filmmaking, originally designed to record the common occurrences of daily life, could have become such a potent propaganda vehicle for encouraging not only racism but also mass destruction?

In searching for an explanation of racism's more recent and modern manifestations, one notes that an expanding faith in the power of the state to exert social control over its citizenry marked much of early twentieth-century Progressive thought (Leonard, 2005). The eugenics movement, which had adherents for many decades but became especially popular in the first early years of the twentieth century and included many luminaries in addition to Terman, was one beneficiary of this belief. The later enactment of Nazi racist beliefs became a logical extension of such an attitude. What was unique in the twentieth century was the state's exercise of its power to control and disseminate information in ways that were highly effective in propagating systematic forms of violence that culminated in genocide. Both educational institutions and the nascent German film industry were culpable in allowing, indeed at times encouraging, the state to exercise such power. However, the relationships between the ways in which ideas are formulated, the conditions under which they receive broad support, how they are circulated, when they encourage, and when they resist specific courses of action are complex.

The thoughts and actions, theories and practices, that contributed to the racist depictions described earlier were certainly related to one another, albeit not always in a direct, causal, or unilateral manner. But if one would be mistaken to separate racist ideology as propagated by text or film from the tragic consequences of racist practice, one would be equally in error to view those ideas as solely dependent upon external conditions and factors or mere by-products of political, socioeconomic, and historical circumstance. As noted in the introduction to this volume, the promise of applying affect theory to comparative work is the possibility of understanding existing interconnections and discovering new ones, but only through resisting the temptation of minimizing or seeking to eliminate complexity and ambiguity. In noting the existence of racist ideas within these different domains, it is thus perhaps useful to comment upon the more general ways in which comparative acts articulate symbolic forms of violence.

There are three types of symbolic violence that can occur when engaging in acts of comparison. They include erasure, self-projection and self-substitution, and domination. Erasure involves a failure to initiate comparison with subjects viewed as being so different from oneself as to even merit recognition. The presumed dissimilarity attributed to these subjects renders any effort to even engage in comparison with them fruitless in the minds of those pursuing the comparative project. Within the educational field, the curricular subjects that are not taught, the population groups whose presence is ignored, and the dismissal of alternative institutional arrangements that might provide for educational delivery in some form offer common examples of symbolic violence through erasure (Bourdieu and Passeron, 1977). Within the comparative education context, projects that are Global North-centric in the curricula they survey, in the institutional policies they analyze, and in the cultural and linguistic groups they identify demonstrate a similar proclivity. In the area of film study, with particular regard to those international films seeking to attract a global audience, the subjects whose stories remain untold also are forced to confront the symbolic violence that arises from their erasure. It should be stressed that such forms of symbolic violence need not be conscious or intentional but reflect an uncritical acceptance of power relations by all involved parties.

A second if related form of symbolic violence involves self-substitution and self-projection. In this case, otherness is perceived as an opportunity to insert oneself or one's values onto the other without concern for who the other is, what the other believes, or how the other is politically and socially engaged. Edward Said's understanding of "orientalism," as a manufactured, stereotypical depiction of Asian and Middle Eastern cultures for the purposes of Westerners furthering their own world view, is one example of the phenomenon (Said, 1978). Boaventura De Sousa Santos's notion of epistemicide, where Western knowledge traditions are consciously promoted as being universally applicable while encouraging the rejection of alternative modes of thinking as being pedestrian or lacking significance, is another example (Santos, 2014). Within the comparative education field, critiques of international development strategies often point to their displacement of local values and norms in favor of Western educational practices as a consequence of Global North assistance strategies. The promotion of English as a global lingua franca to the exclusion of vernacular language use in schools is another example of this trend. There are, of course, numerous examples of similar patterns regarding the terms through which international films are circulated, not only with regard to character portrayal but also with respect to plotlines, settings, techniques, and so on.

A third form of symbolic violence involves categorization and classification for the purpose of exerting domination over the other. It is most evident when rigid classification further encourages a degree of hierarchical positioning that codifies the unequal status of the participants. Homi Bhabha, in referring to Franz Fanon's writing, examined the notion of mimicry as a key component of colonialism, the colonized being forced to mimic the colonizer but never achieving equivalent status in their attempts to do so. Indeed, as Bhabha notes, we implicitly understand that the generic mimic can never be viewed as having the capacity to exactly replicate the subject of one's mimicry; it is a recognition that the distance that codifies the oppressive nature of the colonizer/colonized relationship is ultimately unbreachable, even when the colonized are initially promised the opportunity to achieve the recognition and respect afforded the colonizer (Bhabha, 1984). The North/South global divisions that characterize much of modern schooling follow such a pattern, particularly with regard to the differential degrees of status afforded to Global South institutions in the higher education sector. One could note similar patterns when comparing the status of Global South international filmmaking with that of the Global North.

Although our musings regarding the darker side of comparison have illuminated some of the destructive tendencies that can be attributed to the process itself, they don't offer a complete picture. As has been noted, because comparison plays such an important role in facilitating learning and in influencing our daily interpersonal interactions, one must examine its creative possibilities even while cognizant of its potential harms. Those possibilities are clearly in evidence within the fields of education and film study and by highlighting their presence, the case for studying their interrelationships becomes clearer.

Comparison and Creativity

The promise of modern education has always been embedded within its claim that it contributes not only to the public good but to social improvement more broadly conceived as well. The possibilities for contributing to positive social change are connected to efforts not simply of reform but also of reconceptualization. In response to the neoliberal values and policies that have come to characterize education globally, there have been a number of grassroots initiatives that have recognized the imperative for and are engaging in the reconceptualization process. It is interesting to note a few of these initiatives that are representative of a growing trend. For example, the Ecoversities Alliance involves educator/practitioners who are committed to a reimagining of higher education. As its members state on their website,

> There is an emerging knowledge movement that is slowly building all over the world, though it often goes unnoticed by the media and most formal education systems. A part of this movement can be described as a network of "eco-versities"—people, organizations and communities who are reclaiming knowledge systems and a cultural imaginary to restore and re-envision learning processes that are meaningful and relevant to the challenges of our times.
>
> Although diverse in its origins, these different pedagogical initiatives both critique the existing education systems, and cultivate new practices to regenerate ecological, social and cultural ecosystems, whilst also reflecting on the meanings of "home" as locality and as an "economy": hence the name "eco-versities." Eco-versities, n.d.)

Its members have engaged in establishing regional networks in India, Latin America, and Europe, have held international and regional gatherings, have created short-term residencies for members to visit different project sites, and have created publications, films, and podcasts.

Similarly, the Global Tapestry of Alternatives includes three networks: Vikalp Sangam (Alternative Confluence, India), Crianza Mutua Mexico, and Crianza Mutua Colombia that aim to dismantle hierarchies, encourage autonomy from the market and the state, and connect groups through constructing communal webs (Global Tapestry of Alternatives, n.d.). The Crianza Mutua Mexico, in particular, has interesting roots, originating within the Universidad de la Tierra, a coalition of Indigenous and non-Indigenous communities that created "Unitierra" in reaction to the formal Mexican educational system, which is viewed as having contributed to cultural genocide (Universidad De La Tierra Oaxaca, n.d.). A third example of a similarly minded global initiative is the Wellbeing Economic Alliance. The Wellbeing Economic Alliance seeks to reframe global economic policy to promote, in holistic terms, ecological well-being rather than the more narrow and conventional goal of economic growth while seeking collaboration between government, business, and civil society entities (Wellbeing Economic Alliance, n.d.). It includes approximately 200 members, including individuals, organizations, and social movements that work to redesign economic systems to become fair and redistributive. One of their aims is to replace GDP with more accurate measures of well-being while chronicling sectors that deserve to grow along with those that should experience de-growth.

These initiatives share a number of common features. For the most part, they emphasize horizontal connectivity rather than vertically induced, centralized, bureaucratic relationships. As befits the nature of networking, they dismiss conventional leadership positioning and depend upon grassroots organizing and collective decision-making. Their focus tends to be community-based and includes action items that relate to both educational and broader social concerns. Although their members certainly include educators, writers, and scholars, they make a conscious effort to include those who work and live outside of conventional educational environments. In short, they affirm the core principles of assemblage, intensity of encounter, and meaning-making that comprise an embrace of affect.

In addition to these initiatives, UNESCO, in its *Reimagining Our Futures Together: A New Social Contract* document, examines possibilities for global educational reform at a macro level. The International Commission on the Futures in Education was established in 2019 and was tasked with the goal of "reimagin[ing] how knowledge and learning can shape the future of humanity and the planet" (International Commission on the Futures of Education,

2021). *The Reimagining Our Futures Together* report represents the thinking of commission members, and its publication complements previous periodic efforts on the part of UNESCO to comment upon the role of education globally and to make recommendations for its reconceptualization. At first glance, the report is very much a product of its times, the equity issues exacerbated by the Covid-19 pandemic, the global growth of right-wing populism and authoritarianism, and the need to seriously address climate change and climate injustice offering compelling reasons for envisioning substantive educational transformation. In their view, current educational efforts are inadequate responses to these challenges. Instead, the commission members offer a much more expansive vision of what education should entail, arguing in favor of a capabilities approach that would enhance educational opportunity throughout one's life while developing a "knowledge commons," where access to information and knowledge is made more widely accessible.

> Long interpreted as the right to schooling for children and youth, going forward, the right to education must assure education at all ages and in all areas of life. From this broader perspective, the right to education is closely connected to the right to information, to culture, and to science. It requires a deep commitment to building human capabilities. It is also closely linked to the right to access and contribute to the knowledge commons, humanity's shared and expanding resources of information, knowledge and wisdom. The ongoing cycle of knowledge creation that occurs through contest, dialogue and debate is what helps to coordinate action, produce scientific truths, and foment innovation. It is one of humanity's most valuable, inexhaustible resources, and a key aspect of education. The more people that have access to the knowledge commons, the more abundant it becomes. The development of language, numeracy and systems of writing has facilitated the spread of knowledge across time and space. This, in turn, has allowed human societies to attain extraordinary heights of collective flourishing and civilization-building. The possibilities of the knowledge commons are theoretically infinite. The diversity and innovation unleashed by the knowledge commons comes from borrowings and lendings, from experimentation that crosses disciplinary boundaries, as well as from reinterpretation of the old and generation of the new. (International Commission on the Futures of Education, 2021, 12)

The report specifically calls for pedagogical innovations that promote cooperative learning and problem-solving opportunities for students, enhanced support for professionalizing teaching and teacher training, curricular innovations that invite greater interdisciplinarity and exposure to diverse and Indigenous cultural and knowledge traditions, greater access to information including scientific knowledge and the requisite tools for combatting misinformation, and prioritizing the teaching of lifelong skills rather than focusing solely upon vocational training or limiting one's aims solely to the acquisition of basic literacy and numeracy skills. In addition, there is a recognition that educational institutions, be they public or private, need to do a better job of working together, that universities need to better support other educational sectors, that a community-based education requires educational institutions to work with other noneducational agencies, and that better levels of local, regional, national, and international cooperation will need to be initiated if these goals are to be realized.

The guiding principles behind the report include the view that educational provision is a basic human right and that its delivery as a public good is part of a larger social contract that needs to be made with humanity in its entirety. The authors of the report are thus calling for an expansive notion of educational mission that would extend beyond its traditional role in servicing the state (promoting citizenship) and the economy (teaching necessary skills as dictated by the market). A view embracing the capabilities approach to development, a human rights perspective regarding the importance of education, and an adherence to a social contract framework, all of which serve as a basis for the committee's recommendations, offer a significant rationale for educational reform, but also invite some skepticism. The capabilities approach has been criticized for its vagueness and its emphasis upon individual freedom and choice as the primary determinant of what capability entails (James, 2018). It is curious that the report's promotion of educational expansion for the purpose of enhancing capability has the potential of rationalizing increased global governmentality while simultaneously failing to address the reasons why historic and contemporary educational provisions have proved to be so inadequate (Chandler, 2013). Similarly, the universality embedded in human rights and social contract language belies a reliance upon a global nation-state governance structure that defers to the nation-state as primary protector and guarantor of basic rights. Such a deference has of course at times proven detrimental to the preservation of existing rights and the expansion of newly recognized rights that receive global protection. UNESCO, of course, is discretely positioned within the international system and functions in support of that system. *Reimagining Our Futures Together* thus is an articulate enunciation of future educational possibility, although it reflects the limitations of conceiving of such alternatives within a post-Second World War international order whose assumptions, at least with regard to the primacy of the nation-state, remain largely unchallenged. More importantly, though, the alternatives proposed in the *Reimagining Our Futures Together* report and the international nongovernmental organizations that have been profiled argue that comparative engagement can promote creativity and inclusivity with regard to educational concerns and that such engagement can be a source of dynamism rather than stasis.

This is certainly true of the arts, and more specifically for our purposes, cinema. Art has served as a constant source of interpersonal expression throughout human history, the film being an exceptionally powerful art form because of its appeal to our many senses including the visual, the audio, and the haptic. Not only does it offer the opportunity for direct interpersonal communication and exchange, it is a generically inclusive art form, transcending the hierarchical classifications of certain art labeled "high-brow" as opposed to so-called pedestrian forms of artistic expression, defined as craftsmanship. As will be discussed more fully in Chapter 3, filmmakers operate within structured globalized spaces not dissimilar to those that have governed educational experiences. But within those constraints, they have been able to raise questions and offer insights that are both imaginative and compelling. Technological innovations have democratized the filmmaking process. As a result, the mechanics of production and editing, especially within video formats, have become more accessible to larger numbers of people than ever before. Yet the tension between individual and audience, self, and other that has been previously noted remains an important factor that is characteristic of filmmaking. At their best, successful artists are able to both tap into shared sensibilities that evoke common reactions and offer insights that are new and unexplored. The same can be said for successful filmmakers.

Affect speaks to us specifically when we investigate comparative education and film study and theory, as its usage highlights many of the characteristics that make these domains distinctive as well as comparable. Aside from the acknowledged similarities and differences among the two areas, it is through a recognition of the importance of affect that the fields can be more closely tied together. That goal can best be pursued by digging deeper into examining the distinctive patterns that have marked the evolution of each field.

2

Film, Comparative and International Education, and Affect

Some Theoretical Considerations

In order to further explore the proposition that CIE and film study are worthy of comparative analysis, I believe it is useful to look more closely at some of the salient theoretical perspectives that have come to characterize each field. Upon doing so, the case for engaging in comparison becomes even more robust. That case is made even stronger when noting the ways in which theories of affect speak to the concerns in both knowledge domains. Being cognizant of the fact that volumes have been written about the nature of film theory, it is impossible to do full justice to an academic field that is so rich and vibrant by summarizing some of its concepts in a short space. Nonetheless, it is fascinating to read about the ways in which film theoreticians and CIE scholars have wrestled with basic questions that speak so broadly to our sensibilities and social concerns. Those concerns include the nature of representation with regard to time, movement, and causality; the role of filmmakers and/or researchers and their relationship to audience; their choice of subjects for investigation; and the degree of autonomy with which they operate in a larger social universe.

Evolution of Film Theory: The Photograph Versus the Moving Image

Discussion about film naturally begins with consideration of the photograph and its historically important social impact. The development of photography had a revolutionary influence upon the visual arts when it became clear that artistic representations of objects could never compete with the photographic image with regard to the accuracy of the depiction. The visual artist, then freed from the expectation that one's work must be evaluated primarily on the basis of the realism of object representation, was able to construct art that touched upon broader creative concerns. But what of the photograph, the photographer, and the camera? How did this "new technology" change our understanding of the world around us and the social interactions we experience?

In addressing these issues, it is important to note that meanings ascribed to the photograph differ from that of the artistic pictorial representation, not only because of the accuracy of its depiction but because the image it portrays is decontextualized. There is a sense of timelessness and permanence that we attribute to the photographic image, as we tend to affirm the realism of its depiction independent of the conditions under which it occurred. The fact that the image can be continually and easily reproduced, viewed, and then circulated under radically differing conditions separates the photograph from portraiture or other similarly constructed visual images, whose authority lies in the specific conditions of its creation which can't be replicated. Thus, critical theorist Walter Benjamin argued that the photograph lacked the authenticity and the aura of the painting.

> Even the most perfect reproduction of a work of art is lacking in one element: its presence in time and space, its unique existence at the place where it happens to be. This unique existence of the work of art determined the history to which it was subject throughout the time of its existence. This includes the changes which it may have suffered in physical condition over the years as well as the various changes in its ownership.
>
> One might subsume the eliminated element in the term "aura" and go on to say: that which withers in the age of mechanical reproduction is the aura of the work of art. This is a symptomatic process whose significance points beyond the realm of art. One might generalize by saying: the technique of reproduction detaches the reproduced object from the domain of tradition. By making many reproductions it substitutes a plurality of copies for a unique existence. And in permitting the reproduction to meet the beholder or listener in his own particular situation, it reactivates the object reproduced. These two processes lead to a tremendous shattering of tradition which is the obverse of the contemporary crisis and renewal of mankind. Both processes are intimately connected with the contemporary mass movements. Their most powerful agent is the film. Its social significance, particularly in its most positive form, is inconceivable without its destructive, cathartic aspect, that is, the liquidation of the traditional value of the cultural heritage. (Benjamin, 1935, 2005)

In echoing these sentiments, critic Susan Sontag further noted that because of its accessibility, and because of the likeness of the photographic image to its subject, the photograph has become a desirable item worthy of collection and consumption. Through collecting photographs, she argued that we assert control over the subjects they represent, the experiences they depict, and the information they convey.

> Our irrepressible feeling that the photographic process is something magical has a genuine basis. No one takes an easel painting to be in any sense co-substantial with its subject; it only represents or refers. But a photograph is not only like its subject, a homage to the subject. It is part of, an extension of the subject; and a potent means of acquiring it, of gaining control over it.
>
> Photography is acquisition in several forms. In its simplest form, we have in a photograph surrogate possession of a cherished person or thing, a possession which gives photographs some of the character of unique objects. Through photographs, we also have a consumer's relation to events, both to events which are part of our experience and to those which we are not—a distinction between types of experience that such habit-forming consumership blurs. A third form of acquisition is that, through image-making and image-duplicating machines, we can acquire something as information (rather than experience). Indeed, the importance of photographic images as a medium through which more and more events enter our experience is, finally, only a by-product of their effectiveness in furnishing knowledge dissociated from and independent of experience. (Sontag, 1973, 155–6)

Both Benjamin and Sontag viewed photography as being important because its usage compels us to consider the nature of representation and its relationship to what is real. For Benjamin, the photograph obliterates the uniqueness and creativity inherent in artistic vision because of its common accessibility and the ease with which it can be reproduced. What becomes popularly accessible sacrifices authenticity. For Sontag, the accuracy of photographic likeness encourages viewers to seek control over an imaged relationship with the other, often through engaging in collection, consumerism, and consumption. But both authors also viewed the photograph as a mechanism that asks us to address a larger question regarding the relationship of image representation to reality. Such a concern is not new; it in fact is a fundamental philosophical question first posed in Plato's Republic through his cave allegory. In Book VII, Socrates is speaking with his students, one of whom is Glaucon, Plato's brother, about the nature of the human condition.

> See human beings as though they were in an underground cave-like dwelling with its entrance, a long one, open to the light, across the whole width of the cave. They are in it from childhood with their legs and necks in bonds so that they are fixed, seeing only in front of them, unable because of the bond to turn

their heads all the way around. Their light is from a fire burning far above and beyond them. Between the fire and the prisoners, there is a road above, along which see a wall, built like the partition's puppet-handlers set in front of human beings and over which they show the puppets.

Then also see along this wall human beings carrying all sorts of artifacts, which project above the wall, and statues of men and other animals wrought from stone, wood, and every kind of material; as it is to be expected, some of the carriers utter sounds while others are silent.

"It's a strange image," he [Glaucon] said, "and strange prisoners you're telling of."

"They're like us," I [Socrates] said. (Anderson, 2014, 36)

Nathan Anderson further concludes,

Socrates explains that the men in the cave see nothing of themselves or each other, only shadows cast by statues on the wall in front of them. Their heads are bound motionless, but they can hear each other's voices. The only other sounds they hear are echoes from the puppeteers who parade behind them, which they consider to be voices and sounds from the shadows before them, the only reality they know.

It is a strange image. An image of us, claims Socrates, an allegory of the human condition in the absence of a genuine philosophical education. What we take to be most real, what we encounter all around us is like shadows on a wall, and our so-called common sense and understanding of the world is nothing more than prejudice, untrustworthy opinions rooted in false assumptions. (Anderson, 2014, 36–7)

The cave allegory has been viewed as applicable to the cinematic experience by theorists and critics for many generations, particularly with regard to the protocols that are observed in the collective viewing of film within the movie theater setting. As is true of Plato's cave dwellers, our backs are to one another, we tend not to interact with one another, and our focus is narrowly concentrated upon a set of images that purport to faithfully record human experience, even though they are at best representations of what we understand to be real. Benjamin and Sontag both expressed concerns for how the evolution of the photograph influenced modern social relationships. For Benjamin, the camera itself was a mechanical device whose usage upended the more conventional ways in which we interacted with human subjects and objects around us. For Sontag, the insipid commodification that accompanied the circulation of photographic images was representative of neoliberal tendencies that can be profoundly alienating. However, their basic concerns, regarding the power of image representation, how such images affect our thinking and behavior, and how we as viewers actively imbue those images with meaning, characterize much of film theory and criticism, from its early origins to the present. To be clear, a Platonist worldview that posits a clear demarcation between appearance and reality, and that views reality as being fixed if ultimately unreachable, is certainly controversial and does not speak to contemporary sensibilities. However, exploring the nexus between what constitutes the real as opposed to the representational lies at the core of film theory and study.

There are of course important differences between film and the photograph, the most obvious involving the use of movement. When the first film, *The Horse in Motion*, was created in 1878, multiple cameras took individual shots of a horse galloping, in order to answer the popular question of the time as to whether all four hooves were concurrently in the air while the horse was running. The fascination with the power of the camera was not simply one of being able to see what was obscured before the naked eye but also included the possibility of projecting our understanding of movement onto a living object—the recording of the galloping horse expanding our appreciation of its full capability as a living creature. Such has always been the promise of film, as our exposure to the moving image enhances our appreciation of the realism of the projection.

It is the editing process that gives film its distinctiveness, for the possibility of creating a story line is only realized when camera shots are collected, edited, and reformulated into a holistic narrative structure. But whether one observes movement through exposure to the tracking shot or witnesses its presence between shots, it is through our general recognition of the chronicling of movement that makes film especially distinctive. It is thus not surprising that the nature of montage, or "the process or technique of selecting, editing, and piecing together separate sections of film to form a continuous whole," has been a key area in the history of film study and criticism.

Russian filmmaker Sergei Eisenstein was one of the early masters of montage. Eisenstein, known for his quick edits that juxtaposed shots from parallel scenes with one another, was also one of cinema's leading theoreticians. Influenced by Marxist theory, he viewed the editing process as an exercise in applied dialectics, arguing that the editing of opposing shots whereby they were then placed next to one another led to the viewer's appreciation of film holistically. As he stated,

> But in my view montage is not an idea composed of successive shots stuck together but an idea that DERIVES from the collision between two shots that are independent of one another ("the dramatic" principle). ("Epic" and "dramatic"

in relation to the methodology of form and not content or plot!!). As in Japanese hieroglyphics in which two independent ideographic characters ("shots") are juxtaposed and explode into a concept.

Sophistry? Not at all! Because we are trying here to derive the whole essence, the stylistic principle and the character of film from its technical (-optical) foundations.

We know that the phenomenon of movement in film resides in the fact that still pictures of a moved body blend into movement when they are shown in quick succession after one another.

What does the dynamic effect of a picture consist of?

The eye follows the direction of an element. It retains a visual impression which then collides with the impression derived from following the direction of a second element. The conflict between these directions creates the dynamic effect in the apprehension of the whole. (Eisenstein, 2016, 26–7)

Eisenstein's emphasis upon the importance of montage as a general concept to the exclusion of what he called film's "technical (-optical) foundations" proved to be controversial. Later, critics such as Siegfried Kracauer reacted negatively to the ways in which German expressionist filmmakers intentionally used editing techniques to distort realistic depictions in order to induce psychological reactions among their viewers. Such techniques, which were copied by Nazi filmmakers, led Kracauer to argue that filmmakers are morally compelled to instead focus their efforts upon recording objective movement in realistic ways rather than staging and then editing shots in support of a specific artistic vision (Kracauer, 2016).

After the Second World War, though, there was a critical reaffirmation of the importance of filmmaker independence as a key component of creative artistic expression. Kracauer's more restrictive view of what the filmmaker's role should be was thus rejected. Andre Bazin, founder of the periodical *Cahiers du Cinema* and later author of the classic text *What Is Cinema?*, drew attention to the numerous artistic choices filmmakers made in constructing their works. His analysis of elements of mise-en-scene—composition, sets, props, lighting, costumes, actors, camera shots and angles, depth of field—that acclaimed filmmakers actively took responsibility for shaping and controlling led to focused commentary about the ways in which filmmakers created their own styles, demonstrating independence from the conventional approaches of Hollywood studios (Bazin, 2016).

Two of the more prominent movements with which post-Second World War filmmakers were associated included Italian neorealism and later, in the 1950s, the French New Wave. In the former case, Italian directors, often using nonprofessional actors, portrayed the lives of characters confronting poverty and social injustice in the aftermath of the war. Bazin demonstrated how deliberate and concerted their efforts were in creating in the viewers' minds realistic depictions of working-class suffering. In the latter case, noted French directors such as Francois Truffaut were not only influenced by Bazin's film criticism but also wrote for the *Cahiers du Cinema*. New Wave directors deliberately promoted unconventional story lines, challenging traditional narrative structure while employing experimental techniques including the use of long shots and discontinuous editing which resulted in ambiguous endings. In his writing, Truffaut himself promoted auteur theory, later popularized by film critic Andrew Sarris, where the unique styles of individual filmmakers were chronicled and scrutinized according to the specific techniques and artistic choices they employed (Sarris, 2016).

During the late 1960s and 1970s, as film theory continued to evolve, there was a new effort to examine the nature of film systematically. Christian Metz in particular applied concepts derived from the study of language as a means of analyzing the ways in which meanings were communicated from filmmaker to viewer. Although admitting that rules governing the use of signs within film were not as elaborate as those that govern formal linguistics, Metz still saw merit in analyzing film structure in a similar manner. Metz was influenced by Fernando de Saussere's insights regarding the ways in which we cognitively construct linguistic signs, composed of signifiers and the signified, to create a language structure that allows us to communicate with one another (Metz, 2016). What is most noteworthy for our purposes is that the application of structuralist principles to film theory became indicative of a more comprehensive effort to understand the relationship between filmmaker and viewer than that posed by auteur theory or the critical emphasis that focused on filmmaker style and technique.

Indeed, the fascination with structuralism later evolved into even more expansive discussions regarding the nature of representation and viewer response that incorporated versions of Marxist and psychoanalytic theory into film analysis and criticism. The notion that filmmaking was inherently ideological was supported by the claim that in the process of viewing a film, spectators are compelled into associating the camera's version of reality with their own. Through referencing the theoretical contributions of Louis Althusser, film theorists argued that viewers not only give up their own agency in linking cinematic representation with reality, but they allow themselves to be manipulated by capitalist interests in service of the state, even when the film industry lies outside of the direct jurisdiction of the state. Their willingness to identify with the camera's perspective of what is real by viewing it as their own speaks to a general process of interpellation that makes the state's use of ideological apparatuses effective. The significance of filmmaking was thus linked to its role as an ideological apparatus that bolstered the legitimacy of the capitalist state through presenting a view of reality that affirmed those cultural values that support capitalism (Baudry, J.L., 2016).

The link between filmmaking and psychoanalysis is also historically strong. The surrealist fascination with the unconscious and the irrational, for example, was clearly in evidence in the work of 1920s filmmakers. But in an even more generic sense, the ability to address the "real" as well as the "fantastical," the "actual" and the "imaginary," is part of the expansive nature of cinema's artistic mission. To the extent that psychoanalytic theory also attempts to bridge and integrate these polarities, the attraction to its use as an explanatory device is easily understood. In the mid-1980s, such an attraction became visible. Althusser himself saw benefit in merging the notion of ideological apparatus with key concepts in psychoanalytic theory as resurrected and reinterpreted by theorist Jacques Lacan. Of special importance was Lacan's emphasis upon the mirror stage of human development, where the infant, at the age of six months or after, recognizes one's own image in the mirror. Because the image depicts a fully formed body, at variance with the infant's own underdevelopment, the infant views the mirror image as an ideal, which sets the stage for further forms of external dependency through the association of self with the external object. In his later writings, Lacan reexamined the Freudian notion of scopophilia, or the pleasure of looking as well as the pleasure of being looked at. In Lacan's rendering, the narcissistic pleasure in looking at the other is balanced by an apprehension that the object of our gaze looks back at us, reminding us that we are not in total control of the relationship.

Both the Lacanian notions of the mirror and the gaze were applied to the viewer's experience. Most notably, Laura Mulvey, in her classic piece "Visual Pleasure and the Narrative Cinema," invoked Freudian and Lacanian concepts to construct a feminist critique of filmmaking, noting that at that time, directors of record were almost exclusively male. She specifically argued that the stereotypical trope of the active male/passive female is enhanced within film, as the female image is constructed as a sexual object, satisfying the desire that helps fuel the male gaze. Such objectification leads to the creation of spectacle, an extreme focus upon the female image that competes with the imperative to advance narrative structure. As a result, it is left to the image of the male character, the person of action, to assert responsibility for advancing the story line. As she stated,

> An active/passive heterosexual division of labor has similarly controlled narrative structure. According to the principles of the ruling ideology and the psychical structures that back it up, the male figure cannot bear the burden of sexual objectification. Man is reluctant to gaze at his exhibitionist like. Hence the split between spectacle and narrative supports the man's role as the active one of forwarding the story, making things happen. The man controls the film phantasy and also emerges as the representative of power in a further sense: as the bearer of the look of the spectator, transferring it behind the screen to neutralize the extra-diegetic tendencies represented by woman as spectacle. This is made possible through the processes set in motion by structuring the film around a main controlling figure with whom the spectator can identify. As the spectator identifies with the main male protagonist, he projects his look on to that of his like, his screen surrogate, so that the power of the male protagonist as he controls events coincides with the active power of the erotic look, both giving a satisfying sense of omnipotence. A male movie star's glamourous characterizations are thus not those of the erotic object of the gaze, but those of the more perfect, more complete, more powerful ideal ego conceived in the original moment of recognition in front of the mirror. (Mulvey, 2016, 625–6)

The perpetuation of patriarchy through the use of film was one example of the way in which the industry contributed to marginalization of group identity. Richard Dyer, in examining the use of lighting in film, has pointed to its glorification of whiteness as a default cultural norm. In so doing, he has noted the ways in which lighting is differentially applied to white and Black actors to accentuate the centrality of the former as well as the ways in which lighting is used to associate positivity with whiteness. As he states,

> Movie lighting focuses on the individual. Each person has lighting tailored to his or her personality (character, star image, actorly attributes). Each important person that is. At a minimum, in a culture in which whites are the important people, in which those who have, rather than are, servants, occupy center stage, one would expect movie lighting to discriminate against non-white people in terms of visibility, individualism, and centrality. I want however to push the argument a bit further. Movie lighting valorizes the notion of the unique and special character of the individual, of the individuality of the individual. It is at the least arguable that white society has found it hard to see non-white people as individuals; the very notion of the individual, of the freely developing autonomous human person, is only applicable to those who are seen to be

free and autonomous, who are not slaves or subject peoples. Movie lighting discriminates against non-white people because it is used in a cinema and a culture that finds it hard to recognize those as appropriate subjects for such lighting, that is, as individuals. (Dyer, 2016, 666)

In recent years, the structuralist perspectives that have led to the trenchant critiques of the film industry, with regard to its perpetuation of state capitalism, misogyny and patriarchy, racism and white privilege, have themselves received some criticism. Viewing film as an ideological apparatus of the state does not take into account the globalization flows that are redefining what state is and what boundaries dictate its authority. It further fails to adequately assess how state capitalism transforms itself in different settings. Mulvey's use of psychoanalytic theory as an analytical tool for examining misogyny and patriarchy has also been criticized for not withstanding the test of time. The essentialist and decontextualized nature with which gender roles are ascribed is viewed as being problematic; the rise of the LGBTQ+ civil rights movement and the awareness its presence has created, along with increased recognition of the importance of gender fluidity, challenge some of the traditional assumptions of psychoanalytic theory as applied to film. Similarly, the essentialist assumptions inherent in whiteness theory when applied to cinema studies have also raised similar questions. More generally, there has been a generic reconsideration of the degree of agency inherent in the viewer role. Be it Benjamin or Althusser, Metz or Mulvey, theorists have repeatedly questioned the extent to which the viewer is conscious and aware of the filmmaker's efforts to manipulate images in support of one's agenda(s). More recently, Daniel Morgan has argued, in contrast, that viewers are aware of camera manipulation and that they don't simply view the camera as an extension of their own perceptions. In making his argument, he notes that the camera can never replicate with a strong degree of exactitude the visual process we naturally experience. He further notes that there are a variety of camera shots to which viewers are exposed, belying the assumption that we are only viewing reality through the eyes of the characters upon whom the camera is focused. Indeed, according to Morgan, the tension between experiencing broad camera movement and specific point of view focus upon individual characters is only resolved through the viewer's appreciation of one's own independence in processing the information received on the screen (Morgan, 2021).

Laura Marks has offered an even broader critique of conventional film criticism, arguing that a preoccupation with the mechanical processes of visual perception has skewed analysis in an unfortunate direction. From Marks's perspective, the power of film lies in its triggering of haptic associations. In her view, the critical emphasis on visual imaging to the exclusion of the ways in which all of our senses are activated when viewing a film is misplaced, although it is the appeal to the sense of touch which creates the most powerful of memories. She further argues that at its best, international film can be especially provocative to audiences unfamiliar with the cultural norms they express, particularly because of their holistic appeal to all of our senses (Marks, 2000).

Morgan's and Marks's writings represent efforts to move away from the rigid determinism implicit in structuralist explanations of the filmmaker/spectator relationship. In so doing, Marks explicitly notes the importance of affect in constructing the essence of that relationship. Taken together, their work exemplifies contemporary sensibilities that reject overly prescriptive and rigid explanations for human interactions. At the same time, their presence is indicative of the evolution of film criticism, from its early emphasis upon director prerogative, aim, and behavior (montage, devotion to realistic representation, personalized style, and adherence to structuralist rule-governing norms) to a more sophisticated explanation of viewer perception of and active determination of cinematic meaning.

Evolution of the Documentary

Five of the twelve films discussed in this volume are nonfiction films or what we would generally consider to be documentaries, in the sense that they display images of live events. As was noted in Chapter 1, film, in its earliest inundations, as produced by the Lumiere Brothers, was little more than short recordings of daily incidents. Documentaries were popularized by Russian filmmakers and in particular Dziga Vertov, who in the aftermath of the Russian Revolution edited the newsreel series called *Kino-Pravda* (film truth) using aesthetic techniques to convey political messages (Wells, 1999, 216). American filmmaker Robert Flaherty produced the first commercially viable film in 1922, *Nanook of the North*, followed by *Moana* in 1925 and *Man of Aran* in 1934. In these works, Flaherty framed his subjects as struggling against natural forces in order to survive. In so doing, he used the camera to create for his audiences a traveler's gaze that romanticized and exoticized his subjects. Although he depicted some actual events in live time, he staged other events that failed to correspond to contemporary practice, in order to reinforce his thematic perspectives with his audience (Wells, 1999, 217–18).

As the example of Flaherty's film attests, and as Vertov's films demonstrated, the line between fiction and nonfiction within the documentary genre has always been ambiguous. In the 1930s, the use of live images in support of political messaging was pervasive. Film historians have cited Scottish documentarian John Grierson's work as initially employing the form in the service of social commentary, but later working to produce propaganda in support of the British war effort during the Second World War. Leni Reifenstahl's *Triumph of the Will*, noted in Chapter 1, was an egregious example of documentary propaganda but certainly not the only one of its kind. Indeed, even after the war, Grierson was instrumental in helping to produce instructional films in support of British colonialist policies, blurring the distinction between commercial and publicly funded documentaries (Rice, 2019, 16–20).

With advances in technology including the use of shoulder and handheld cameras, proponents of direct cinema created documentaries in the 1960s and 1970s that appeared to be less overtly controlled and scripted than their alternatives. Subjects frequently ignored or lacked awareness of the camera's presence which operated as a "fly on the wall." Cinema vérité proponents, on the other hand, following in Vertov's footsteps, believed it is necessary to acknowledge the subjective nature of the documentary process, viewing the recording of actual events as an expression of the filmmaker's vision (Wells, 1999, 225–6). Suffice it to note that the questions involving the authenticity of visual representation, the relationship of filmmaker to audience, and the difference between creative expression and viewer manipulation, all of which have characterized critical discussions of fictional projects, have remained salient to a discussion of the documentary form as well.

International Film

As this is a book about international film, it is appropriate to return to Laura Marks's assertion that international films have the potential to be creatively disruptive, encouraging their viewers to grapple with the unfamiliar, expanding their awareness in the process. But is this in fact true? Does the act of viewing a film that expresses distinct cultural difference compel us to examine existing assumptions we hold about ourselves and the world in which we engage, or does the act of viewing encourage us to reflexively reassert the primacy of our own beliefs when we are exposed to profound cultural difference? Rey Chow has written persuasively about the promotion of Orientalism through the act of film viewership, particularly when one brings to the cinema screen a lack of deep understanding of or appreciation for historical and cultural contexts. In writing specifically about the viewing of Chinese film, but in terms of reference that are generically applicable, Chow questions whether the viewing of international film under such circumstances gives permission to the outside spectator to shape one's view of Chinese society in one's own image, reinforcing a form of cultural domination Edward Said so eloquently critiqued, as the displays of gender roles and other depictions of traditional forms of repression become essentialized (Chow, 2016).

Although even in its origins, film production was characterized by its international diversity, the influence of the Hollywood studio system cannot be underestimated in dictating its content and form. Dudley Andrew has argued that film production evolved in distinct phases he labels as cosmopolitan, national, federated, world, and global. In the cosmopolitan phase, although the Hollywood studio system had achieved dominance by the 1920s, an audience of sophisticated international elites, situated in major international cities, was able to access US and European films shortly after their initial showings. During the national phase, films became closely associated with their countries and regions of origin, supposedly exemplifying the linguistic, cultural, and stylistic influences specific to the location. The discovery and use of sound as a key element in film production, enhancing the importance of linguistic distinctiveness, contributed to the creation of national cinemas, with respected actors prominent in national theaters being recruited to the nascent film industries. In Andrews's view, the federated phase of cinematic development occurred after the Second World War, in reaction to the destructive excesses of nationalism that had encouraged mass destruction. Film festivals, which had begun in the 1930s, became federated with the creation of organizations such as the International Federation of Film Producers Associations and the Fédération Internationale de la Presse Cinématagrophique (for film critics). At the same time, the promotion of UNESCO's universalist and humanitarian values at film festivals proved to serve as a counterweight to those who continued to view film as only representative of nationalist sentiment. By the 1970s, new film festivals were established and existing ones made concerted efforts to better showcase offerings from newly emerging and previously ignored national cinemas. Finally, Andrew notes that the effects of globalization, including the ability to more easily network and share film products, the speed with which films can now be distributed through internet and other platforms, and the increased ease of making one's own films, have transformed world cinema into a more inclusive global variant (Andrew, 2016).

Other film critics, while not necessarily agreeing with Andrew's exact typology, point to certain trends in the development of various national cinemas that reiterate a number of his general themes. Certainly, the growth of art cinema in post-Second World War Europe can be viewed as an effort to break away from Hollywood studio hegemony. Similarly, in the 1960s and the 1970s, proponents of Third Cinema argued for using cinema in support of national liberation, rejecting the hegemonic influences of both Hollywood and Europe (Solanas and Getino, 1969, 1983). Nonetheless, as will be discussed more fully in Chapter 3, the power differentials that favor the Global North in the global circulation of cultural artifacts such as film continue to operate in contemporary settings.

Affect Theory and Film

The evolution of film theory and criticism as outlined earlier offers a further case for applying the principles of affect theory to the study of film. The issues film critics and theorists have tackled are not only consequential, but they touch upon ontological questions that have been raised for centuries. To what extent is what we see on the screen real as opposed to a series of manipulations? How active are we in creating meaning from what we see rather than simply reacting to screen images in a passive way? And how conscious are we of the efforts to manipulate our sensibilities? All of these questions touch upon the nature of the encounters we experience and their intensities, the acts of meaning-making and assemblage with which we engage, and the condition of contingency that characterizes so much of contemporary life. The theorist most associated with affect theory, who has written extensively about the nature of film from a set of philosophical perspectives, is Gilles Deleuze, who in his two-volumed series, *Cinema 1* and *Cinema 2*, argued that one can see in the history of film an evolution from an emphasis upon movement to an emphasis upon time. The concepts that buttress his analysis are also key to an understanding of the importance of affect.

In *Cinema 1*, Deleuze borrows heavily from the writings of Henri Bergson, who made a distinction between the use of the intellect and the use of intuition in comprehending reality. Bergson argued that through use of our intellect, we analyze reality in static terms, and the viewing of film mirrors that process. As Donato Totaro notes,

> In several essays and in the final chapter of Creative Evolution (1907), Bergson employs what he calls the "cinematographical apparatus" as an analogy for how the intellect approaches reality. The analogy appears within Bergson's

epistemological dualism, where intuition is placed alongside the intellect as a means of acquiring absolute knowledge. According to Bergson, "movement is reality itself" (*The Creative Mind*, 169). The intellect is by nature a spatializing mechanism, which means to acquire knowledge it employs concepts, symbols, abstraction, analysis, and fragmentation. Hence, the intellect can only express movement—reality itself—in static terms.... Bergson likens this process to the cinema apparatus. The camera begins with a real movement, breaks it down mechanically into a series of static single frames and then returns the movement through the projecting apparatus. The movement that we see is a reconstituted illusion. (Totaro, 2001)

Interestingly, Bergson's skepticism of the cinematic experience echoes Benjamin's mistrust of the camera as an artificial, mechanical device whose usage intrudes upon the creative process. Deleuze, however, was less pessimistic about the possibilities of cinema representing movement realistically. He saw this in evolutionary terms, noting that the use of montage, a mobile camera, and the implementation of disparate viewpoints rather than reliance upon the single shot contributed to the camera's increasingly realistic depiction of movement, claiming that these were advances through the 1930s and 1940s that Bergson was not able to witness (Deleuze, 1986a, 2017, 3). For theorists such as Deleuze, traditional shots such as the close-up demand viewers' immediate attention without allowing them to interact with the image at a deep level of engagement. Images that were constructed to create tight narrative structures similarly left little to the viewer's imagination. Thus, Deleuze viewed the experimental directors of the 1930s and 1940s as creating new possibilities in the portrayal of movement. Reflecting Eisenstein's understanding of montage, it was understood that filmmaking could become more than the mechanical sequencing of edited images, but instead, an artform that encouraged viewer active engagement and response. In *Cinema 2*, Deleuze argues that post-Second World War filmmakers, particularly those who are associated with Italian neorealism and the French New Wave, were able to move away from the association of movement with reality and instead focused upon time rather than movement as a way of encouraging viewer engagement. Previously, our cinematic experience of time was developed as a subset of our experience of movement, but after the Second World War, the time image became predominant. Time, of course, can mean many things but for Deleuze it is a concept that evokes transcendence. As a result of efforts that emphasize spatial discontinuities and disjuncture, the viewer becomes compelled to question what one is seeing rather than simply reacting to what is presented. The answer to such a question involves the assertion of meaning that transcends segmented and discrete measures of time. Deleuze thus states,

> But precisely what brings the cinema of action into question after the war is the very breakup of the sensory-motor schema; the rise of situations to which one can no longer react, of environments of which there are now only chance relations, of empty any space-whatevers replacing qualified extended space. It is here that situations no longer extend into action or reaction in accordance with the requirements of the movement-image. These are pure optical and sound situations, in which the character does not know how to respond, abandoned spaces in which he ceases to experience and to act so he enters into flight, goes on a trip, comes and goes, vaguely indifferent to what happens to him, undecided as to what must be done. But he has gained an ability to see what he has lost in action or reaction: he SEES so that the viewer's problem becomes "What is there to see in the image?" (and not now "What are we going to see in the next image?"). (Deleuze, 1989, 2013, 272)

To a degree, Deleuze's commentary foreshadows the writings of those who rejected structuralist interpretations of the viewer role. But more importantly, the principles of affect theory, which he helped define, are present in his commentary on film. It is the intensity of encounter that results in viewers establishing an embodied relationship with the art form. It is through assemblage that filmmakers construct and deconstruct images that push forward the creative process, and it is through assemblage that viewers themselves share and give meaning to an art form on a mass scale. The time image is so important to Deleuze's analysis, specifically because it encourages viewers to make meaning rather than simply react to what they experience. And, it is the embrace of contingency, as expressed through irrationality and uncertainty, that offers the opportunity for film to be experienced in ways that are exciting and illuminating. In writing about cinema, Deleuze clearly views the concepts derived from the study of cinema to be applicable to all forms of social practice. As he notes,

> A theory of cinema is not "about" cinema, but about the concepts that cinema gives rise to and which are themselves related to other concepts corresponding to other practices, the practice of concepts in general having no privilege over others, any more than one object has over others. It is at the level of the interference of many practices that things happen, beings, images, concepts, all kinds of events. (Deleuze, 1986b, 280)

It thus makes sense at this point to briefly revisit comparative and international education theory, in light of what we have seen with regard to film theory and affect.

Comparative and International Education Theory Revisited

When scholars write about CIE theory, they are compelled to address fundamental questions involving the nature of education and its relationship to other forms of social experience. What does it mean to be educated? Is education necessarily a social good? How do we know if and why educational endeavors are or are not effective? In order to address such questions, they have relied upon dominant social science and international development paradigms that speak not only to educational practices but to the nature of social relations more generally. How do we evaluate causality and randomness when determining how, when, and why educational events occur? Is conflict endemic to all forms of social interaction? How are identities shaped and how do they become transformed? In spite of the importance of application to the CIE field, it is through the invocation of theory that CIE scholars attempt to make sense of so many different educational experiences that can appear on their face to be as fragmented and disjointed as they are interconnected.

Causality

We rely upon a belief in causality to make order out of our world, and in the case of CIE scholars, such a reliance has been present since its earliest origins. But is such an impulse a realistic rendering of educational experience? Is our reliance upon causation in educational settings natural or self-serving? Historically, the impetus to learn from educational systems and practices different from one's own was coupled with a belief that the acquisition of this knowledge could lead to beneficial educational reform. By discovering educational patterns, practices, policies, and institutions different from one's own that produced varying degrees of effectiveness, one could, through comparison, improve one's own educational system. In calling for a systematic compilation and then analysis of educational data from sources outside of those with which one is most conversant and familiar, nineteenth-century CIE scholars viewed such engagement as an advantageous intellectual response to more informal ways of gathering information about different educational systems, which often occurred through short-term travel and excursion, accompanied by personal observation (jules, 2021). The positivism associated with such a stance is clear, and it has remained a defining characteristic of much of conventional CIE literature since its origins.

But how do you identify what makes a cause or an effect significant, especially when multiple causes and effects are often at play? How does one account for randomness, for causes that are not immediately discernible, for effects that are not readily discoverable? For much of its history, CIE scholars have relied upon conventional social science paradigms to address these questions. Through the first part of the twentieth century, scholars working within the nascent social sciences argued that nations distinguished themselves according to the common traits that their majoritarian groups expressed. Institutions, constructed under such terms, operated in ways that were reflective of the cultural values of such national groups. Thus, in the CIE field, scholars such as Isaac Kandel and Nicholas Hans argued that national systems of education represented the character and values of the citizenry residing within nation-state borders and should be studied in order to better understand the significance of the policies and practices that expressed those values (Marquis, 2021, 30). A unilateral cause/effect deductive relationship was thus assumed.

After the Second World War, the study of public policy grew in importance, as a concerted effort was made to study the nature of policy design, evaluation, analysis, and process. Within the CIE field, one saw a gradual transference of emphasis from the general and normative concept of national system to one that privileged methods for determining causality borrowed from the sciences. Analyses of the various components of educational policy employed deductive methods as a means of understanding their importance. The prospect was one of isolating factors that contributed to policy formation or impacted its execution and effectiveness. Brian Holmes, for example, argued that Karl Popper's notion of science as falsification, whereby we look to disconfirm what might be theoretically posited in order to verify its truth, should be employed as a means of deducing what types of educational policies should be employed, which ones were useful and why. All policies should thus be subject to rigorous testing based upon adherence to scientific method (Holmes, 1977; Trethewey, 1976). Others, such as Noah and Eckstein, while still proponents of a deductive approach, relied upon the work of M. R. Cohen and E. Nagel in arguing that scholars should analyze patterns of covariation among the variables they were investigating, as a means of discovering salient nomothetic principles that could be applied more generally (Noah and Eckstein, 1969; Holmes, 1977). In their view, the beauty of comparison resided in its possibilities for creating scientifically valid generalization. At the same time, they implicitly recognized that an embrace of covariation was necessary in order to avoid the challenges of defending a search for unilateral cause/effect relationships, which was both an overly simplistic and artificial means of depicting social interactions. Today, a reliance upon the "scientific" aspects of conventional social science methodologies remains a significant component in CIE research. Nonetheless, the affirmation of deduction as the best tool for conducting comparative investigation has never been universally embraced.

George Bereday, for example, writing in the early post-Second World War era, believed that one should conduct comparative inquiry through induction, positing a four-step process including description, interpretation, juxtaposition, and comparison, a model for which German scholar Franz Hilker was also a proponent (Adick, 2018). Although his system proved to be overly complex and impractical for many engaged in the comparative research act, his perspective is still notable for its rejection of deduction at a time when there was considerable pressure to apply the deductive principles of scientific method to educational issues. Others, in the 1970s, noted the unintended consequences of negative factors given little initial attention in the prediction of positive educational outcomes such as credentialism in assessing the limits of global educational provision (Dore, 1976). In the United States, Christopher Jencks's use of path analysis to chart the connection between educational attainment and social inequality found that the most important set of factors responsible for determining one's social position ultimately involved luck (Jencks, 1972). And, in more recent years, others have viewed the difficulty in replicating research findings as a more generic weakness in educational research of all types (Makel and Plucker, 2014). Such skepticism begs the question as to how one should appropriately recognize the randomness of educational interaction, acknowledging that even when unpredictable, such interaction can still be extremely consequential. Throughout the late twentieth and early twenty-first centuries, a number of scholars have at least recognized such unpredictability as an endemic feature of globalization, be it through the notion of "scape," to describe the fluid nature of various cultural, technological, and economic flows (Appadurai, 1996), or "risk" (Beck, 1992; Giddens, 1991). Zygmunt Bauman's notion of "liquid modernity" further captured the incessant nature of change and flux in all aspects of social experience (Bauman, 2012). But, as has been previously noted, a comprehensive rejection of the more rigid conceptions of causality associated with empirical social science inquiry is evident within the principles of affect theory. The mere recognition of affective intensities of varying duration and effect, the notions of assemblage and dis-assemblage that posit a more dynamic accounting of social interconnection, and the overall embrace of contingency that characterizes much of affect theory offer a forceful refutation to the views of causality that have been embedded in some of the CIE research.

Conflict

Determining whether conflict is endemic to various forms of social, political, and economic interaction lies at the heart of social science research. Making such a determination has ramifications for one's view of a society's cohesiveness, how power is exercised, and how wealth is acquired and distributed. It has further implications for deciding whether education is an intrinsic social good and whether educational failures can be ameliorated or rectified. The tensions that arise from the way in which one addresses the nature of social conflict have correspondingly been a part of CIE research and scholarship as well.

In the aftermath of the Second World War II, social scientists reiterated their faith in the power of the state to initiate social reform through use of the social scientific methods. Their form of positivism became a key component in newly arising international development strategies, reflecting the Cold War assumptions of the Western powers with regard to the role of education in various aspects of economic, political, and social development. It is for this reason that proponents of human capital theory, modernization theory, and structural functionalism all coalesced around the same time period to express a shared set of nomothetic assertions. Together, such beliefs embraced the basic assumptions that in a society that was becoming more complex, productivity was based upon the creation of an increasingly skilled workforce, that societies in their natural state operated under conditions of equilibrium, that social conflict was an unnatural by-product of institutional ineffectiveness, easily correctable through modest policy reform, and that a well-informed, well-educated citizenry was essential to the creation of democratically responsive government. Education was of course asserted to be a key element in contributing to social cohesiveness, political stability, and economic productivity. However, given the Cold War setting in which these theories were propagated, when applied to international development considerations, their ideological imprint was clearly visible. In the race for global political influence, investing in education would not only allow a developing country to progress economically, but would immunize it from Soviet influence. Investing in schools would speed up a country's democratic trajectory, encouraging its political modernization in ways that would ameliorate internal political conflict and divisiveness. If educational opportunity was inequitably distributed, it could be expanded upon or be reallocated. If there were systemic inequities within an educational system that privileged some individuals over others, those inequities could be redressed. Such was the promise of educational expansion and/or educational reform (Karabel and Halsey, 1977; Tonini, 2021).

The premise that holds social interaction to be nonconflicting in its natural state has outlasted the Cold War era; it is evident in updated human capital and structural functionalist orientations, but also in other perspectives that examine global educational interrelationships. Niklas Luhmann's systems theory approach, for example, has been used in ways that seek to explain how education sectors complement and distinguish themselves from other institutions in social spaces. He has emphasized the notion of autopoiesis in discussing the ways in which social systems maintain and renew themselves, a process expedited not simply through the influence of external sectors but through communicative events, whereby meanings are negotiated and socially constructed. CIE scholar Jurgen Schreiwer has relied upon Luhmann's insights in arguing that national education policymakers, when exposed to external policies circulating within global spaces, pursue a process of externalization, whereby they reshape and reinterpret such policies to insure their national contextual relevance (Parreira Do Amaral and Erfurth, 2021). Gita Steiner-Khamsi (2004) has further applied Schreiwer's notion of externalization to educational borrowing and lending processes, arguing that national ministries don't mechanically accept the dictates of external international funding agencies and resist engaging in a dependency relationship with such units as they actively negotiate and reframe the terms of educational borrowing and lending.

Human capital and structural functionalist orientations have been largely applied to groups operating within discrete boundaries, often at the national or regional level. Systems theory has been applied to the interface between those operating within national education systems and international funding agencies, organizations, and institutions. Neo-institutionalism is a third perspective that views social organization in consensus rather than conflict-oriented terms, and it asserts its relevance to educational institutions operating at local, regional, national, and global levels. Conceived as an alternative to rational choice theory, neo-institutionalists have sought to examine how institutional norms (in our case involving the education sector) have spread globally, coupling or decoupling with local, regional, and national policies and practices (Wiseman, 2021).

The alternative to consensus-oriented frameworks is one that asserts that conflict is a natural function to group social interaction and is endemic to all societies. An understanding of racism, sexism, sexual orientation, classism, ableism, religious discrimination, and so on, cannot be fully realized without appreciating its pervasive nature. Within the educational context, social conflict is evident not only in the disparate allocation of educational resources and in the denial of educational opportunity, but it can be perpetuated and exacerbated by educational policies and practices themselves. On a global level, the consensus-oriented theories that were invoked to support the liberal world order that was constructed by the United States and its Global North partners in the aftermath of the Second World War II were directly challenged for their embrace of superpower hegemony at the expense of peripheral countries and their creation of compliant elites within those countries. Thus, the writings of scholars who championed dependency theory and world systems analysis, such as Andres Gunder-Frank (1966) and Immanuel Wallerstein (1989), were applied to policy issues involving educational development assistance, scholarly research, language usage, and academic training (Altbach, 1977; Arnove, 1980; Kelly and Altbach, 1984). Proponents of social reproduction theories argued that schools played a direct role in encouraging working-class students to pursue working-class jobs (Bowles and Gintis, 1976) or were structured in ways that favored middle and upper-class students to the detriment of their working-class counterparts. Theorists with post-structural orientations, such as Basil Bernstein and Pierre Bourdieu, examined the ways in which the possession of linguistic codes and cultural capital, in relation to the use of curricular and pedagogical styles and choices, privileged middle-class students and families (Bernstein, 1977; Bourdieu and Passeron, 1971). But even those who rejected structuralist and post-structuralist approaches viewed schooling as directly complicit in perpetuating class conflict. Paul Willis, in his classic work *Learning to Labor*, for example, argued that working-class youth in the UK consciously and intentionally rejected the meritocratic values schools were propagating because they clashed with the working-class notions of performative masculinity to which they had been socialized. His point was that these "lads" were not simply victims of an oppressive educational structure but resisted the conformist pressures of schooling rituals through expressing their own agency (Willis, 1977).

In more recent years, considerable attention has been paid to an examination of the effects of neoliberalism upon educational practice and policy. Although enabled by globalization trends, neoliberalism has its own specific ideological proclivities: encouraging consumption fueled by financial investment and speculation over the traditional production of goods and services as a driver of economic wealth; eliminating some basic public services and privatizing others for the purposes of facilitating structural adjustment; supporting government interference to promote selected private entities in the name of efficiency while also paying lip service to the importance of competition, and so on. Critiques of those international organizations encouraging privatization in the midst of structural adjustment have been part of the CIE literature for decades

(Klees, Samoff, and Stromquist, 2012) but such criticism has tended to focus upon the inequitable consequences of such policies. It has been left to others to test the core assumption that educational provision in its purest form provides generic benefit. For example, education's role in perpetuating global inequality has been explored by those investigating its role in helping to produce state-sponsored knowledge-based economies in competition with one another (Sum and Jessop, 2013). And, in recent years, some CIE scholars are calling for an even more fundamental rejection of the modernist assumptions involving education through their embrace of decoloniality, as a theoretical option that categorically rejects educational modernism for its complicity in fostering Global South educational subservience to the Global North (Andreotti, 2011).

Within the affect theory literature, issues of conflict are also addressed within the assemblage/dis-assemblage frame. To the extent that assemblage and dis-assemblage are viewed as naturally occurring processes, they don't fall into stasis or conflict polarities given their impermanence. The importance of intensity in conceiving of what one's social positioning means is also significant insofar as it gives focus to the ways in which affiliations become embodied. Such a recognition offers a more comprehensive sense of the nature of social acceptance, privilege, marginalization, and oppression (Emery, Powell, and Crookes, 2023). It thus becomes implausible to separate issues of identity from those of causality and conflict within the affect of an axiom that also holds true for affect theory and CIE.

Identity

Issues of identity within the CIE literature are evident when one analyzes how scholars address questions involving the appropriate scale of comparison to be pursued, the ways in which objects deemed worthy of comparison are identified, and the degree to which educational actors are viewed as having the potential to successfully express their agency. The field has historically shown deference to the nation-state, geographical region, and cultural group as defined units worthy of educational comparison. But scholars in the field have also invoked patterns of even broader generalization and classification on a macro level. The tension that has resulted from a failure to address these polarities has resulted in contrasting methodological approaches. On the one hand, much of CIE research is conducted in case study form representing the units described earlier. The fact that one may be writing for an audience different and/or broader than one's own has traditionally offered justification as to why the work is generically comparative. Nonetheless, an appreciation for the implications of transnationalism, with political conflict, economic dislocation, and environmental uncertainty contributing to large population groups suffering severe and lasting displacement, demonstrates the limitation of relying upon traditional boundaries for units of comparative analysis (Bartlett, Oliviera, and Ungemath, 2018; Oliviera, 2018; Bartlett and Ghaffar-Kucher, 2013).

On the other hand, there is a significant segment of CIE literature that focuses upon larger scale research, be it through assessment data (such as PISA), higher education university rankings regimes, or international development indicators. Skeptics have noted that there has been a fetishization of data collection, to the point whereby educational data accumulation has taken on a life of its own, without due appreciation for its limitations, in efforts to drive educational policies in certain directions (Gorur, 2011). Scale, of course, has implications for determining who and what is deserving of attention as part of the comparative project. Is an emphasis upon the decision-making of a policymaker working on behalf of a large international funding organization more warranted than that placed upon the day-to-day experiences of a school teacher working in a developing country? Is tracing the ways in which national ministries of education share information with one another more significant than examining which top-down educational initiatives are embraced or ignored at the local level within a specific country? Is an emphasis placed upon the effectiveness of formal educational institutions on a global level warranted when so many marginalized populations never have an opportunity to engage with said institutions on a sustained basis? Such are the larger dilemmas that CIE scholars regularly confront but are rarely able to reconcile, and in this vein, Lesley Bartlett, Fran Vavrus, and their associates have attempted to balance the specificity generic to the case study approach with the generalizability that a truly global approach demands (Vavrus and Bartlett, 2022; Bartlett and Vavrus, 2017).

The way in which personal agency is framed has serious implications for the ways in which issues of identity are analyzed. Are educational institutions simply appendages of the state or of global governance regimes, or are they actual or potential sources of emancipation? In the 1970s, Paolo Freire, in *Pedagogy of the Oppressed* (1970), as well as in subsequent writings, argued that literacy training was an effective tool for creating personal empowerment, social reform, and political change. Unlike other critics who excoriated educational policies that were viewed as enabling Western domination, Freire's voice expressed a degree of unique authenticity, because it was directly shaped by the experiences of his work in the Third World. Not surprisingly, his consciousness-raising methodology synergized with liberation theology perspectives promoted by Gustavo Gutierrez and others (Kirylo, 2011), and became widely popularized. More recently, CIE scholars have embraced Amytra Sen and Martha Nussbaum's capabilities approach to international development. In viewing the success of international development strategies not simply in terms of discrete indicators that measure the attainment of affluence, health, and well-being, but according to how well those strategies assist individuals in achieving their potential, a broader conception affirming the importance of education as an enabler of agency has been articulated (DeJaeghere and Walker, 2021). But questions remain as to whether either the Freirean or the capabilities approach lose their significance when their applications are overly generalized and decontextualized.

CIE and Affect Theory

The major themes CIE scholars have explored since the field's inception are ones with which affect theorists also engage. The framing of causality is essential to CIE thought because it touches upon questions of structure, agency, free will, determinism, moral efficacy, consequence, and accountability. This is not surprising for a field where the assumption that education is a generic public good and an agent of social reform has rarely been contested. If that assumption were to hold true, then there should be a way of demonstrating how the positive effects of one's educational efforts arise. From the perspective of affect theory proponents, though, an acknowledgment of the random nature of social experience is a more realistic way of examining educational interaction. The rigidity in the structure/agency dichotomy is replaced with an emphasis upon intensity that allows for a broader appreciation of the range of educational interactions that can be as ephemeral as they are transformative, but are not necessarily explainable or reduplicative. Embracing such unpredictability can feel discomforting in the immediate sense, but the possibility of conceiving of educational experience in more expansive terms allows for a more realistic appreciation of their complexity.

For affect theorists, the conflict/consensus divide is most directly addressed through their notions of assemblage and dis-assemblage. Here again, while aspects of both consensus and conflict are acknowledged as characterizing how social groups operate, it is the impermanence of either tendency that is of crucial importance. In addition, there is a sense of flexibility attached to notions of assemblage and dis-assemblage that is absent in traditional discussions of group affiliation, stratification, cohesiveness, and dysfunctionality. For example, the assemblage/dis-assemblage model holds particular salience when analyzing twenty-first-century social movements, which are more frequent and intense but of shorter duration than earlier counterparts (Butler, 2018; Epstein, 2019, 145–70). In the second part of this work, the prevalence of conflict as part of our social experience is directly acknowledged in the form of discussions focusing upon social class, racism, coloniality, environmental justice, and their relationship to education. But when one examines the importance of affect as represented in film, it is possible to at least occasionally see more nuanced views of social conflict than those that are typically depicted in the educational literature.

Questions of identity lie at the heart of CIE research as they speak to the importance of scale, the appropriate subjects for inquiry, and the nature of empowerment. In their discussions of intensity, assemblage, and meaning-making, affect theorists also address similar concerns although with distinct perspectives. Is the act of reducing educational experience to a set of data points a suitable means of accurately representing the nature of that experience? Void of a recognition of the importance of the intensities that comprise that experience, affect theorists would respond in the negative. Can one legitimately focus upon the functioning of institutions operating at macro or micro levels without examining how they connect to and interact with one another? Affect theorists would again offer a negative response but would point to notions of assemblage and dis-assemblage as a better way of examining such interconnections, a stance more recently espoused by CIE scholars Florin D. Salajan and tavis d. jules (Salajan and jules, 2023). The connection between affect and meaning-making also finds resonance in the CIE literature that speaks to agency and personal empowerment, in the voices of Freire, Sen, and Nussbaum, although affect theorists would include in their analyses an acknowledgment of contingency that is not evident in other writings.

Conclusion

We have noted that the areas of film theory and CIE theory have broad similarities. As these are fields that are centered around different domains of social practice, the questions that they compel us to address are substantive. How do we know that what we represent as being true is authentic? What makes the relationship between filmmaker and viewer or scholar and research subject affirming, as opposed to constricting or harmful? Who really controls the production and exchange of images, of ideas, and in what ways are these entities reshaped in space and time? We have argued that theories of affect hold the promise of energizing both of these fields. In the case of film theory, the reconsiderations of how movement and time are represented have opened up creative possibilities for encouraging artistic creativity while actively engaging viewers. Other elements of affect theory contribute to a reconceptualization of the field that takes into account the ways in which we use all of our senses to make meaning from an art form that has mass appeal. In the case of the comparative and international education field, a reconceptualization of what causality, conflict, and identity mean for educational policies and practices is fundamentally important, at a time when traditional notions of educational theory and practice have become increasingly contested, while certain aspects of affect theory, including intensity of encounter, meaning-making, assemblage, and contingency, speak directly to the embodied characteristics of education as a social practice in the twenty-first century.

3

Globalization, Commodification, and Affect

Throughout this project, comparative and international education discourse and film theory and study have been depicted as being cultural objects. We have noted the similar intellectual trajectories that characterized theoretical developments in both areas, but have yet to fully explore how as cultural objects, they are created and then globally disseminated. In rectifying this omission, we concede that they exist in global settings that foster the ambiguity, precarity, and contingency affect theoreticians emphasize. Given the speed with which cultural products are circulated, conventional assumptions regarding the discrete and bounded nature of time and space are questioned, as is our ability to understand the past, control the present, predict the future, and protect sense of place (Bauman, 2012). At the same time, we also live in a world that perpetuates neoliberal hegemonic practices, practices that foster exclusion and marginalization in support of Global North domination. The film industries and the creation of various forms of educational provision reflect these realities, as do the knowledge domains that frame our understandings of their operations. It thus becomes a challenging task to reconcile the dueling experiences of precarity and hegemony that characterize contemporary global interactions. We approach the task by first tracing the development of film study and comparative and international education as academic disciplines. We then examine how they have been transformed into commodified cultural products, and finally, we analyze the ways in which they have been affected by the globalization cross-currents that mark contemporary social experiences. In so doing, we reiterate the importance of theories of affect in aiding our analysis. Rather than viewing the construction of identity solely in terms of the commodities we acquire, be they in film or in the educational practices to which we are exposed, affect theorists, through their emphasis upon intensity, meaning-making, and assemblage, view commodification processes as significant but not entirely determinative in shaping our beliefs and actions. Rather than viewing global neoliberalism as an uncontested hegemonic force, affect theoreticians focus upon its complexities and the varying intensities while chronicling the ways in which various actors assemble and disassemble from one another within its various permutations. And, rather than viewing the contingency that commodification processes invite as being inherently alienating, affect theorists embrace the creative possibilities that contingency necessitates.

Initial Elements in the Construction of the Academic Study of Film

The history of film is marked by a number of seminal events, two of the most important being the aftermath of the First World War, and with the discovery and implementation of new technology, the transition from the silent film era to the production of films using sound. In its early years, a number of centers, including those in Paris, New York, Italy, Japan, and Scandinavia, promoted the creation and distribution of commercial film. Over time, Paris and New York began to take over the field, with Hollywood supplanting New York in importance after the First World War, as the US film industry asserted its global dominance. One consequence of the war was that European film industries were unable to secure the resources necessary to compete with their Hollywood counterparts on an international level. As a result, Hollywood studios took advantage of the situation (Bakker, 2008). "During 1913, the United States exported 32 million feet of film; by 1925, this figure had risen to 235 million feet" (Shao, cited in Lee, 2008, 373). Between these years, US film exports to Europe increased by 500 percent, and by the 1920s, Hollywood accounted for four-fifths of all film screenings in the world (Shao as cited in Lee, 2008, 379).

To be clear, French filmmaking continued to play an influential role in film production in the 1920s, as did German filmmaking. The newly established Soviet Union provided the space for film artists who developed an ideological counterweight to Western initiatives. However, the US film industry had the financial resources and means to create products that generated mass appeal, and as a result, even noted German and French filmmakers migrated to Hollywood to further their careers. A key factor in the growth of the studio system was the ability to control both the production and distribution of film, and as the five most important studios were able to vertically integrate their operations, their influence grew accordingly. Others point to the size and wealth of the English-speaking market when examining reasons for the ascending US global domination of the film industry (Lee, 2008, 374). It is not surprising that by the mid-1920s, leaders within the European film industries lobbied for the trade protectionist relief from their own governments, while Hollywood leadership pressed the US government for free trade accommodations.

In 1923, short films using synchronized sound technology began to be produced, and in 1927, *The Jazz Singer* became the first major feature-length film to use sound with dialogue. The ramifications of the transition from silent to sound-incorporated films were global in nature. Silent films implicitly asserted that their images conveyed a universality of understanding, with their emphasis on gestures and movements that audiences could recognize regardless of one's specific linguistic or cultural background. With the use of sound, there were new opportunities to invest in and promote national film industries, which could more directly serve the interests of their audiences (Druick, 2008, 71–2). As a result, there were two competing trends that influenced the global development of film in the 1920s and 1930s. On the one hand, Hollywood studios capitalized upon the synchronization of sound with image and enhanced the medium's commercialization. On the other hand, the "talking" picture promoted the notion of supporting a liberal world order, grounded in nationalist cultural expression, exemplified through the emergence and in some cases reemergence of national film industries. Even if nascent national film industries could not compete on a resource basis with their Hollywood counterparts, their presence reiterated post–First World War beliefs in the power of national self-determination to promote such a new world order. The shift, from its cosmopolitan origins, to Hollywood domination, to the cultivation of national cinemas in different regions, reaffirms Andrew's analysis of the early stages of cinematic development (Andrew, 2016).

One of the more visible ways in which national cinemas were promoted was through the creation of the film festival. The first international film festival originated in Venice in 1932 and was followed by other European counterparts such as Brussels (1935) and Cannes (1939). From its beginnings, the Venice Film Festival displayed nationalist and fascist influences. Benito Mussolini viewed the motion picture as a useful propaganda tool and worked to sponsor a state-run Italian film industry that would be immune to Hollywood control and would confront the growing importance of Soviet experimentalism. With this goal in mind, the International Exhibit of Cinematographic Art, formed as a part of the Venice Biennial Exhibition of Italian Art in 1932, was created with the intent of making the latter more diverse and eclectic. Venice became an annually scheduled event in 1935, and as its pro-fascist ideological bent became increasingly clear, the notion of creating an international film festival in Cannes was explicitly promoted as a counterweight to Venice. When pro-Nazi

German films were repeatedly recognized for their artistry in its international film category to the exclusion of French and other noteworthy submissions, the necessity of finding credible alternatives to the Venice Film Festival became particularly pressing (Film Reference, n.d.). Unfortunately, one day after the first international festival in Cannes began, Germany invaded Poland, launching the Second World War. The Cannes festival as we now know it was ultimately resurrected in 1946.

The film festival was only one of many ways in which film began to be taken seriously as an important social phenomenon as opposed to being conceived of simply as a mundane form of popular entertainment. From its origins, intertwined with the goal of promoting national film industries, there was a recognition of the importance of embracing the educational and artistic function of film in contradistinction to its commercialism. Initial efforts to research and study film from an educational perspective emphasized the importance of understanding the medium's influence upon mass behavior with particular attention paid to its impact upon children and youth. In the United States, the Payne Fund Studies, established in 1929, relied upon sociological research emanating from the University of Chicago to investigate problems of urban decay, publishing a twelve-volume study, *Motion Pictures and Youth*, in 1933. The sociologists viewed these problems as emanating from the failure of immigrants to successfully socially assimilate, but also viewed film as one of many factors in negatively influencing youth behavior (Anderson, 2008, 42–3). The widespread dissemination of the Payne Fund Studies report emphasized the importance of film as a form of mass communication. As has been previously noted, the moral panic concerning its deleterious effects upon the public was a key element in its findings, although fear of the potential harm film viewership could create was certainly not limited to the United States and in fact was also shared in other national settings. However, the Payne Fund Studies projects served to influence the development of film study as a discipline in an important way: it highlighted the importance of conducting social research in the area of film and in creating film experts who could authoritatively speak to film's social significance. The fact that such expertise was broadly based upon what was then considered to be the social sciences and was not simply confined to the dissemination of the technical mastery of film production was especially noteworthy.

There are other elements that are involved in the creation of an academic discipline, and their presence in the 1920s and 1930s was significant. In order to conduct research, for example, there must be a recognition of the need to collect, store, archive, and safely preserve and protect information. In the cases of the United States and the United Kingdom, the Museum of Modern Art (established in 1929) created its Film Library in 1935, and the British Film Institute created its National Library also in 1935, setting the precedent for the professional collection and preservation of film. The creation of a curriculum not only gives existing knowledge an institutional imprimatur, but its presence shapes its boundaries and directs its positioning in reference to other knowledge forms. In Chapter 1, we noted that the University of Southern California established its School of Cinema in 1929, following by a decade the creation of the Moscow film school. In USC's case in particular, the curricular emphasis was focused upon the technical mastery of film production. Further curricular efforts in the United States demonstrated a willingness to broaden the field. In the 1930s, courses initiated at the New School for Social Research (1932), the City College of New York (1933), New York University (1933), Syracuse University (1934), and the University of Illinois Urbana-Champaign (1938) began offering a more expansive range of topics to include film appreciation and history. In 1938, Columbia University, in association with the Museum of Modern Art, began to offer a four-year course of study through its extension division (Groening, 2008).

Curricular innovation does not occur in a vacuum and is often configured as a response to external factors. In this instance, the development of 16 mm film, initially created in 1923 by Eastman Kodak, with a colorized version made available in 1929, made film production more accessible on a mass level. Not only did its invention encourage popular home movies to be produced, but it gave impetus to educational and documentary filmmaking as well. As a result, the divide between the dissemination of commercial film, controlled through the Hollywood studio system, and noncommercial alternatives, labeled as documentaries and/or educational films, grew. Such a divide was not limited to the United States and North America, though, for in their efforts to create national film industries, European countries embraced noncommercial films for their contributions to national cultures, while international organizations, such as the League of Nations, reiterated their importance through its sponsorship of the International Cinematographic Institute from 1928 to 1937 (Druick, 2007). In 1929, the institute founded the *International Review of Educational Cinematography*, which published articles devoted to the promotion and exchange of educational films between various countries. The *IREC* was one of a number of periodicals that focused upon film, a trend that began in 1920 in the United States that included *Visual Education* and *Educational Screen* (in Chicago), *Film Spectator* (Los Angeles) and *Visual Review* (Chicago) in 1926,

Experimental Cinema (Philadelphia) in 1930, and the *Motion Picture Herald* (New York) in 1931. Outside of the United States, *Close Up* (Switzerland) in 1927 and *Film Art* (London) in 1933 represented international efforts to examine film from literary and aesthetic perspectives (Groening, 2008).

The invention of the film festival, the creation of the "film expert" as a result of the Payne Fund Studies, the technological advances that made film more popularly accessible, the construction of formal curricula that extended beyond the teaching of technique and skill mastery, the development of film libraries, repositories, and archives, and the production and dissemination of journals and magazines devoted to the broader discussion of film topics all played important roles in creating disciplinary components for the study of film. The creation of film societies and organizations devoted to a wider, popular distribution of films with accompanying discussions of their importance cannot be underestimated as an additional factor that contributed to film study development. The London Film Society, founded in 1925, was accompanied by similar European iterations, while in New York, Film Associates, Inc., part of the "little theater movement," exhibited international films in more intimate spaces than those reserved for commercial productions. The British Film Institute, founded in 1933, the New York City Film Forum and Film Society, also founded in 1933, the National Film Society of Canada (1935), and the American Film Center (New York, 1938) all centralized efforts to resist the influence of commercialism while promoting alternatives deemed as creative, independent, and educationally beneficial counterparts to the Hollywood mainstream (Groening, 2008). It is important to note that in total, these efforts spoke to a widespread popular fascination with film, regardless of the degree of elite sponsorship or centralized administrative control that some of such efforts invited.

When we think of the role of the academy in disciplining knowledge, we tend to view the process as one requiring the exercise of institutional control initiated within the university. What is apparent in examining the film study example, however, is that periodic efforts to limit the shape and scope of the field were met with external resistance. Attempts to narrow the teaching of cinematic knowledge to the technical aspects of filmmaking were rejected as the popular fascination with the new technology demanded a more robust view of its social importance. Film meant more than the training of workers in support of a newly emerging powerful commercial industry. On the other hand, efforts to attribute the importance of film *only* to its amplification of existing social problems or its potential to remediate their negative consequences were also rejected, in favor of a more expansive view of film as an artistic product. To be clear, film study as an academic discipline fully came into fruition in the 1970s. But these 1920s and 1930s antecedents were influential in shaping later precedents.

There are two general trends that characterized the growing fascination with film that deserve emphasis. First, the fact that film as a subject matter held popular appeal prior to being incorporated into the ivory tower and maintained its appeal afterwards guaranteed that discourse regarding film would be generically public. Critics, commentators, and film historians, when writing in film journals and magazines or speaking at film society events, thus eventually were able to take on the role of public intellectual. Indeed, it has been argued that Gramsci's notion of organic intellectual is appropriate here, insofar as film comment became inextricably bound to social criticism (Acland, 2008, 152–3). Second, film discourse occurred within the boundaries of a liberal world order in the aftermath of the First World War, where personal freedom and self-determination were conflated with nationalism and its assertion of the primacy of the nation-state. The economic tensions between Hollywood and its national film industry counterparts, and the embrace of nonfiction filmmaking as an alternative to Hollywood's commercial dominance arose in such a setting. But the liberalism that characterized the 1920s and 1930s contained important internal contradictions, contradictions that could encourage, dependent upon setting and time period, the use of the medium to promote not only creative independent expression but colonialism, racism, and rabid nationalism as well. By way of example, as was noted in Chapter 2, the use of nonfiction films to promote colonialist agendas was an important part of film history, and its origins, which began in the interwar period, are indicative of such contradictions.

Tom Rice has written the definitive volume on British efforts to use film in support of colonialist policies and the British case is instructive on a number of accounts. The Colonial Film Unit, established in 1939 as a part of the Ministry of Information, was created in anticipation of the Second World War, for the purposes of affirming the continuing global importance of the British Empire. Its initiation was preceded by the creation of nonfiction films in the 1920s and 1930s that incorporated elements of documentary, educational, and instructional genres, with both British and colonized peoples as their target audiences. Their aims included a desire to affirm the vibrancy of the empire to British citizens by chronicling different experiences within the colonies, offering educational instruction to colonial peoples on various topics including health, hygiene, and agriculture, and portraying an idealized version of life in the UK to colonial audiences. John Grierson, noted in Chapter 2 as a founder of the British Documentary Movement, gravitated to the use of both documentary and educational filmmaking, working with the Empire Marketing Board for the purposes of promoting government trade policies (Rice, 2019, 14). In so doing, he was supported by a Conservative government that was fearful of its citizens becoming "Americanized" or at least susceptible to the positive imagery of US life portrayed in Hollywood films. William Sellers, a sanitary inspector who moved to Nigeria in 1926 and later became head of the Colonial Film Unit, produced numerous training films dealing with local health concerns. He was innovative in filming on-site, using local help, and in traveling to remote communities in Africa where he showed his films, ostensibly for altruistic purposes. Upon becoming head of the CFU, the publication *Documentary News Letter* borrowed from his earlier writings and published in 1940 a list of rules that he argued should be observed in making films for colonial subjects. Their appearance spoke to insipid racism directed toward colonial subjects that was evident in Sellers's thinking.

1. The general tempo must be slow, and the length of individual scenes must be twice or three times as long as is usually considered necessary for English school audiences.
2. The content of any given scene must be very simple in its composition, because natives view all objects on the screen with equal interest, unless the important object is clearly explained. Close and mid shots are therefore preferable to long shots.
3. Strict accuracy is vital in portraying native habits and customs. Mistakes at once turn a serious film into a comedy.
4. No camera tricks of any sort. Continuity must be clearly maintained in all changes of scene, even if it means using three shots elsewhere one would normally do for audiences more used to film technique.
5. Films must be made as silent. A master commentary is then written and is added by a native commentator, or by disc records, through a microphone during each performance. The system is vital, owing to great variation in local dialects. (Sellers, 1940 as cited in Rice, 2019, 65–6)

The racism implicit in the UK colonial agenda is but one of the many elements that contributed to the transition of the study of film into an academic discipline. Those elements did not congeal into a coherent set of practices and understandings until the 1970s, although their origins can clearly be seen during the 1920s and 1930s. As we have repeatedly noted, the growth of interest in film at an international level occurred within a post-First World War, Wilsonian world, marked by conflicting appeals for free trade and protectionism in lieu of US global ascendancy, accompanied by political interests professing various commitments to nationalism, colonialism, and (in the case of Europe) nation-state self-determination. Film, a global cultural object, evolved into a modernist signifier. The League of Nations played an important role in supporting the liberal, colonialist, and nationalist agenda by sponsoring conferences, publications, and offering support for the establishment of film archives and repositories, viewing film as an effective vehicle for transmitting traditional European cultural values. Not surprisingly, its efforts laid the foundation for the creation of UNESCO, with many League officials playing important roles in UNESCO's formation. The decisions to explicitly include the term "culture" as part of its name and to headquarter UNESCO in Paris were testimonies not only of French influence in the formation of the new organization but to the recognition that it was important to explicitly facilitate the global dissemination of knowledge that included European humanist perspectives in addition to scientific and educational knowledge domains. Film was widely acknowledged to play an essential role in this project (Druick, 2008, 80–7).

The Construction of Comparative and International Education as an Academic Field

In the broadest terms, the evolution of CIE during the late nineteenth and early twentieth centuries resembled Andrew's analysis of film theory and practice to which we have previously referred. Early comparative education founders, such as Marc-Antoine Jullien de Paris and Michael Sadler, sought to systematically compile information about educational practices in political and cultural settings different from their own, for the purpose of chronicling shared commonalities and similarities that could be generally applied. Their efforts to record observations of "other" educational practices resemble the cosmopolitanism that Andrew described as governing early perspectives involving international film. Travelers' tales, where individuals would visit and then anecdotally report their observations to home audiences, were common during the nineteenth century, and the initiatives that sought to chronicle such observations in a systematic way mirrored the positivism that gave rise to the modern social sciences. Their efforts can be labeled as cosmopolitan insofar as they recognized that educational practices in settings different from their own had value that deserved to be acknowledged. In some ways, such cosmopolitan instincts never left the field, as the utility of engaging in travel for purposes of educational investigation has been repeatedly acknowledged throughout the twentieth century, and in the United States, it was crucial in highlighting the importance of international education description and analysis.

After the First World War, a shift in emphasis occurred, with greater consideration given to better understanding of national educational systems. Such an emphasis was buttressed with the creation of institutions including the International Institute of Columbia University's Teacher College, supported by funding from the Rockefeller Foundation, the Institute of International Education in New York, where offering international students study opportunities in the United States was promoted, and the University of London Institute of Education. In these years, annual yearbooks, edited by Isaac Kandel of Teacher's College International Institute (1922–44) and by Lord Eustice Percy, of the University of London Institute of Education (1932–40), were important vehicles for promoting comparative and international education engagement (Bo, 2020; Mallinson, 1952). Kandel's *Comparative Education*, the first comprehensive publication in the field, reflected the predominant thinking of the time, comparing national education systems holistically from historical perspectives (Kandel, 1933). Contemporaries such as Nicholas Hans took a similar approach (Hans, 1964). Indeed, the League of Nations' International Committee on Intellectual Cooperation, which was also influential in promoting the production and circulation of film as a humanistic enterprise (Druick, 2008, 70), sought to promote the teaching of national histories within an international frame of reference (Osborne, 2016). However, as was true of the attitudes toward noncommercial film, comparative and international education proponents were not immune from invoking colonialist/Western-centric frameworks in their efforts to fuse their internationalist orientations with an embrace of European and Western nationalism. Lord Eustice Percy's comments, upon the publication of the British Yearbook of Education, are instructive in this vein.

> If the common features of British education at home and overseas are to be intelligently observed ... it is necessary to study British education against the background of the educational systems of other nations. There is an educational tradition common to the whole of Western Europe and America, and the student must beware of attributing to British education qualities or defects which the British empire shares with all countries whose cultural origins lie in the Roman Empire, in Roman Christianity and in the Renaissance. He must know something too, of education in other countries, especially in Asia, whose cultural history has been so different. (Percy, 1932, as cited in Mallinson, 1952, 61)

Teacher College International Institute leaders Paul Munro as well as Kandel at times expressed similar sentiments in their writings (Takayama, 2018), although Kandel's *The Making of Nazis* (1935) was an unequivocal refutation of nationalist extremism (Null, 2020, 40). Daniel Friedrich and Nancy Ku Brandt offer an in-depth analysis of the ways in which such colonialist attitudes began to permeate the field through analyzing international students' doctoral dissertations completed at Teachers College from 1900 to 1920. They place the dissertations into three categories: the encyclopedic, the comparative, and the psychometric. The encyclopedic dissertation asserted a degree of universal comprehensiveness that belied the authors' decision-making in including or excluding certain information, gearing the dissertation writing toward a Western audience. The comparative dissertation focused upon an educational problem or issue across national boundaries, ensuring that the Western-influenced subject initiating the project remained the authority determining not only the scope of the investigation but also the efficacy of suggested problem-solving solutions. The psychometric dissertation invoked scientism and privileged measurement as universalist factors contributing to the authority of the researcher, which was asserted in accordance with one's expertise in employing such methods (Friedrich and Brandt, 2021). These themes, as has been previously discussed in Chapter 1, continue to be visible to differing degrees within contemporary CIE scholarship.

It is important to note, though, that as a product of the interwar years, they were reflective of a liberal/modernist world order that also influenced the noncommercial elements of the film industry and their academic beginnings. What globalization meant at this time involved a mixture of viewpoints that were often contradictory. The fascination with new technologies that allowed for expedited travel across borders and continents and the enhancement of mass communication created an embrace of education as a key to better international understanding, along with an allure for film as a potentially powerful educational device. Such enthusiasm, though, was counterbalanced with efforts to preserve a European-dominated world order, seriously shaken as a result of the First World War. The reflexive appeals to nationalism and colonialism that characterized many of the frames through which education and film were portrayed defined the limits through which liberal internationalism would be pursued. We also see those limits in the contradictory reactions to the growth of fascism in the 1930s. The Venice Film Festival's increasingly blatant embrace of fascism was matched by the move to create the Cannes Film Festival as an alternative; the transformation of the *International Education Review* into a pro-Nazi propaganda journal (as noted in Chapter One) occurred only a year before Isaac Kandel's antifascist *The Making of a Nazi* was published. Not surprisingly, "experts" who channeled their advocacy for noncommercial film dissemination and comparative and international educational inquiry worked with both the League of Nations and later the United Nations in seeking support for their aims.

Systemic changes that occurred in the aftermath of the Second World War produced lasting consequences for film industries on a global basis. They additionally created trajectories that reshaped the comparative and international education field. To a certain extent, the practices enumerated in our discussion of the interwar years were reinforced. In other ways, they were replaced with those that were more accommodating to the exigencies of a Cold War and post-Cold War environment.

Post-Second World War Cinema

The dissolution of the Hollywood studio system was one of the more important events that occurred in the early post-Second World War era. In 1948, the US Supreme Court ruled in the *U.S. vs. Paramount* that studios had to divest their theater chains because their ownership was in violation of antitrust law. The power of the system lay in the ability of the studios to vertically integrate all aspects of filmmaking including production, distribution, and exhibition. With the 1948 ruling and Howard Hughes's subsequent sale of RKO studios to the General Tire and Rubber Company in 1955, the Hollywood studios began the process of relinquishing their control over film exhibition. Some of the other components of vertical integration were transformed as well. Eventually, actors no longer were required to sign contracts obligating them to complete multiple films over a seven-year period. Instead, they were now contracted on a film-by-film basis. Studios also began to at least partially relinquish control over film production, ceding more control to independent producers and production companies, focusing more exclusively upon financing and distribution responsibilities (Bakker, 2008). At the same time, as suburban neighborhoods expanded, and as television became more popularly accessible to middle-class families, interest in cinema viewing became stagnant. Together, these factors contributed to increased competition for viewership, with producers catering to a variety of niche markets in order to appeal to audience interest while maximizing profit. As a result, the cinema experience became redefined as a form of cultural engagement associated with a higher level of status than that afforded radio and television.

There was a considerable level of financial support for reemerging national film industries in postwar Europe, as their governments viewed film as a catalyst for promoting reconstruction and social cohesiveness. Access to television occurred later in Europe than in the United States, as did opportunities for homeownership and suburban residential growth. The confluence of these factors gave impetus to the development of national cinemas supporting both commercial and noncommercial endeavors. National film industries could now survive without being consigned only to documentary and educational film genres.

It is not surprising that, given these trends, the international film festival grew and reestablished itself as an important vehicle for the global circulation of film in the 1950s and 1960s. The Venice Film Festival, suspended completely in 1942, was reestablished in 1946. The Cannes Film festival in its modern iteration also was started in 1946, and in 1951, the Berlin Film Festival was created, intending to bridge the ideological Cold War gap between Soviet and capitalist filmmaking. The London Film Festival was initiated in 1953, at the behest of British film critics, and the New York Film Festival, modeling itself after its London counterpart, was established in 1963. Cannes, Venice, and Berlin established themselves as the premier international film festivals but in 1978, the Toronto Film Festival was created, succeeded by what would be later labeled the Sundance Film Festival. Today, there are thousands of film festivals that are held around the world, many but not all organized according to theme, genre or region of origin (Film Reference, n.d.)

Although they are generally operated by nonprofit associations, prestigious film festivals have forged links with production companies who are constantly looking to secure potentially profit-making projects. The tensions that occur as a result of supporting independent artistic creation because of its importance as a social benefit and investing in profitable ventures because of their commercial viability may have always existed within the film industry but now became apparent at this level. At least through the 1990s, the film festival's growing popularity demonstrated how film industries, particularly in the United States but also in other Global North countries, extended their ability to control the production, dissemination, and marketing of films relying upon the techniques of modern global capitalism. On the one hand, festivals invoked the ideology of capitalism: encouraging independent filmmakers to compete for festival admission through an open submissions process subject to jury screening and evaluation. The promise was that designation as an official festival selection and perhaps afterwards, further recognition gained through receipt of a festival prize or award would lead to a contract with a major production company, enhancing the possibilities for even wider distribution. On the other hand, the fact that in some cases films were preselected for public viewing on the basis of director notoriety or the publicity the film had already received belied an unequivocal commitment to open competition and unbiased critical review. The growth of the film festival was but one affection of what globalization came to entail in the 1970s and 1980s. As the dissolution of the studio system meant that US production companies could no longer directly control the film products they created and distributed, so the competition for access to resources that would allow them to reassert their dominance became intense and reached global proportions. As European film industries began to prosper with the support of their national governments, US companies started to make films on location in Europe as a way of reducing production costs. At the same time, in the 1960s and 1970s, some filmmakers consciously adapted Hollywood production values and styles even as they crafted works embedded within their own national and cultural settings, the Italian Spaghetti Western, and the explosion of Bollywood musical spectacles being noteworthy examples. To be clear, a recognition of what globalization implied during this time period meant negotiating the demands of a global/local dichotomy: creating a cultural object reflective of one's own sense of identity and sense of place but cognizant of the need to appeal to broader international audiences (conditioned by North American proclivities), in order to obtain maximum recognition and transnational value for one's product. Certainly, the transformation of English into a global lingua franca made the use of English subtitles for films produced in non-English speaking countries an absolute necessity. Even so, the struggle to obtain global recognition for one's work was always a precarious undertaking, although as leaders of the Third Cinema movement noted, Global North bias in determining what films rose to the level of deserving international respect, let alone acclaim, was (and continues to be) prevalent.

The Emergence of Film Study as a Discipline

Dudley Andrew traces the contemporary origins of film study as an academic discipline to the efforts of French film advocate Gilbert Cohn-Séat, who, after starting the journal *La Revue internationale de filmologie* in 1948, secured the support of the Sorbonne in 1950 to create an institute that would bring together scholars who would write and give lectures about film. From the start, his ambition was to apply interdisciplinary perspectives involving the humanities and social sciences to investigations involving film (Andrew, 2009, 889). Given the fact that film critics, independent film societies, and journals played an important historical role in promoting French film, the promotion of *filmologie* as a separate academic discipline was met with a certain degree of ambivalence, if not all out hostility and by the 1960s, the journal ceased to exist. The notion of restricting the study of film to within the walls of the academy ran counter to this tradition. As Andrew notes,

> An emergent *filmologie* foundered after a single decade because it was linked to the changing profile of higher education and research rather than to that of its subject; cinema's value ballooned worldwide, and especially in France, in the 1950s, yet *filmologie* took little note of this and did not try to abet it. Aiming to analyze the everyday experience of film, not to contribute to its advancement, *filmologie* set itself at a distance from such growing cultural manifestations as international film festivals, federations of ciné-clubs, upstart journals, and repertory movie theaters that brought an art form out of the circus of mass entertainment and into the high life of discriminating culture. As cinema attained its majority, its place in the university seemed reserved in advance. And so it happened; cinema infiltrated the universities of France, as well as the U.S., Britain, and elsewhere. However, student interest in this newly available academic subject came not from *filmologie* but was incubated in the (chiefly French) ciné-club movement and the journals that fed cinephilia, especially *Cahiers du cinema*. These in turn were tied to the growth of cinema as an art. (Andrew, 2009, 890–1)

However, in spite of such tension, film study became increasingly popular as an academic endeavor during the 1970s in France, the United Kingdom, and the United States. In further examining its evolution as an academic discipline, there are factors worth considering. In the United States, the effects of student protest in support of civil rights and in opposition to the Vietnam War created pressure for educational reform, insofar as broad critiques of mainstream institutions included those of the academy and their distance from the social and political struggles of the day. One can see a similar phenomenon in examining the effects of the May 1968 protests in France. The widespread expansion of the film studies major spoke to students' broader demands for coursework within the academy that would be more socially relevant. Within formal academic circles, film theory gained legitimacy when scholars began applying structuralist principles to the study of film, merging interests in linguistics with psychoanalysis and neo-Marxist thought (see Chapter 2; Andrew, 2009). As the field of cultural studies gained momentum, its commitment to interdisciplinarity and its embrace of both humanities and social science concepts also offered those pursuing film studies a comfortable location within the academy to pursue their interests. The accompanying changes to the industry that we have described, which encouraged a recognition that the importance of film could not be appreciated by simply considering its formal geographical and cultural origins, but had as a cultural product obtained global significance, further served to establish film study as a legitimate area of inquiry worthy of research and teaching at the higher levels within the academy.

The Emergence of Modern Comparative and International Education

As has been noted, comparative and international education was established as an academic field prior to the Second World War, but its visibility grew significantly afterwards. A number of exogenous factors contributed to its ascendancy. The World Bank and International Monetary Fund were created in 1944 as a result of the Bretton Woods Conference, which established the parameters of the postwar international monetary system. In 1945, UNESCO was created, with comparative education scholars playing a significant role in the formation of its education sector, and in 1946, the Fulbright Program was initiated in the United States, supporting international educational exchange among US and international scholars and students. Of crucial importance to US higher education institutions was the passage of the National Defense and Education Act of 1958, which offered federal funding at the higher education level for language and area studies training. Asian, African, Latin American, Russian and East European, and Middle Eastern study centers were created with national support as a result. The Peace Corps, established in 1961, which sent US youth to developing world countries, proved to be an incubator for future CIE students and scholars. All of these initiatives supported CIE development in the United States. The World Bank and UNESCO, which set the terms for international educational development assistance, became important sources for CIE knowledge generation and dissemination. The types of international exchanges the Fulbright Program supported facilitated graduate student enrollment and faculty research in CIE areas. Select institutions built upon the area studies model and created their own CIE academic centers, with multiple faculties offering coursework covering educational issues in different geographical and cultural regions (Altbach, 1991).

Higher education in the United States was changing significantly after the Second World War as well. With the passage of the G.I. bill, university enrollments increased, graduate-level curricular specializations proliferated, research universities were able to secure significant federal funding as their numbers grew, and former state-based teacher-training institutions were transformed into comprehensive universities. While CIE in the United States benefited from these trends, the field became closely tied to international development policies and strategies, influenced by US dominance within the world order. Institutional and programmatic formation at this time must therefore be viewed within the Cold War context that shaped international relations during ensuing postwar decades with many of the institutions we have described played a role in furthering the interests of the US and other western capitalist governments.

The massification of higher education also occurred in the United Kingdom, although somewhat later than in the United States. As a result of the Robbin Report in 1963, colleges of advanced technology were given university status, establishing a trend that culminated with the granting of university status to thirty-five polytechnics and other colleges in 1992. Student enrollment grew as well. In the early 1960s, there were approximately 400,000 full and part-time students attending UK universities. By 2003, there were over 2,000,000 students in attendance (Greenaway and Haynes, 2003). The possibility of including comparative education coursework as a part of teacher training, whose institutional status within the academy was improved as a result of these trends, augured well for the field's growing popularity (Sutherland, Watson, and Crossley, 2008). And, as former British colonies gained their independence throughout the 1950s, international educational development became an area of interest and focus, as was true in the US example.

The 1950s and 1960s also witnessed the growth of comparative and international education societies. In 1956, the US Comparative Education Society was born during the third annual meeting of a Comparative Education conference, held at New York University. The impetus to form the society came from the decision to hold a seminar with educators who would be studying and visiting Western European educational systems, as it was felt that if sponsored by an official educational organization, the seminar's status would be enhanced (Brickman, 1977, 397). In 1968, the society amended its name to include the term "international" in its title in an effort to inclusively reflect the differing theoretical and professional proclivities of its membership.

A proliferation of comparative education societies occurred after Comparative and International Education Society (CIES) was established. In 1961, the Comparative Education Society of Europe (CESE) was inaugurated, and in 1966, a British section was started. It eventually became the British Comparative Education Society in 1979, changed its name to the British Comparative and International Education Society in 1983, and after an affiliation with another organization, is now known as the British Association of International and Comparative Education (BAICE) (Manzon and Bray, 2006, 72). Together with CIES and CESE, the Japan Comparative Education Society, founded in 1965, the Comparative and International Education Society of Canada, founded in 1967, and the Korean Comparative Education Society, founded in 1968, comprised the five national societies that were the founding members of the World Congress of Comparative Education Societies, founded in 1970 (Manzon and Bray, 2006, 3). It is noteworthy that these societies served to support academic scholarship and teaching in the field, rather than compete against them. Unlike the tensions present in France regarding the academic embrace of film studies, comparative and international education societies were viewed as useful in making a relatively small academic field more internationally visible. The current annual membership of the Comparative and International Education Society, the largest of its type, for example, now exceeds 3,000, while as of 2006, there were thirty-five different national, subnational, regional, and language-based societies that formed part of the World Council of Comparative Education Societies (Manzon and Bray, 2006, 1).

A major purpose of professional societies is to disseminate ideas through conferencing and publication. In the case of comparative and international education, the periodic academic conference, sponsored by various professional societies, serves such a purpose. In so doing, it has played a similar role to that of the film festival in showcasing works in progress and work products. The various conference formats, with their reliance upon both the peer-review process for proposal submissions and their sponsorship of select invited presentations, echo the use of juried-approved submissions along with those predesignated for showing during film festivals. With the exception of local or regional conferences, the use of English as the global lingua franca dominates. The publication of scholarship is another important function of the academic society. In the case of CIE, the *Comparative Education Review*, the official publication of CIES, was started in 1957, one year after the society was founded, while *Comparative Education*, associated with CESE, was founded in 1964, and *Compare*, associated with BAICE, began publication in 1975. Here too, the major publications in the field have been in English with some noteworthy exceptions (Wilson, 2003).

Film study became a formalized academic discipline in the 1970s; comparative and international education expanded its academic footprint during the same time period. Interestingly, CIE grew as sister subdisciplines declined in popularity and suffered from dwindling institutional support. Independent areas of inquiry such as the history, sociology, politics, and anthropology of education, separated by their distinctive methodological approaches, were combined into educational policy programs and departments that obfuscated their distinctive perspectives, at least in the United States. And while employment prospects were and have been extremely limited within academia for scholars in CIE as well as these other areas, the growing importance of international development work has served as an employment channel for CIE graduates seeking to remain engaged in CIE issues.

We have noted that through the 1980s and 1990s, for those involved in the film industry, globalization was defined by the continuing domination of Global North institutions dictating the terms with which local, regional, and national films received international attention and support. At the same time, with state support at the national level, independent filmmakers were given increased opportunity to pursue their creative visions. In the case of the international education development sector, one sees the continuing influence of intergovernmental organizations with Global North origins, such as the World Bank, UNESCO, US Agency for International Development (AID), the Organization for Economic Cooperation and Development (OECD), and so on, as well as the expanded number of nonprofit organizations (in 2022 numbering over 40,000) all operating within a global environment where neoliberal policies were in ascendance (Leverty, n.d.). Within the education sector, such policies included efforts to privatize education, measure educational attainment on a comparative basis, eliminate inefficiencies and corruption while providing resources for economies that were increasingly becoming knowledge-based. As was discussed in Chapter 2, comparative education scholarship has often been critical of such policies as well as their neoliberal assumptions more generally. At the same time, though, the field as a whole profited from the consequences of those assumptions: through the growth of international student study and exchange in the Global North, enhanced funding opportunities IGOs and NGOs provided to universities for research and policy, and increased employment opportunities with international development agencies provided to qualified graduates. As altruistic as the intent of some of such practices may have been—expanding educational opportunity to alleviate poverty, promoting literacy, reducing gender discrimination, and supporting public health and safety—CIE scholars, students, and practitioners operated with a worldview that accepted the unequal power dynamics of Global North/Global South interactions as a given; in many cases, they profited from the results of such interactions.

Commodification

For both the film industries and various educational sectors, an evolving understanding of what globalization entailed meant acknowledging the existence of forces that extended beyond conventional local, regional, and national borders. Those forces coexisted with neoliberal policy-making agendas that served to reassert institutional dominance in the Global North. If the Hollywood studio system no longer controlled the international film industry in as direct a way as it did prior to the Second World War, film industries in the Global North continued to exert significant if more indirect influence over international film content, production, and distribution through the 1970s and 1980s. At the very least, central to the growing awareness of the power of globalization was an understanding that there was an international audience willing to view one's work wherever one was situated, irrespective of where and to whom one's artistic product was immediately directed. However, the terms of such engagement would remain dictated by market forces favoring Global North industries.

Within educational sectors, upon becoming popular in the Global North, neoliberal educational policies were transferred to Global South regions, with public/private funding and administrative educational partnerships, *Teach for All* teacher-training projects, and international efforts to comparatively assess educational achievement being noteworthy examples of the trend. However, with the proliferation of NGOs and IGOs, the kinds of unilateral and bilateral arrangements common in the 1960s and 1970s among such organizations and national education ministries became less clear-cut, even if institutional Global North influence remained potent. As was true of the film study case, while the presence of globalization trends became increasingly appreciated, the *nature* of globalization interactions began to change in the late twentieth century as basic assumptions governing the dynamics of global capitalism became increasingly contested.

Technological change and shifting consumer preferences heavily impacted film industries in the 1980s and continue to do so in the twenty-first century. Within the United States, the relationship between television usage and cinema viewing became more complicated with the growth of cable television, as well as with initially VHS and later DVD options. One result was that a clear hierarchical demarcation between television and cinema with regard to their signifiers as forms of low brow versus higher order cultural expression became muddied. Another result was that as media consumers were afforded more viewing opportunities, niche programming exacerbated audience fragmentation. In more recent years, the ascendancy of the internet and the growth of streaming companies have shaded the difference between television and cinema to an even greater degree, with such companies actively producing media in both venues (Scott, 2002).

Certainly, the experience of attending cinema as a valued social event has been challenged, with the arrival of radically increased opportunity to view film in the privacy of one's home, on one's computer screen, or even on one's tablet or cell phone. But what is perhaps even more significant than the increased ease of access to film viewing is the changing understanding of what film means, with the cinema experience in its entirety having become increasingly commodified. The proliferation of films that are internationally circulated enhances a consumerism that heightens a consumptive mentality on the part of viewership. With the exercise of choice so highly valued, one's viewing pleasure becomes tied to what is fashionable, current, or in receipt of international recognition. On the other hand, filmmakers confront the truism that the heightened competition for international acclaim becomes a factor in defining professional success and the worth of one's work product. Commodification thus occurs as these considerations define cinematic interactions, even if they are so alien as to and separate from the interpersonal nature of the viewing experience or the creative elements of the production process.

It is not surprising that in light of the speed and volume with which cultural flows have increased, the nature of film study as an academic discipline correspondingly has changed in the late twentieth and twenty-first centuries. Currently, academic units place film studies under the more general umbrella of media studies, in deference to the technological advances that have democratized film production, enhanced its accessibility, and accelerated its delivery. To be sure, film is being viewed as one of a number of texts, be they electronic or otherwise; the influences of the internet and social media, with particular regard to image capture and sharing, have significantly influenced and repositioned the study of film per se. In some ways, the reframing of film as one of a number of communicative devices reverts to the early history of film study, with its emphasis upon analyzing the nature of mass communication with its social scientific rather than humanistic repercussions.

Changing educational policies have also reflected the increasing tendency to view educational provision as a series of commodified objects. As was noted in Chapter 2, a long-standing infatuation with the importance of measurement as a key factor in determining and evaluating educational policy has encouraged participation in international efforts to assess comparative student performance among national educational systems with particular regard to the Program of International Student Assessment (PISA) and the Trends in International Mathematics and Science Study (TIMSS) projects. The increased popularity of global university rankings regimes at the higher education level is another example of efforts to quantify, categorize, and label institutional quality. In these cases, the notion of education being a process of intrinsic value is rejected in favor of a view that attaches its worth to performative outcome. Comparative and international education scholarship has both reflected and expressed criticism of these trends but as is true of the film study field, there is a recognition of the increasing importance of commodification in defining what globalization entails.

Commodification involves the process of turning a relationship into something that can be bought, sold, exchanged, and consumed. It has always existed in some form as an essential component of economic activity, but its application to social and cultural spaces has, in the late twentieth and twenty-first centuries, become directly tied to globalization forces. How so? To begin with, the very nature of global capitalism has changed as a result of enhanced information access and the speed with which global transactions are now negotiated. The growth of financial industries and their displacement of traditional modes of capitalist production is one consequence of such a change. As a result, investment has become increasingly speculative, as incentives for short-term profit as opposed to long-term investment in production and manufacturing proliferate. Indeed, the search for short-term profit has encouraged the hollowing out and elimination of businesses, rather than efforts to preserve, protect, and enhance their long-term viability, for which we have traditionally become accustomed. What has also fundamentally changed is an embrace of the uncertainty that accompanies such speculative activity. Because capital is so easily movable and because access to information is so fluid, there is little consequence to investment failure, with new ventures and opportunities in the digital economy arising. The global repercussions of such economic behavior have been felt in social and cultural realms as well. As has been noted, globalization flows, in mimicking economic behavior, have created increased individual freedom to choose and consume products made valuable through their global circulation. But the uncertainty and unpredictability that characterize their duration influence our relationship to these objects as well as our social relationships more generally. As Zygmunt Bauman so eloquently notes,

> In a world in which deliberately unstable things are the raw building material of identities that are by necessity unstable, one needs to be constantly on the alert; but above all one needs to guard one's own flexibility and speed of readjustment to follow swiftly the changing patterns of the world "out there." (Bauman, 2012, 85)

> Whether genuine or putative to the eye of the analyst, the loose, "associative" status of identity, the opportunity to "shop around," to pick and shed one's "true self," to "be on the move," has come in present day consumer society to signify freedom. Consumer choice is now a value in its own right; the activity of choosing matters more than what is being chosen, and the situations are praised or censured, enjoyed or resented depending upon the range of choices on display. (Bauman, 2012, 87)

It is one of the important paradoxes of globalization that the urge to exercise freedom of choice through engaging in consumerist selection leads to uncertainty and unpredictability. Bauman's contention is that the drive to engage in such behavior is rooted in the fantasy that one can exert control over one's life, if even for the short term, when one acquires consumptive objects. This is the point whereby one associates one's identity with these desirable objects. To be clear, processes of commodification as related to consumerist behavior of course did not begin in the late twentieth century. Nor has such behavior been contingent upon the strength of globalization trends. As was mentioned in Chapter 2, Walter Benjamin and Susan Sontag independently expressed caution about the way in which the photographic image influenced social behavior because of what they viewed as its inherently consumptive character. And, as was also noted in Chapter 1 within the educational realm, efforts to commodify cognitive ability through the use of intelligence testing have had a long and sordid history predating contemporary globalization interactions. What makes contemporary commodification processes distinct, and what ties them more directly to what we think of as globalization, is the way in which they have reordered conventional understandings of time and space. The diminishing respect for routine and the faded reliance upon time as a control mechanism over daily experience are consequences of twentieth and twenty-first-century globalization. The heightened degree of movement and rejection of place permanence is an additional attribute (Bauman, 2012, 91–129).

Ironically, if the aim of projecting a sense of personal identity onto the material object of desire that one wishes to consume is to produce a degree of control over one's life, such an aim is never fulfilled or realized under such conditions. Indeed, the opposite feelings of general impotence, generated by global conditions beyond one's control, tend to percolate and fester.

Affect, Globalization, and Identity: Moving Forward

Throughout this volume, we have argued that an embrace of affect theory offers a compelling alternative to Bauman's notion of "liquid modernity." Instead of fearing uncertainty and contingency, affect theorists argue that it is natural to embrace its presence. Instead of viewing the world through the lenses of individual choice as posited in opposition to communitarian obligation, theorists embrace the notion of assemblage as a more flexible way of negotiating these polarized categorizations. And, rather than viewing our relationship with material things as items we seek to acquire and then devour and destroy, proponents of affect theory view the human relationship with material things to be much like our relationships with living things insofar as such relationships are dynamic, interactive, and much less one-sided. Although it is difficult to reconcile these competing versions of human experience, the larger and more important question is whether one needs to do so.

If we look closely at the vicissitudes within our daily encounters, one might conclude that the contradictory desires we have noted: to exercise choice or submit to passivity, to exert overt control over our interactions or to embrace contingency, to accede or to challenge authority, to view oneself in a state of transiency or permanence, to identify with or remove oneself from institutional association all play a role in characterizing what human experience entails. Recalling the work of Graeber and Wengrow, discussed in Chapter 1, a fair reading of our collective history reiterates the variety of ways in which we have pursued differing and at times contradictory strategies for negotiating relationships with one another and our natural world without any one set of actions consistently predominating over time. It is my personal view that theories of affect offer a more inclusive view of how to best understand such interactions, but insofar as the ways in which we seek to formulate and express our identities are myriad, Bauman's insights regarding globalization's challenges must be taken into account.

In examining more broadly how the study and practice of film and filmmaking have evolved, and in analyzing how we address questions regarding the ways in which educational practice has manifested itself on a global basis, it is clear that there are a number of considerations that should be recognized. For example, in spite of the enhanced possibilities for worldwide recognition that have been actualized as a result of the potency of contemporary globalization forces, neoliberal structures governing film production, marketing, distribution, and recognition continue to be powerful. English remains the global lingua franca with regard to subtitle dialogue; the festival system continues to serve Global North industries who pick and choose what they hope will be commercially viable for their audiences, and aspiring filmmakers must continue to negotiate the demands of filmmaking within national contexts while cultivating global recognition. In reflecting these tensions, the study of film as an academic discipline has necessarily been forced to make accommodations to the power and influence of new media, where image-making has become more democratized, the venues for display of one's work more varied, and the theoretical threads connecting these various forms of artistic expression more fragmented.

When analyzing changes in global educational practice, and examining the ways in which the comparative and international education field has reacted to such changes, it is clear that scholars are well aware of the creative and intellectual limitations of modernist perspectives that continue to place their faith in Western social science-driven policy prescriptions. Critical scholarship that makes the case for decolonizing educational provision and decolonizing the academy, noted in Chapter 2, is supportive of such a critique. However, it remains paradoxical that the conditions under which such critical scholarship is produced continue to perpetuate Global North institutional domination while the audiences for whom such scholarship is directed continue to also be centered within the Global North.

In examining comparative and international education scholarship, and in analyzing international films that address issues of common concern as articulated within that scholarship, a Global North-dominated world order that continues to perpetuate neoliberal sensibility places limitations upon the ways in which education and education-related experiences are framed and depicted. We have made the case that even while acknowledging the presence of these limitations, there are spaces for creative insight and alternative viewpoint that are worth exploring. It is the premise of this volume that such an exploration can best be achieved through using the tools of comparison to note the similarities and differences in the ways that CIE scholarship and selected international films treat topics of similar concern. In Part II, we focus upon twelve works that use the moving image to investigate aspects of social experience that have educational resonances. In comparing their perspectives with those expressed within existing CIE scholarship, we hope to question existing assumptions, gain new insights, and further pursue evolving understandings. The themes that are discussed in Part II of this project, involving the relationship between education and social class, race, colonialism and indigeneity, and environmental justice, speak to the issues involving affect, identity, social structure, agency, and globalization that have heretofore informed our discussions in the first part of this project. They reiterate the importance of and the creative possibilities for engaging in comparison.

Part II

Case Studies

4

Social Class

Oppression and Aspiration

Social Class and Education

The academic literature that focuses upon the relationship between education and social class is robust and is indicative of the centrality educational provision has played in framing our understanding of the nature of social interaction and its relationship to the state. It is difficult to name a more important concept within the social sciences than that of social class as its presence speaks directly to how societies are organized, how the state is constructed, and how globalization forces are activated. Although our understanding of its meaning has evolved over time, the presence of education's role in contributing to what social class is and how it functions has been consistently acknowledged. The films selected for discussion and analysis in this section highlight the importance of affect in considering what social class means and how it impacts our daily lives. In these works, social class becomes more than an intellectual construct. Instead, it becomes a marker for the alienation, pain, violence, and uncertainty their characters regularly experience. Although depicted as a social class marker, education in these films is far from a panacea for the repression and social inequality their characters confront.

Karl Marx and Friedrich Engels were the first great modern thinkers to invoke the notion of social class as an explanatory device that spoke to how societies are structured and why social conflict occurs. Their analysis defined the concept in terms of the means of production, or the ability to exercise control over the nature of one's work, and explained that throughout history, social conflict arose over who exercised such control and under what conditions such control was enforced. Not only was class conflict endemic to and a natural characteristic of social interaction, but social progress only occurred through its temporal resolution. Thus, when comparing earlier historical epochs where social classes were defined by the slave/master and then the serf/lord relationships, the class division endemic to industrial capitalism, involving workers and factory owners, or the proletariat and the bourgeoisie, represented a form of historic social progress. This was true because the proletariat exercised more freedom of movement and control over their lives than did their slave/serf predecessors, while the collective nature of their factory working conditions set the predicate for a future socialist revolution, whereby the proletariat would finally gain control over their own work.

As capitalism has experienced a number of iterations, traditional understandings as to what social class entails have correspondingly evolved. The growth of corporate capitalism in the twentieth century, along with the development of the bureaucratic state, influenced the creation of a professional managerial class which positioned itself between the proletariat and bourgeoisie. As the work of the managerial class involved mental as opposed to physical labor, the importance of education as a vehicle for professional training became increasingly tied to class positioning. An embrace of bureaucratism as a positive set of values meant accepting the desirability and inevitability of meritocracy as an "advanced" form of social organization, and here too, meritocratic principles were embedded within the ethos of modern schooling. During the late twentieth century, financial capitalism became ascendant, whereby financial institutions set the terms for global investment in various companies and enterprises. The financier class, far removed from engaging in the production of goods or services, has obtained inordinate wealth through its focus upon wealth accumulation, attained through evaluating risk and engaging in practices designed to obtain short-term profit (as previously noted in Chapter 3). Its members include elites who promote the benefits of knowledge-based economies on a global level.

The meaning of social class extends beyond social positioning based upon economic determinants, however. The concept has come to include cultural, linguistic, spatial, and psychological attributes, and its presence is equally visible in the worlds of the political as it is in social and economic spheres. It is for this reason that it is not surprising that education would be implicated in any serious discussion of what social class means and how it operates.

For those who saw value in the historical Marxist analysis of class conflict, the unresolved question that one was compelled to address focused upon the reasons why the proletariat proved unsuccessful in creating a durable socialist revolution that would lead to a classless society. Indeed, the leading revolutions of the twentieth century, in Russia and China, took place in societies undergoing nascent industrialization whose proletariat were less well developed than their

Western counterparts. One theoretical thread emphasized the centralization of state power and the ability of the modern state to use its resources to maintain the privileged position of capitalist elites. As was true of some of the film theorists noted in Chapter 2, scholars writing from this perspective, including Louis Althusser (2014) and Nicos Poulantzas (2014), examined the use of state apparatuses to solidify class domination. Educational institutions constitute one type of apparatus implicated in the preservation of class position and the perpetuation of class division. On a broader level, Gramsci's notion of ideological hegemony offered an explanation as to how control over institutions such as schools and the knowledge they transmitted created a widespread subservience to class domination, with privileged classes using educational apparatuses to legitimize and frame their class privilege as being commonsensical. Schools thus became implicated not only as a functional apparatus but as a primary site for class conflict (Giroux, 1981). Other scholarship has emphasized the fact that the state is not a static, unitary entity, and there are contradictions within and among the spaces where its apparatuses operate (Jessop, 1990). Educational institutions correspondingly function in dynamic ways that offer both support of and in opposition to such spaces but not necessarily in coherent ways. As has been repeatedly noted, the widespread circulation of capital has in more recent decades also impacted class formation on a global basis. Theorists looking for explanations as to how capitalism has evolved to emphasize the monetization of labor value have pointed to Rosa Luxemburg's Theory of Accumulation as having foreshadowed late twentieth-century trends (Ypi, 2022), further calling into question the primacy of the unitary state. It is definitely the case that as a result of global capital flows, international elites are less bounded by geographical constraint in accumulating their wealth.

The sociology of education literature offers a more focused and contextualized reiteration of these themes. In Chapter 2, reference was made to the work of Bowles and Gintis (1976), who directly implicated US schools for their complicity in creating class distinctions. In *Schooling in Capitalist America*, they answered the question as to why working-class children were limited to obtaining working-class jobs by highlighting the role their parents played in steering them into the vocational curricular tracks that would foreclose alternative employment possibilities. The authors reasoned that their parents, aware of the limited employment opportunities traditionally available within their communities, guided children into curricular areas that would assure their children of secure employment, regardless of the status or long-term income potential of the jobs for which they were being trained. In his classic work *Learning to Labor*, Paul Willis (1977), as noted in Chapter 2, focused upon schooling in the UK as a site where working-class "lads" consciously rejected the middle-class values enunciated through school rituals, curricula, and interactions. They did so because these values, through asserting the importance of competition, individual achievement, and academic learning, were at variance with the working-class cultural attributes with which the lads identified: physical prowess, sexism, group affiliation, and loyalty. Male teachers were especially disrespected in their efforts to exert control over classroom behavior because the values they represented were considered to be illegitimate, so directly in opposition to the working-class culture with which the lads identified.

As powerful as the writings of Bowles and Gintis and Willis may have been, the work of Basil Bernstein and Pierre Bourdieu was even more influential in focusing upon the structural mechanisms within schools that contributed to social class formation and reproduction. Bernstein (1971), along with Shirley Brice Heath (1983), explained how teachers tended to favor students with middle-class backgrounds, who came to the classroom utilizing elaborated as opposed to restricted linguistic codes. The distinction, based upon parenting styles and family structure, harmed working-class students, as their intellectual capabilities were denigrated by teachers and administrators who assumed that the elaborated linguistic codes, a common feature of middle-class parenting, were unbiased and universally applicable. Bernstein further reflected upon how middle-class parents imposed curricular and pedagogical styles upon all students through manipulating collection codes (the way information was categorized within curricula) and framing (the forms of pedagogical distancing between teacher and student). Working-class parents had little say or recourse to the curricular and pedagogical decisions that were formulated. Bernstein's explanations were written with regard to the UK context but could be applied more generally to other societies experiencing similar class distinctions and conflict.

The view that school was an active site where class conflict played itself out as well as an independent incubator of class formation was forcefully articulated in Pierre Bourdieu's work (previously mentioned in Chapters 1 and 2). Among Bourdieu's important insights was his view that the distinction between the personal and the social was an artificial construct and that one's so-called personal preferences and choices involved an internalization of external conditions, leading to the formation of habituses, or dispositions that framed one's interpretation of human experience. Those habituses were instrumental in students' ability to acquire cultural and social capital, essential components in determining social class affiliation and position. Cultural capital refers to the beliefs, ideas, and knowledge forms that hold broad social value, while social capital refers to the power of social connections with friends and family members that influence class positionality. Schools play the role of gatekeeper, disseminating cultural capital that is deemed valuable by those in power, and they serve as a site where, through personal friendships and associations, social capital of varying value can be acquired. As the cultural capital schools create tends to be more distant from the habituses working classes experience, and as the social connections within school also tend to reflect existing class affiliations, schools function in ways that reproduce class inequality according to Bourdieu (Bourdieu and Passeron, 1971).

Critics of Bernstein and Bourdieu's post-structuralist perspectives focus upon the determinism implicit in their analyses as well as the inflexibility of their approaches. But one of the important benefits of their work is that they were able to view social class in terms that were more expansive than being defined solely in terms of the conditions of work and economic power. They certainly viewed schooling as an important site where class identity was partially shaped and where class conflict was enabled, but the walls defining that site were permeable, reflecting wider currents of class conflict germinating from external sources. It is thus important to reiterate that the meritocratic values promoted by contemporary schooling, including specialization of task as one proceeds through the educational ladder, competition for individual recognition on the basis of graded academic achievement, and rule-governing procedures universalizing behavioral expectations, implicitly favor those who identify with or aspire to be part of the professional/managerial class.

Two questions remain. First, does it make sense to think of the professional/managerial or middle class as a unified, coherent, bounded entity? Erik Olin Wright, in his classic work on contradictory locations within class, argued that the professional/managerial class was unique insofar as its members relied upon the labor of other workers for income in part but did not have the same degree of independence as did traditional capitalists; they themselves were also forced into working at the behest of others (Wright, 1985). The ambiguous nature of teacher work and the overall social treatment of the teaching profession in the United States, whose members experience evolving restrictions placed upon their autonomy and an increasingly limited opportunity to exercise choice with regard to their pedagogical and curricular options, offer an applied example of such a contradiction (Apple and Jungck, 1990). For Wright and his followers, the condition of being middle class thus presented an inherent degree of instability.

A second question forces us to wonder whether it makes any sense at all to conceive of social class as a universal constant. Certainly, proponents of affect theory and assemblage theory more specifically would be critical of efforts to rigidly define or apply the concept in a non-contextualized manner. They would further question whether it is even conceivable to imagine an elasticity to the concept that would continue to preserve allegiance to the notion of class distinction. It is my contention that an examination of three films—*Parasite, A Separation*, and *Still Life*—may offer us a more nuanced appreciation for what social class entails and what its relationship to education may portend. An analysis of these three films may not fully satisfy theoretical critiques as to what social class is and what its relationship to education involves, but they can shine light on these concerns.

Parasite (Gisaenchung)

Synopsis

Parasite, the 2019 South Korean film, directed by Bong Joon-Ho, who also cowrote the screenplay and coproduced the film, was the first non-English film to win the Academy Award for best picture of the year during the 92nd Academy Awards ceremony. In addition, this widely acclaimed film won Academy Awards for best director, best original screenplay, and best international feature film, and won the Palme d'Or award at the Cannes Film Festival, also in 2019. As of 2020, it had won 138 prizes and 167 nominations from prestigious festivals and film societies (Koehler, 2019). Director Bong had previously received international acclaim for his films *Snowpiercer* (2013) and *Okja* (2017), his prominence indicative of a robust South Korean film industry that came of age during the mid-twentieth century (known as its Golden Age). Severely restricted during years of dictatorship, the film industry was resurrected in the late 1990s and now has achieved global status and recognition. Directors and actors such as Bong have formed associations with US studios, which have also established subsidiaries in South Korea.

The plot of *Parasite* is somewhat complicated, but in its essence is a tale critiquing capitalism and social class exploitation. At the beginning of the film, the viewership is introduced to the Kim family, who struggle to make ends meet through engaging in temporary work and living in a small semi-basement apartment. Ki-woo, who lives with his father, Ki-taek, mother, Chung-sook, and sister, Ki-jung, is encouraged by friend Min-hyuk to pose as a university student and help Da-hye, the daughter of an affluent family, the Parks, prepare for the English portion of the university entrance examination. Min-hyuk is about to travel to study abroad and thus suggests that Ki-woo take the job. As engaging in such tutoring is generally reserved for students already enrolled in the university, Ki-woo, with the help of his sister, forges university credentials and lands the position. Eventually, in addition to Ki-woo, other family members take on service positions for members of the Park family. This occurs as the Parks are manipulated into firing or forcing the current position holders out of their positions. Ki-woo's sister is hired to teach art therapy to the Park's young son, Da-song, his mother becomes the Park family housekeeper, and his father takes over as the Park family chauffeur. In spite of their scheming and dishonesty, and their exploitation of the unsuspecting Park family employees, we feel a sympathy for the Kims. Many of their exploits are framed within comedic contexts, as their actions illustrate the hypocritical nature of Korean capitalism and social class privilege. At the very least, we feel little sympathy for the Park family members, who are extremely dependent upon their employees in order to function, let alone maintain their class position, and tend to be spoiled and self-indulgent.

During the second half of the film, the plotlines become darker. When the Park family goes on a short vacation, the Kims indulge themselves in the affluence to which the Parks are accustomed, taking over the main part of the house and entertaining themselves at will with luxury items typically beyond their economic reach. Their activities are disrupted when the former Park family housekeeper, Moon-gwang, arrives and informs Kim matriarch Chung-sook that she left a personal item in the house basement. In reality, Moon-gwang's husband, Geun-sae, has been living in a bunker attached to the basement for the past four years, hiding from loan sharks after having failed to repay debts. When Chung-sook discovers Geun-sae's presence, she threatens to tell Moon-gwang's secret to the Parks, but as the other members of the Kim family eavesdrop upon their encounter, Moon-gwang threatens to expose them as well. The Kims engage in a physical struggle with Moon-gwang and Geun-sae, who are subsequently assaulted and are tied up in the bunker. When the Park family returns unexpectedly, the Kims quickly try to clean up the mess they have made in the house. Hiding after the Parks arrive, the Kim family members eventually sneak out of the house, but not before they hear the Park patriarch complain about father Ki-taek's body odor (Ki-taek having served as his chauffeur).

The final part of *Parasite* includes even greater violence and tragedy. Upon leaving the Park home in the rain, the Kim family members see their own semi-basement apartment residence flooded and are forced into sheltering with other homeless victims. However, as Mrs. Park has planned an elaborate birthday party for her son, Da-song, the Kim family is forced to attend and provide service for the occasion the next day. When Ki-woo returns to the Park residence and goes to the bunker to check on Moon-gwang and Geun-sae, he discovers that Moon-gwang has died from her wounds due to the previous assault. He is severely beaten by Geun-sae, who seeks revenge for his wife's death. Geun-sae then intrudes into the birthday celebration and stabs Kim daughter Ki-jung in a further act of revenge for his wife's death. Da-song, the young son in the Park family, suffers a seizure, and Geun-sae is killed by Chung-sook with a skewer. Commanded by the Park father to take his son to the hospital, even though daughter Ki-jung is lying on the ground bleeding to death, Ki-taek refuses to obey and initially fails to give the Park father the keys to the car. Upon hearing the father's reference to Guen-sae's smell (triggering his previous reference to Ki-taek's own body odor), Ki-taek kills him and flees.

At the end of the film, we learn that the Kim family has been decimated. Ki-jung (the sister) has died, brother Ki-woo and mother Chung-sook have been convicted of fraud but are put on probation, and father Ki-taek has escaped but has not been located. The Park house has been sold to a German family but when Ki-woo sees a coded message communicated through flashing light emanating from the house bunker, he realizes that his father, Ki-taek, is living in the bunker, sheltered from police authorities. He communicates his intention to make enough money to free his father from the bunker, but given his status and economic prospects, it is clear that this is an extremely unrealistic proposition, as it would take 564 years for him to earn enough money to buy the property (Vashchuck, 2021; Wikipedia, 2022).

Analysis

Many have recognized that *Parasite* offers a devastating critique of modern capitalism. But that fact, in and of itself, does not explain the film's widespread popularity and international recognition. Part of its success lies in director and co-screenwriter Bong's depiction of both the comedic and violent in characterizing the practice of capitalism. In many societies, certainly in the United States, for example, the harsh consequences of class structure and class conflict when discussed and depicted are intentionally obfuscated; the material violence they perpetuate is not typically presented as a series of daily or regular occurrences. To the degree that we tend to view capitalism as an ideological abstraction, *Parasite* forces us to question such a depiction. In an extremely perceptive essay, Minjung Noh applies Walter Benjamin's categorization of capitalism as a religion to Bong's treatment of the topic. As summarized by Noh, Benjamin argues that capitalism shares four characteristics with certain forms of religious observance. He believed that capitalism is based upon utilitarian practice rather than adherence to pure doctrine; its presence is constant on a daily basis and is never paused; its practice leads to feelings of guilt resulting in despair; and its hidden "god" (consumption) is only revealed after guilt is expressed (Noh, 2020).

Throughout the film, its characters act in ways that are transactional rather than ethical. There is no overriding ethical belief system or set of principles to which they are attached. Instead, it is material consumption that they collectively value, regardless of their specific class position. Nor do any of the characters remove themselves from the exigencies of daily life; they never pause or reflect upon their actions or attitudes. In the case of the Kim family, their class position is defined by its precariousness; they live moment to moment and are often involved in situations seemingly beyond their control. For the Park family, their class position affords them the luxury of self-absorption as they easily fulfill their material desires. However, in a capitalist society, no one is ever totally secure, and the consequences of their failure to acknowledge the destructive tendencies of consumptive capitalism are tragic. Ultimately, neither family engages in thought or action that allows them to separate themselves from the demands of capitalist consumerism. The guilt or despair that the surviving members of both families do experience is expressed only in the midst of the tragedy that occurs during the end of the film. In the film's denouement, there are no lessons learned, and the class positioning of the two families remains the same. Ki-woo's pledge to earn enough money to free his father from the former Park family house bunker is not only unrealistic but demonstrates his unwavering faith in the liberatory possibilities of consumer capitalism, a faith that can never be realized (Noh, 2020).

When we analyze the way class position is depicted in *Parasite*, a number of anomalies become apparent. If there is internal instability within one's class position, one's standing vis-à-vis other social classes is quite permanent. Note that there is little chance of the Kims uniting with the former Park servants to transform a system that is mutually exploitative, and there is no chance that they will ever advance beyond their poverty and marginal class status in the long term. Correspondingly, there is no indication that the Parks will ever be forced into giving up their class standing even after the tragedies they experience.

At the same time, the two classes, as depicted by the Parks and the Kims, are mutually dependent upon one another, their dependency encapsulated by the title of the film.

Class position is also portrayed through conscious cinematic technique. Director Bong has commented upon the vertical depictions of space in the film to connote class separation and positioning. The semi-basement apartment where the Kim family resides is small, claustrophobic, and below street level. However, it includes a little window that allows them to see the outside world and perhaps aspire to some degree of upward mobility (Bong). At the same time, their desperation is foreshadowed at the very beginning of the film, when Ki-woo is sent to chase away a vagrant who is urinating on the street in front of their apartment window. The Park family home, by contrast, is spacious and situated on a hill, protected from external intrusion. Until he arrives at the Park residence, Ki-woo is filmed with the camera looking down on him, our perception of his diminutive stature corresponding to his class position. Once in the Park residence, the camera lens no longer looks down upon him. Within the household, the staircase plays an important role throughout the film, as cinematographer Hong Kyung-pyo notes,

> Walking up some stairs, you become infinitely elegant, while walking down another, you fall endlessly or enter into an ominous mood. . . . Stairs also function as a tool that makes one realize their true identity after basking in the momentary "highness." They walk up with excitement, but run down endlessly in the pouring rain. What they see at the end of the stairs is their house drowned in water. (Desowitz, 2019)

Similarly, lighting is used to also emphasize class difference, the Park mansion being fully lit as a result of its being able to take advantage of sunshine while the Kim semi-basement apartment is much darker, with residents experiencing limited exposure to sunlight (Desowitz, 2019).

There are numerous cultural references in the film, but there are two that especially stand out. When Ki-woo first meets his friend, Min-hyuk, he brings with him a scholar stone or viewing stone (suseok). Such stones traditionally have been kept for the purpose of bringing about good luck. As Min-hyuk reports that his family has many of them, he gives one as a gift to Ki-woo and the Kim family. Although venerated by older members of Korean society, Ki-woo and the Kims really don't know what to do with the gift. Eventually, however, Ki-woo brings it to the Park household, and in his struggle with Guen-sae, he is struck and suffers brain damage as a result of the altercation. Not only does the placement of the scholar stone in the screenplay indicate a rejection of traditional symbols of authority within the family dynamic, but it functions to demonstrate that any hope of achieving a better future for the impoverished results in a destructive outcome.

The treatment of the scholar stone can be compared with the display of the Native American headdress, which Ki-taek is forced to wear during the birthday party scene. Throughout the film, Park son Da-song "plays cowboys and Indians." When we are first introduced to the character, Da-song is shooting plastic bows and arrows inside his house; later, he builds a teepee outside his home in preparation for his birthday celebration, organized around the cowboy/Indian theme. We also learn that he is a member of the South Korean cub scouts, his ability to pitch the teepee associated with his membership in that group. At one level, the acquisition and use of these cultural symbols and consumptive objects signify the ways in which globalization helps to mark class position. Da-song's playful use of the walkie talkie with his parents is another example of this theme. However, the Native American paraphernalia are indicative of more than the desire to acquire and consume global cultural objects. The act of "playing Indian" involves the practice of the intentional appropriation and dehumanization of the other, as a means of engaging in masculine fantasizing (Springwood and King, 2001). That such a practice extends onto a Korean setting doesn't change its intent or impact; it universalizes it. But more importantly, it signifies that one of the important aspects of class conflict is the theft of one's dignity when one's class position is too low to offer self-protection and resistance. In their classic work *The Hidden Injuries of Class*, Richard Sennett and Jonathan Cobb noted how members of the working class in the United States were made to feel ashamed for engaging in work that was less prestigious and more likely to involve manual as opposed to mental labor (Sennett and Cobb, 1972). In this case, by being forced to wear the headdress, the assault is even more direct. While both Mr. Park and Ki-taek wear headdresses to accommodate the birthday party theme, Ki-taek has no choice in the matter and is forced into becoming an infantized, dehumanized object of Da-song's desire. When he takes off the headdress and kills Mr. Park with an ax, this act of agency can be viewed as his effort to reclaim his humanity (Cea, 2019).

Ki-taek is motivated to kill Mr. Park, not simply because of the Park family's indifference to the plight of his family and his dying daughter but because Mr. Park notes the dying Geun-sae's smell, triggering Ki-taek's memory of Mr. Park having previously negatively commented upon his own body odor while he and his family were surreptitiously hiding in the Park residence. The vehemence with which smell is used to express disgust for the lower classes is evident in the dialogue between Mr. and Mrs. Park that Ki-taek overhears when in hiding. Note the dialogue from the screenplay (Korean romanization of character names differs slightly from aforementioned subtitles).

> DONG-IK [MR. PARK]
> Hold on.
> sniffs
> I know that smell.
> Yon-Kyo [MRS. PARK]
> What?
> DONG-IK [MR. PARK]
> This is Mr. Kim's smell.
> Yon-Kyo [MRS. PARK]
> Mr. Kim? Are you sure?
> sniffs
> I don't know what you're talking about.
> DONG-IK [MR PARK] and Yon-Kyo [MRS. PARK] both sniff the air.
> DONG-IK [Mr Park] becomes nervous. He smells his T-shirt.
> DONG-IK [MR. PARK]
> I guess you don't know. I sit behind him every day so I know the smell.
> Yon-Kyo [MRS. PARK]
> Like poor people smell?
> DONG-IK [MR. PARK]
> No. It's not that strong. It's more like a subtle aroma that seeps into the air—
> [Yon-Kyo] MRS PARK
> Like old people smell?
> DONG-IK [MR. PARK] No, no. How should I put it—Maybe the smell of an old radish pickle? Or that smell when you're washing a dirty rag? (Bedard, 2021).

We recall that in Chapter 2, we referenced the work of Laura Marks, who has argued that the most powerful scenes in film arise when associations are made with all of the different senses and that the visual is certainly not the only sense that triggers memory or depth of feeling. The sense of smell fulfills that function in *Parasite*. It illustrates the message that belonging to the poor and marginal working-class strata in South Korea means being thought of as a consumable object, worthy of being discarded, rather than receiving recognition as a living human being. In addition to smell, taste is also used effectively to trigger emotion in the film. Upon analyzing the outdoor garden birthday party scene, for example, a barbeque is being prepared when the physical struggles commence and the ensuing violence occurs. The association of the burnt skewered meat with the victims of the birthday party violence is direct and compelling. For Marks, touch is among the most important of the senses that triggers the viewer's memories and previous associations. In *Parasite*, it is worth noting that the graphic nature of the violence that is portrayed deeply involves objects that evoke the sense of touch. Ki-woo consciously takes his gifted scholar stone with him, hugging it, and believing that it is following him around and will give him good luck. Eventually, Geun-sae smashes the stone on his head during their altercation. He then uses a normal kitchen knife to stab Ki-woo's sister, Ki-jung. The use of these ordinary implements for violent purposes makes the violence that is portrayed even more graphic than would ordinarily be the case. Thus, what makes both the description of class affiliation and the dynamics of class conflict so visceral in the film is Bong's eclectic use of symbols that trigger the many senses, which then allow us to form associations with these themes.

Social Class Revisited

How does Bong's treatment of social class and class conflict compare with the academic literature we summarized at the beginning of the chapter? It is clear that Bong's view of social class extends beyond the traditional association of class with ownership of the means of production. In *Parasite*, the dimensions of class affiliation include spatial, cultural, and sensory dimensions in addition to the economic. Certainly, the poor/working class is not a unified entity nor is it a stable cohort. Marx and Engels negatively described those who in their poverty could not or refused to work as the lumpen proletariat. Yet, in this picture of contemporary South Korean society, the precarity that defines their existence prevents the lower working class from ever protecting themselves from the threat of descending into abject poverty, and it prevents them from becoming a unified cohort. Nor is social class beholden to the state in the film's portrayal of South Korean society. With the possible exception of education as a state apparatus, we don't see the state involved at all in the lives of either the Kims or the Parks. It offers little in the way of social support for its most indigent members, nor is its bureaucracy so overwhelming or overbearing so as to overtly control the lives of its citizenry. It is curious that we don't see the characters in the film directly interacting with other entrenched bureaucracies that are typically associated with corporate capitalism either. Mr. Park, for example, is the chief executive officer of a virtual reality technology company, which could be characterized as a small business start-up company, as opposed to a large corporation. One could assume that he has amassed his wealth somewhat quickly rather than having laboriously risen through the bureaucratic ranks.

One of the more interesting factors that involves the way in which the Kim family is portrayed is that their limited cultural capital does not prevent them from earning the trust of the Park family. There are no linguistic or cultural deficits that impede them from playing roles for which they were not trained, and they are able to perform their jobs without difficulty. As a result, their lack of cultural capital does not prevent them from temporarily improving their dire economic situation. Although they do lack the amount of social capital that would have been necessary to advance their class position, it is because of Ki-woo's connection to friend Min-hyuk that they are able to maximize the social capital they do possess in landing their jobs with the Park family. Connections do matter in this society, although the Kims are unsuccessful in ultimately acquiring enough social capital to permanently alter their class position.

It is globalization and consumption that define the class status of both families in the film. With regard to globalization, the tutoring opening within the Park household occurs because Min-hyuk is taking the opportunity to study abroad, while the subject matter he is helping the Park daughter (Da-hae) to master is English. Indeed, when Ki-woo takes over as English tutor, he is given the English name Kevin, while sister Ki-jung, who is a supposed art teacher, becomes "Jessica," having studied art therapy in Illinois. Combined with the depiction of the "playing cowboy/Indian theme," the United States and the West more generally are always present, as an idealized site where one finds the source of the desirable consumerist products that are highly valued by the Parks but out of reach for the Kims. The juxtaposition of Park son Da-song dressing up in his headdress and playing with his US made toy ax, or father Park having a chauffeur drive him around in his Mercedes, with the Kim family members struggling to steal a Wi-Fi connection near their apartment because they are too poor to pay for internet access, informs us about the depth of the class divide between the two families that colors their day-to-day consumerist experiences. Both families understand the logic of globalization and consumerism, which is why the Kims are able to gain the trust of the Parks. The ultimate destructive nature of these forces also creates tragic consequences for both families.

Education Revisited

What, though, does *Parasite* tell us about the way in which education is implicated in social class formation and conflict? The South Korean educational system is structured to include four years of primary school, three years of middle school, three years of high school, and four years at the university level. As is true of other East Asian countries, the university entrance examination system drives much of the high school curriculum, and university selection to elite institutions can be extremely competitive. However, over 70 percent of all students enroll in a university, and South Korean students have consistently performed well on the OECD's Programme for International Student Assessment (OECD, 2019). It is also true that over 70 percent of South Korean students participate in some form of private education, be it through afterschool study classes or individual tutoring (Yonlap, 2019). Shadow education thus plays an important role in students' education from their primary years through high school. From an international perspective, the South Korean educational system is judged to be quite successful and is viewed as an important contributing factor to the country's impressive economic growth and development (Shim, 2012).

Within the film, however, education is portrayed in a less favorable light. We recall that when we are introduced to Ki-woo, we become aware of the fact that he has failed his university entrance examination four times, twice before and twice after having entered the army. As has been previously noted, his examination performance is not a reflection of his intelligence, nor is his sister's educational status a reflection upon her ability to play the role of art therapist without having achieved the requisite credentials. Educational attainment seems to be a secondary factor in the Park's favorable class position as well, as Mrs. Park is portrayed as being particularly dimwitted, and there is little comment about Mr. Park's education or its importance in his ascendancy to the chief executive officer of his virtual reality technology company. The role the educational system plays in *Parasite* is that of a screening function through its issuance of credentials, but the credentials it rewards are not indicative of the level of knowledge or skills that it transmits. Criticisms of modern educational systems for their excessive perpetuation of credentialism are not new (Collins, 1979; Dore, 1976). What *Parasite* brings to the discussion, though, is a recognition that there are costs for excluding the poor from the opportunities to succeed within the system; such exclusion is a form of violence and results in violence. It thus offers a devastating critique of meritocracy and the meritocratic values modern schools promote. The social relations *Parasite* portrays are not rule-governed but are entirely transactional. It is for this reason that the members of the Park family illegitimately obtain and maintain their class position. During the first portion of the film, the audience finds humor in their family dysfunctionality apparent in spite of their wealth, but especially in their obliviousness to the world around them. The violence that they eventually experience cannot be contained or ameliorated by their educational standing or by meritocratic rules of conduct to which few actually adhere. Instead, it is the power of consumerism that shapes the values of both families and inevitably leads to tragedy. But beyond tragedy, in depicting Ki-taek entrapped in the house bunker, in the same way that Geun-sae was held captive, the permanence of class position and the inability to successfully engage in social class mobility is confirmed with an exclamation point. Education certainly is no panacea here.

Why, then, has *Parasite* become such a popular and honored film, particularly among Global North audiences? I believe that there are three reasons why the film has received its acclaim. First, the juxtaposition of comedy and tragedy, humor and violence, as essential components of the film's narrative structure offers an expansive understanding of social experience that is not often explored within commercial film. Second, a recognition of the power of globalization and consumption speaks to audiences from many backgrounds. Audiences able to see this film who reside outside of South Korea are certainly aware of these dynamics, often in intimate ways.

Finally, I believe that the sensibilities apparent in the film speak to aspects of affect theory that have broad resonance. The appeal to the various senses that trigger our emotions, and the graphic nature with which violence is depicted, speaks to the intensities of encounter that create affect. The efforts, unsuccessful as they may be, of the Kims and the Parks to make sense of their worlds through fortifying their consumerist behaviors speak to the ways in which they negotiate meaning in a world marked by consumptive capitalism. In spite of internal pressures, their loyalties to their respective family members speak to their need for assemblage, while their inability to bridge class division and the Kims' inability to form stronger class solidarity with the former service workers for the Parks speak to the realities of dis-assemblage. And, most importantly, the precarity that marks the Kims' class position, moving in and out of poverty on a regular basis, and the explosive end to the Park family's dominance speak to the overriding contingency that marks all social relations and is a key for those who are proponents of affect theory.

A Separation (Jodaeiye Nader az Simin)

A Separation, written and directed by Ashgar Farhadi and released in 2011, won the Academy Award for best foreign film in 2012. Farhadi also won an Academy Award in the same category in 2016 for his film *The Salesman*, and he received the Cannes Festival Grand Prix award for his film, *A Hero*, in 2021. His films are noteworthy for their emphasis upon the way in which characters negotiate the moral ambiguity and ethical dilemmas of everyday life. For many, the "New Wave" period of Iranian cinema, in the 1960s and 1970s, was especially noteworthy as filmmakers incorporated various elements of both social realism and magical realism into artistic products that were "lyrical" and "self-reflexive" (Cross, 2019). Although some have argued that in the aftermath of the Iranian Revolution of 1978–9, a new and distinct cinematic culture arose in opposition to the ensconced theocracy, others have argued that many of the qualities of contemporary Iranian cinema have their roots in the prerevolutionary "New Wave" era. Farhadi's work is thus viewed by many as a product of this legacy. Critics are also cognizant of the differences between "art-house" and "popular" cinemas, and note that many of the Iranian films that have received international acclaim are restricted from being widely shown in their home country and/or have less widespread domestic appeal. Ashgar Farhadi's films, though, tend to transcend the art house/popular dichotomy and are viewed as including elements that have met with domestic as well as international approval (Cross, 2019). *A Separation*, recipient of critical as well as popular acclaim, is often viewed as Farhadi's masterpiece. It should be noted, though, that while his artistry has been rarely questioned, Farhadi has been accused of taking ideas and story lines from colleagues and students and using them in his films without giving them credit for their input. *A Separation* is one of a number of films where the director has been accused of this behavior (Aviv, 2022).

Synopsis

In the beginning of the film, the audience is introduced to Simin, who seeks a divorce from her husband of fourteen years, Nader. She wants to leave Iran in order to secure a better future for her eleven-year-old daughter, Termeh, but Nader wishes to stay and care for his elderly father, who is suffering from dementia. The court rejects Simin's request, finding that the couple's marital problems do not rise to a level whereby a divorce deserves to be granted. As a result, Simin separates from Nader and moves in with her parents, while

Termeh stays with Nader. Because Simin is no longer living with Nader, there is no one to permanently attend to his father, who needs constant care while Nader is at work. Simin then hires Razieh, a religiously observant woman, to help care for Nader's father. Razieh, who is in difficult financial straits and is four months pregnant, takes her daughter, Somayeh, with her on the job. Once on the job, it becomes challenging for Razieh to take care of the father, who at one point wanders outside on the street after being left temporarily unattended.

The next day, when Nader returns home with Termeh, they find his father unconscious, on the ground tied to a bed. Razieh is not present. Nader also notices that some money is missing and upon her return to the apartment, Nader accuses Razieh of neglecting to care for his father while stealing funds from the premises. Razieh refuses to leave the apartment until she is paid for her time, denying that she has stolen any money. Later it is revealed that Nader's wife Simin took the disputed money to pay movers to take her furniture to her parents' residence. Nader pushes Razieh out of the apartment, she falls down the stairs, and ends up in the hospital, where she miscarries.

According to Iranian law, causing the death of an unborn is akin to committing murder and is punishable by a possible one to three-year prison sentence. Nader is thus investigated by the authorities where he denies knowing that Razieh was pregnant. During court proceedings, Nader comes into contact with Razieh's husband Hojjat, who is unemployed and is facing the prospect of being incarcerated himself in debtors' prison. Hojjat is depicted as being aggressive and at times out of control, and at a later point, Razieh notes to the court judge that Hojjat suffers from mental illness and is on medication.

As events proceed, Nader's claim of ignorance regarding Razieh's condition is called into question, and he is eventually forced to admit to Termeh, his daughter, that this was a lie. After Termeh's teacher/tutor withdraws a statement of support, having originally attested to Nader's lack of knowledge regarding Razieh's pregnancy, Nader tells the judge that he eventually was told of her condition by Termeh. A skeptical judge interrogates Termeh, who is also forced to lie and offer official support for her father's claim. Eventually, Simin convinces Nader to offer a payment to Hojjat and Razieh, settling the matter. However, Razieh confides to Simin that it is quite possible that the miscarriage occurred before the apartment incident with Nader took place. Nader offers payment to Hojjat and Razieh on the condition that she swear on the Qur'an that she is telling the truth, an act with which she is ultimately unable to comply. Hojjat expresses profound anger at his wife's noncompliance.

At the end of the film, Simin and Nader are back in court, and a final separation is granted by the judge. The parents, however, allow Termeh to decide which parent she will live with. Both parents exit the court room and await Termah's decision. The audience is left in the dark, unaware of which choice she ultimately makes.

Analysis

One of Ashgar Farhadi's considerable strengths is his ability to affectively portray social class affiliation and conflict, and one of the ways in which he does so is by linking the dynamics of family interaction to their larger social class ramifications. Simin and Nader's marital difficulties, and Razieh and Hojjat's struggles, for example, are best understood as indicative of their respective class positioning and the degrees of freedom with which each couple operate. When *A Separation* begins and Simin is filing for divorce from Nader, both parties have the luxury of contemplating a future life without the other spouse while preserving their basic material well-being. Nader's concern seems to be primarily focused upon his maintaining parental custody of Termeh, his daughter. From Simin's perspective, it is clear that Nader is not willing to work to improve their personal relationship so that the marriage can be maintained. What is more important from her perspective is that she be able to leave Iran with her daughter in order to give her daughter a better future. Engaging upon such a journey would amount to making a decision based upon choice and personal preference rather than material necessity. Nader argues that he must stay in Iran in order to take care of his infirmed father. Although Simin notes that the father is so incapacitated he can't even recognize Nader, Nader believes that he is duty-bound to stay with his father as a matter of honor. We see much of the dynamics of the relationship through the eyes of their daughter Termeh, who not only seems to be academically successful but appears to be wise beyond her age. Her mother, for example, knows that Termeh's decision to stay with her father for the time being is based upon her calculation that her mother would eventually reconcile with her father and the family unit would be left intact. Their middle-class position does not ameliorate the tensions, disappointments, frustrations, and anger that mark their family dynamics. But it preserves a degree of stability that is not afforded Razieh and Hojjat, their poor working-class counterparts. It is also interesting to note that the ethical considerations that weigh on Nader, with respect to his obligation to care for his father and his desire to maintain a close relationship with his daughter, or on Simin, who wishes for a better life for Termeh outside of Iran, don't involve expressed religious conviction. They represent that segment of Iranian society that embraces modernism rather than religious orthodoxy as they tolerate rather than embody religious observance and fealty to religious doctrine.

Razieh and Hojjat, on the other hand, consistently confront the precarity that defines their class position. Such uncertainty is expressed not only through their dire physical circumstances, but it is also present metaphorically through Hojjat's emotional instability and his expressions of anger and threats of violence. In some ways, Nader exhibits similar emotional conflicts, but his class position immunizes him from the same degree of desperation that Hojjat must regularly confront. For Razieh, in particular, religious faith offers a degree of certainty in an uncertain world, until it doesn't. It is attractive to the Iranian working-class poor, who, unlike their middle-class counterparts, are unable to ever experience the economic benefits that modernism promises.

From Ashgar Farhadi's perspective, neither religious conviction nor an embrace of modernism relieves his characters from the ethical dilemmas they confront, dilemmas that transcend their class standing. Indeed, it is indicative of his artistry that he encourages viewers' attitudes toward his major characters to change as we learn more about the moral choices they make. Simin, for example, initially is depicted in an unsympathetic light, given her dismissive attitude toward Nader's desire to continue caring for his father. But later, we see that she is the one who pressures Nader to offer monetary compensation to Hojjat and Razieh in an effort to resolve their dispute. The audience at first has sympathy for Nader, who is trying to care for his infirmed father and desperately doesn't want to lose his daughter. At one point, when Hojjat faces arrest due to a separate courtroom dispute, Nader intervenes and asks the judge to refrain from sending him to prison, feeling compassion for Hojjat's circumstance. But as the story line proceeds, we learn that Nader indeed has lied and did know that Razieh was pregnant before pushing her out of the apartment, and he manipulates his daughter into further lying before the court in support of his claim. He has always had the monetary means to settle the dispute with Hojjat and Razieh but resists doing so until the end of the film. Razieh's religious conviction doesn't prevent her from failing to disclose the full circumstances that might have affected her miscarriage, although she ultimately refuses to swear on the Qur'an that the injuries suffered as a result of her staircase fall were the sole cause of the tragedy. Hojjat cannot understand how, given the dire nature of their circumstances, she could refuse to take the monetary compensation they so desperately needed. All of these characters lead their lives with a degree of ethical ambiguity that is embedded within their social class positions and is only too human.

It is in this way that Farhadi encourages us to see social class affiliation in intimate terms. It is not simply the case that the characters change their behavior or their attitudes when confronted with new situations. They are continually struggling to come to terms with daily conflicts that resist quick and clearly defined resolutions. Farhadi's repeated use of the close-up, and his positioning of his characters in small, at times even claustrophobic, spaces creates an impression of intimacy that we learn to associate with the social class affiliation and conflict that marks the daily lives of these characters. The social realism that is intrinsic to his filmmaking creates the affect that makes his depiction of Iranian daily life broadly understandable. What is most realistic about his depiction of daily life is that his characters fail to ultimately resolve the tensions and contradictions they experience. At the end of *A Separation*, we fail to learn which parent Termeh decides to join, and in a sense, this is totally appropriate, because we understand that the consequences of her decision will cause unresolved disappointment within the family unit regardless of what the decision may be. Metaphorically speaking, the same can be said about the hybrid reality of Iranian society, with its dual embrace of modernism and Islam. Farhadi's critique suggests that neither perspective is completely satisfactory.

In 1999, there were systemic student protests in Iran after a reformist newspaper was closed. In 2009, there were nation-wide protests after the regime refused to honor the popular vote in a presidential election. As of the writing of this chapter, the country is again experiencing convulsive mass protest, after a twenty-two-year-old Kurdish Iranian woman, Mahsa Amini, died in detention, after having been arrested for supposedly violating the country's dress code and wearing her hijab improperly. The protest participants have included both men and women, and the vehemence of their reaction can be attributed not only to the state's attempt to control and restrict personal behavior in the name of religious orthodoxy but to the selective and inconsistent ways in which such codes of conduct are enforced. At best, they are enforced in ways that are arbitrary and capricious; at worst, lower standards are applied to elite members of the middle class as opposed to the poor and working poor (Moaveni, 2022). In this vein, it is noteworthy that in *A Separation* we are able to see Simin's red hair through her rather loose-fitting hijab, whereas Razieh is more fully covered. The class distinctions that accompany the unequal enforcement of religious dress codes have thus been a basic feature of Iranian society for decades (Kochai, 2017).

But what is also remarkable about Farhadi's depiction of Iranian life, especially in the light of current events, is the role he ascribes to women in making the most consequential of decisions that affect the lives of all of the film's protagonists. Whatever their faults, Simin and Razieh provide the respective moral compasses that anchor their families' experiences. It is also noteworthy that it is left to Termeh, wise beyond her years, to decide which parent she will ultimately live with. Given the fact that Iran has a relatively young population with an average age of 31.7, Farhadi's focus on Termeh highlights the social importance of youth and is significant. Such a focus further exemplifies the modernism, with its futuristic orientation, that plays such a prominent part in the country's outlook. The lack of closure with which the film concludes signifies not only the country's uncertain present but its uncertain future as well.

Such uncertainty is evident in Farhadi's treatment of state institutions. Not only are they fragile, but they are noticeably irresponsive to the daily concerns of the Iranian citizenry, at least until events that reach cataclysmic status arise. One thus notices the chaos that is depicted when respondents are waiting to see an official adjudicate their court proceedings or the unpredictability of those proceedings once they are invoked. The Iran that is depicted in this film is not that of a bureaucratic state whose power is so centralized that it closely dictates the parameters of individual and collective behavior. Instead, the state's presence is mediated by its inefficiencies which limit its effectiveness in offering broad social support to its population.

Its treatment of education is similarly suggestive. Although schooling and educational provision doesn't play an obvious role in constructing social class identification and conflict, its presence is nonetheless significant. In comparing Termeh's life with that of Somayeh (Razieh's daughter), it is obvious that Somayeh will never have access to the educational advantages Termeh has been able to utilize. Accompanying her mother to Nader's father's apartment, Somayeh is at an early age conscripted into helping her mother perform her caregiving responsibilities, rather than having the opportunity to be in school. Eleven-year-old Termeh, on the other hand, already has a tutor who is helping her to study for school exams. It is interesting to note that her teacher/tutor, Miss Ghahraii, is depicted as a voice of conscience in the film. Initially, she swears that Nader did not or could not have known of a conversation she had regarding Razieh's pregnancy and a subsequent recommendation for an affordable physician who could give her a sonogram. Later, Hojjat comes to Termeh's school where he angrily confronts Miss Ghahraii for lying before the court and for suggesting that he may have physically injured his wife, causing her miscarriage. She ultimately recants her statement of support for Nader when made aware of conflicting information. Clearly, Hojjat's anger is exacerbated because he views teachers as possessing an ethical responsibility to tell the truth and believes Miss Ghahraii has failed to fulfill such responsibility. He also views her questioning of his own behavior toward his wife, suggesting possible domestic violence as a reason for the miscarriage, as evidence of her deep social class prejudice. In eventually recanting her initial statement of support for Nader, she offers support for Hojjiat's view that educational purpose is embedded with ethical concern. The irony of course is that Hojjat's travel to Termeh's school is itself a disruptive act. In so doing, he upends a social order where Termeh's middle-class girls' school, safely separated from poor and working-class access, is ensconced in foreign territory, where a person of Hojjat's social standing is not expected to trespass. And, as is true of other social institutions, the ethical importance associated with educational practice does not extend to its ultimate influence upon the future for either family depicted in the film.

As was true in *Parasite*, it is precarity and uncertainty that mark the representatives of the two social classes represented in *A Separation*. However, Farhadi relies upon other aspects of affect in his film too. His characters struggle to make meaning in a society where beliefs in modernism or religiosity fail to completely help them adequately address the ethical conflicts to which they are regularly exposed. But the stakes in resolving such conflicts are heightened by the intensity of the encounters that frame their construction as well. Moreso than in other representations, social class is deeply personal in this film; it is defined in terms involving expressions of identity, aspiration, family survival and cohesiveness, and moral compass. Finally, through the lens of family, we see assemblage and dis-assemblage as a major theme coloring the behaviors of all of the film's central characters.

Still Life (San Xia Hao Ren)

Jia Zhangke is one of China's most admired filmmakers and has been recognized as a leader in his country's sixth-generation film movement. Fifth-generation filmmakers coming of age in the late 1980s became known internationally for their iconoclasm, their focus upon broadly historical themes, their exquisite cinematography, and their political critiques of Chinese society. Many were graduates of the Beijing Film Academy, having studied there after the end of the 1970s, their childhood and early youth having been shaped by Cultural

Revolution events (Clark, 1989). China's sixth-generation filmmakers, who began working in the 1990s and 2000s, have focused more upon contemporary tensions evident within Chinese society, themselves products of China's economic transformation and its integration into the global economy. Their story lines tend to focus upon nondescript individuals rather than larger-than-life heroes and villains; their settings are constructed in ways that frame the inner conflicts their characters confront. Many of their films, at least initially, were produced underground, without the support of official Chinese authorities, and confronted censorship with limited distribution (Linder, 2011).

Jia also graduated from the Beijing Film Academy after having attended Shanxi University as an art student. His initial films were produced independently without state-sanctioned approval, with some state support for his fourth feature film, *The World*, occurring as a result of his previous work receiving international recognition. *Still Life*, his next film, completed in 2006, received the Venice Film Festival's Grand Lion Prize. It was immediately deemed noteworthy for Jia's use of digital video in its filming (which he also used for *The World*), for its occasional reliance upon documentary style, and for his use of nonprofessional actors in a number of scenes. Interestingly, Jia completed *Still Life* while also making the companion documentary, *Dong*, where he chronicled the thoughts and works of artist Liu Xiaodong. *Still Life* and the first portion of *Dong* are set in the Three Gorges River area in rural China, specifically in the historic town of Fengjie, which was being destroyed as a result of the construction of the Three Gorges Dam. That dam, which since 2012 has been designated as the largest hydroelectric power station in the world, became quite controversial during its construction. First, a large number of local inhabitants were forcibly displaced when their local villages were intentionally flooded in order to facilitate the creation of the dam reservoir. In addition, the increased susceptibility to landslides, soil erosion, and the eradication of local plant species were all additional factors that invoked criticism of the project. Jia's original intent was to film artist Liu Xiaodong, who was painting Fengjie inhabitants while their city was being decimated. Concurrent with the filming of his documentary, Jia wrote the screenplay for *A Still Life* in a few days, borrowing from some of what he observed in the making of the documentary and incorporating it into his fictional counterpart (Berry, 2022).

Synopsis

Still Life focuses upon the experiences of two main characters with separate but loosely interconnected stories. Han Sanming is a coal miner from Shanxi

Province who travels to Fengjie looking for his wife (Missy Ma), who ran away with their daughter from their home sixteen years ago. Shen Hong, a nurse also from Shanxi, is introduced later in the film, as she has also arrived in Fengjie looking for her husband, Guo Bin, with whom she has been separated for two years. During the first part of *Still Life*, we see the changes brought about by the Three Gorges Dam project upon the Fengjie area through Han Sanming's eyes. Upon his arrival in Fengjie, he learns that the street and address where he presumes his wife lives, on "Granite Street," no longer exists, demolished with the entire area now under water as a result of the dam's construction. Upon contacting his wife's older brother, he is told that his wife now lives down the river in Yicheng and that she will occasionally return to Fengjie. Waiting while trying to contact his wife, Han befriends a local youth, Brother Mark, and begins working with a group of laborers who demolish buildings by hand, as the bricks and metals they collect are recycled for other purposes. Some of the workers act as enforcers on behalf of Guo Bin, evicting residents prior to their homes and businesses being demolished, or in other ways coercively enforcing his edicts.

It is during the second part of *Still Life* when we are introduced to Shen Hong, who, after traveling to Fengjie, gets in contact with a friend of Guo Bin's, Wang Dongming, as she tries to find her husband. It seems that Guo has become a successful if corrupt entrepreneur while bankrolled by a patron, Ding Yaling, with whom it is suspected he is having an affair. Wang doesn't confirm Shen's suspicion but doesn't offer an unequivocal denial when she asks him if this is true. Eventually, Shen is able to meet Guo, who, after speaking with him briefly, walks away. When he follows her and asks her to come back, she informs him that she is in love with another man and will be leaving to meet him in Yicheng as they plan to relocate in Shanghai. She asks him to sign divorce papers when he has the time to do so. We last see her on the river in a boat, leaving Fengjie.

In its third section, the film returns to Han Sanming and his efforts to meet his wife, Missy Ma. His young friend, Brother Mark, dies as a result of a building collapse, and during a funeral ceremony on the river, Han is told by his brother-in-law that his wife has arrived. Prior to seeing her, we learn that the marriage actually was illegal, occurring as a result of a mercenary transaction. When they meet, he learns that his daughter is working further south and his wife is working on a boat for a boat owner. He asks why she left their home sixteen years ago, and she reflectively states that she was quite young. She asks him why it took so long for him to come and find her. When asked to see a picture of his daughter, she takes him to the boat where she is working, and upon retrieving the photo, he learns that she is working basically as an indentured servant in payment for a debt incurred by her brother. Han asks the boat owner for her release, and an agreement is made if and when he pays off the 30,000 yuan debt. Han informs his demolition worker friends that he intends to do so by returning to Shanxi and working in the coal mines there, so he can then permanently reunite with his wife and daughter. They express a desire to accompany him back home, but he warns them that the work is quite dangerous. As the film ends, they see him off as he makes his way back to Shanxi.

Analysis

At first glance, *Still Life* can be viewed as a meditation about the ways in which two representatives of distinct social classes navigate the challenges of globalization and modernization in contemporary China. Both Han Sanming and Shen Hong are resolute in their efforts to resist the negative consequences of dislocation and separation to which globalization forces have subjected them. Given her more favorable class position, Shen Hong is more likely to successfully assert her independence and actualize personal agency than Han Sanming, although he is no less committed to doing so. However, part of the film's beauty lies in its nuanced treatment of what globalization means and how the main characters understand their changing world.

Jia's depiction of globalization underscores the importance of time, space, and affect in considering its ramifications and consequences. Both in the film and in published dialogue with film critic Michael Berry, Jia mentions the fact that the older part of Fengjie was a city over 3,000 years old, referenced by Tang Dynasty poet Li Bai, who wrote after visiting the area, "The cries of the monkeys from both sides of the shore never cease, as my small boat traverses ten thousand layers of mountains" (Berry, 2022, 96). In *Still Life* and in the accompanying documentary, *Dong*, Jia juxtaposes the permanent beauty of the Three Gorges scenery with the relatively rapid and ugly displacement of human settlement, expedited through demolition and destruction. The inevitability of the total destruction of physical living space is foreshadowed by the camera's repeated focus on 153.3-metre markings, signifying the rise in the water level that will occur as the dam reservoir is constructed and underlying lands are flooded. The immense scale of the natural environment that the camera captures—the Yangtze River itself and the mountains, trees, and foliage that surround it—makes the individual characters who are portrayed appear to be diminutive in contrast, further underscoring the futility of their fighting against the imperative to modernize, which, as the film notes, was a Communist Party goal for generations.

But what is also clear, from Jia's perspective, is that what is replacing the past evokes impermanence and superficiality rather than substance. At one point in the film, Guo Bin points to a new bridge he takes responsibility for creating, turning on a switch which lights up its beams and girders. The neon-like effect highlights the garish ostentatiousness of the man-made project, a particularly striking comparison with the enduring natural beauty that surrounds the edifice.

In *Still Life*, globalization is also depicted in terms of spatial change, dislocation, and loss of a sense of place. Both Han Sanming and Shen Hong travel to Fengjie from Shanxi Province, and both arrive as outsiders, isolated in their incomplete knowledge of how the Three Gorges area has already been transformed. Han Sanming, for example, is unaware of the fact that Fengjie is now under the governmental authority of the Chongqing municipality rather than that of Sichuan Province. When Shen Hong arrives and tries to contact her husband Guo Bin by cell phone, the seven-digit number she was given is no longer in use, having been replaced by an eight-digit number for all inhabitants. In Han's case, his heavy, difficult-to-understand Shanxi accent becomes indicative of his rural isolation; the Fengjie area's dependency upon tourism and commercial exploitation further invites efforts on the part of some to take advantage of outsiders such as Han. Most dramatically for Han, he discovers that the Fengjie residence where his wife once lived and where he assumed she currently resided is now underwater. It is noteworthy that one of Han's local acquaintances identifies his hometown with its image engraved on a banknote, which is additionally reflective of the loss of sense of place as a personal identity marker.

Han Sanming and Shen Hong experience the disruptive consequences of globalization on a personal level, both having seen their respective marriages dissolve in at least part due to the lure of increased economic wealth that directed their spouses to the Three Gorges area in the first place. One of the virtues of the film is that character dialogue is sparse, as the viewership is left to empathize with the characters' plight through focusing upon their physical actions and reactions to the circumstances to which they have been subjected. In so doing, we empathize with their respective plights by identifying with their courage to confront situations created by forces that are seemingly beyond their control. As Jia himself states in his interview with Michael Berry,

> Once the government made the Three Gorges Dam project a priority and decided to make Fengjie the site, individuals had no recourse or means of resisting. One decision ended up bringing about massive change. More than

a million people would be relocated, and a city of more than three thousand years of history would be erased, buried beneath the river. *Still Life* reveals the helplessness of the individual when confronted with rapid change; instead, the individual simply gets pushed aside and swept away. It was within that kind of environment that I stood amid the ruins reflecting on what a person can do when faced with such monumental changes. What can any single individual do? Perhaps we need to start by resolving our own issues as individuals and make some difficult decisions? You may not have any power over whether or not the city will be flooded, but perhaps you can exert control over who you love. While this made me somewhat depressed, it helped me understand just what it meant for someone to truly have a passion for life—it is not that they are able to resist the raging tide of their times, but rather are able to grab hold of themselves as the floodwaters crash down. (Berry, 2022, 97)

In spite of the fact that the agency Han Sanming and Shen Hong express is defined through the ways in which they individually interiorize their reactions to their surrounding circumstances, their respective class affiliations play a role in determining their individual agency and freedom of choice. As has been noted, Han confronts more obstacles than Shen in trying to find his wife and daughter, and ultimately, in being able to reunite his family. His class position is extremely precarious, as is true for his wife and daughter. Being poor, uneducated, and susceptible to family manipulation, Missy Ma (Han's wife) admits when he finally is able to see her that her life has not been good. The demolition workers Han befriends similarly negotiate a precarious existence, susceptible to physical injury and death due to building collapse as well as intergang conflict. In an environment where money is scarce and corruption rampant, they are able to find a degree of peer comradery but it is not necessarily sustainable over the long term. Thus, even when Han decides to return to Shanxi and go back to the coal mines in order to earn enough money to pay back his brother-in-law's debt, freeing his wife and presumably reuniting the entire family, the decision is his and his alone. His fellow demolition workers initially express interest in going with him, especially when learning that the pay is much greater than that they are currently earning, but they are also told of the extreme dangers of the work. They accompany him to his boat as he leaves Fengjie but there is no indication that they will really travel with him.

Shen Hong's journey is also a personal one, made easier by her better class position. A trained nurse, she doesn't experience the economic precarity Han must confront. Seemingly placed in an inferior position, dependent upon her friend Wang Dongming to locate Guo Bin so that she can finally see him, all the while cognizant of the fact that he is probably having an affair with his benefactor, Ding Yaling, it is Shen Hong who ultimately asserts control over her situation, in meeting and then surprising her husband with the news that she has her own lover and wants a divorce. If Han Sanming exudes a kind of quiet stoicism in light of his journey to repair his marriage and locate his daughter, Shen expresses confidence in pursuing her own aims. When looking for her husband, a young sixteen-year-old girl comes up to her and asks if she could help her seek employment as a maid, viewing her as a person of prominence. While waiting for her Guo Bin to appear, one of the youths he employs suffers a head injury in a gang-related altercation. Using her nursing skills, she confidently bandages the wound. Both Han and Shen are resolute in their aims and their class positions, which, while different from each other, do not ultimately significantly force them to change or modify their respective goals.

The overriding theme of the film, though, is that the globalization forces to which these characters have been subjected affect everyone, regardless of class position. As a result, confronting those forces must occur on an individual rather than collective basis. Interestingly, there are a few scenes in the film that evoke magic realism imagery. When Shen first arrives in Fengjie, she looks up at the sky and sees spaceships flying about. Before Han returns to Shanxi, we see a tightrope walker straddling two buildings. And, at one point in the film, a building labeled the Commemorative Tower of the Immigrants, oddly constructed with a modernist design, is morphed into a rocket ship and takes off. Jia explains that these surrealistic images reflect the surreal nature of Fengjie itself as it confronted its demise, but they also reflect the dream-like perceptions of the characters in their efforts to make sense of what they are witnessing around them (Berry, 2022, 99).

There are few direct references to educational institutions or educational practice in *Still Life*. At the beginning of the film, one of the first buildings that we see demolished is the destruction of the education bureau but otherwise, references are much less explicit. In a less overt sense, educational attainment is occasionally associated with class standing and position. When Han Sanming sees his wife Missy Ma after so many years, he notes that her skin is darker, ostensibly because of the difficult manual labor to which she has been exposed. The reference is cultural, reflecting a deep-seeded traditional prejudice against manual labor in favor of those jobs, requiring "mental" labor instead, the darker one's skin color, the more likely one is to be looked at with disfavor. And, as was previously noted, Han's heavy Shanxi accent and his ignorance of the change in jurisdictional authority over Fengjie affairs also speak to his limited formal education, while Shen Hong's nursing background reminds us of her more favorable class position. The fact that education plays such a minimal role in the film's story line is itself noteworthy, given its historical prominence and importance within Chinese culture. As is true of those other traditional identity markers within Chinese society noted in the film—family, home, and sense of place—globalization trends destabilize and displace educational aspirations that are typically associated with a positive future.

The importance of affect transcends any significance attached to social class or education in *Still Life*. The main characters display an internalized search to make meaning in an environment alien to them. The forces that destroy their marriages are the same ones responsible for the physical devastation that is occurring around them. The forces these characters confront are seemingly beyond their control, yet they attempt to survive and find meaning in their lives in spite of their omnipresence. The film works in large part because the intensities of encounter that the characters experience are palpably felt, even with the minimal degree of dialogue with which they engage. Through marriage, separation, recommitment, and divorce, the two main characters engage in varying degrees of assemblage, reflecting the fragile social relationships Fengjie workers and other inhabitants pursue in the face of ongoing demolition and destruction. Interestingly, different thematic arcs are framed within the film through reference to consumable products that are collectively shared: cigarettes, tea, toffee, and so on. Social bonding thus regularly occurs, although it is not necessarily of lasting consequence. The final attribute of affect that is prominent in *Still Life* is precarity. We are never sure whether Han Sanming's plan to return to the Shanxi coal mines and eventually pay off his brother-in-law's debt will actually work. We don't know if Shen Hong will really find personal happiness as a result of her decision to divorce Guo Bin. And of course, we don't know the fates of the demolition workers or other inhabitants of Fengjie who are being forced to relocate without any real guarantees for their future survival. The audience instead is asked to be satisfied knowing that these characters act upon the agency they possess in ways that are life-affirming even when their future fates remain unresolved.

Concluding Remarks

It is clear that the depictions of social class and its relationship to educational provision and practice differ markedly in these three films from what has been expressed within the conventional social science and educational literature. In the first place, there is no uniform set of characteristics which define social class groupings among the films in question. In *Parasite*, for example, there is little that distinguishes the Kim family from the Park family except for the differing material circumstances that affect their respective wealth and status. Neither family is more intelligent, more capable, or more ethical than the other. There is no class solidarity either, as the Kims willingly scheme to exploit their working-class counterparts who are employed by the Parks. For Bong Joon-Ho, social class affiliation is a function of the random nature of economic opportunity in modern South Korea, made more precarious through globalization forces than through the intentional exercise of class consciousness per se. It is thus telling that the Kim and Park families, representing South Korea's working poor and middle-class members, both become victims of the violence perpetuated by the consequences of globalization including exclusion, lack of recognition and respect for the other, the manufacture of desire enhanced through commodification, and intense competition for limited material rewards.

In the Iranian case, Ashgar Farhadi offers a picture of an Iranian population whose class affiliation and division are marked by the country's inability to reconcile the benefits of modernization with a commitment to religious orthodoxy. Simin, Nader, Hojjat, and Razieh all struggle to do what is "right" but are confronted with moral dilemmas that transcend their specific class positions and defy their desires for economic security and a better future. In *Still Life* as well, while corrupt individuals such as Guo Bin are able to take advantage of government-mandated dictates, the effects of modernization and globalization are felt by the entire local population of Fengjie; class affiliation offers no relief to those who seek to resist their impact.

Although the three films question the degree to which distinct social class cohesiveness exists in their respective settings, and although lines are often muddled with regard to the terms through which class conflict is defined and then played out, they present scant evidence that the state, through its institutions, is able to effectively dictate class behavior or positioning. The view of state institutions offered in *Parasite* is one where they are largely absent in the daily lives of the main characters. In *A Separation*, courts are the primary state institutions that do intrude upon the lives of the major characters. But the judicial process is so arbitrary that none of the characters can count on the courts to protect their rights or well-being. In forcing the broad evacuation of millions of inhabitants from the Fengjie region, state institutions depicted in *Still Life* offer little compensation or protection from those who are most susceptible to exploitation. Thus, the social science literature that speaks to the relationship between the state, class formation, and reproduction, and social class conflict in the broad sense, is largely absent in the stories that these films tell. It is thus not surprising that the presence of educational institutions in these works is also circumscribed, but it is certainly noteworthy, particularly with regard to the chronicling of life in modern South Korea and China, two countries with long traditions of venerating educational achievement. The fact that the endings in these films embrace ambiguity or pessimism is also significant, as they differ significantly from the faith placed in educational reform that permeates much of the formal educational literature. The fact that the conflicts their characters confront remain unresolved at the end of these films highlights the precarity that has and will continue to mark each of their lives. As has been noted throughout this volume, the degree of uncertainty these filmmakers are comfortable expressing in the endings of their story lines is not one that has been embraced in the formal academic discourse to which we have previously referred.

What these films do affirm is the centrality of affect in our daily interactions. The plots in all of these films focus upon character development as defined through their relations with one another and with their surrounding environment. They respond to their encounters with a level of intensity that is commensurate with the violence, separation, displacement, and lack of recognition they experience. Although their likeability varies on a personal basis, as viewers, we certainly understand and can empathize with the conditions they are compelled to confront. And while the quality of their responses may vary from overt expressiveness to quiet stoicism, it is their high degree of intensity that contributes to the realism of their stories.

The characters in these films also engage in meaning-making to a significant degree. Meaning-making occurs in the face of precarity, be it based upon economic survival, striving to maintain and/or increase material privilege, surviving separation, loss of personal connection, or physical removal and dislocation. Ethical considerations play a major role in the actions of characters in *A Separation* and *Still Life*; in *Parasite*, the characters attempt to make meaning in a world devoid of ethical commitments. Even so, when many of the characters turn to physical violence, they do so as a way of affirming their dignity in response to their presence being ignored or dismissed. Finally, the characters in these films repeatedly engage in acts of assemblage and dis-assemblage. All three films focus upon the fragility of family and marriage ties; the cohesiveness of these social units is never assumed and is perpetually endangered.

The filmmakers in question are able to illustrate the importance of affect not only by touching upon its intellectual components but by compelling us to make associations with all of our senses in addition to the visual. In *Parasite*, smell becomes a key marker of social class distinction. In *A Separation*, the plot turns on a main character hearing a phone call. In *Still Life*, the appeal to viewers' sense of smell and taste is enhanced through the camera's focus upon cigarettes, tea, noodles, and toffee candies, which serve as props for the human interactions that do occur amid the surrounding dislocation and destruction. In all of these ways, the filmmakers' embrace of affect affirms the universality of their messaging and enhances their films' cross-cultural appeal. In so doing, they present alternative perspectives to the conventional social science and educational literature with which we are most familiar.

5

Racism and the Struggle to Assert Identity

It is difficult to conceive of investigating social relations of any type without considering the central role racism has played and continues to play in defining those relations. Racism's omnipresence is directly implicated in the exercise of power, privilege, exclusion, and elimination. It has been repeatedly used as a tool in determining which living beings are labeled human or inhuman, and its presence is visible in every facet of political, economic, social, and cultural life. It marks our collective histories and current interactions. And, as has been noted in the previous pages of this text, racism's presence is implicated in the study of education and film; its existence is apparent in broad exercises of comparison, and it is closely tied to practices involving slavery, settler colonialism, and postcolonial international development agendas.

In the introduction to this volume, we noted that those who have been critical of affect theory have noted that its Western origins belie its claim of universality, particularly for those living in the Global South, while others remain unimpressed with its emphasis on pluralism, which minimalizes in their view, the enduring consequences of racism and colonialism. Since there are differing perspectives regarding the immutability of racism and colonialism among scholars writing directly about racism and colonialism as well, such criticisms of affect theory are not surprising. We acknowledge that an affect theoretical emphasis may be unable to resolve some of the conceptual tensions regarding what racism and colonialism mean, how they operate, and the degree to which their continuing presence is inevitable. What such a perspective does provide, though, is a heightened awareness of their various inundations, and through the use of film, a more comprehensive and realistic understanding of their consequences.

In some ways, it is easier to comprehend what racism is not, rather than label it according to specific criteria that limit our appreciation for its pervasiveness. Thus, the distinction between what constitutes bias, prejudice, and racism is useful. To the degree that expressions of bias and prejudice at their core connote negative judgments of others based upon individual interactions and experiences, they don't begin to fully explain racism's systematic and violent nature. Perceptions, be they positive or negative, change according to circumstance; they are often amplified or modified as a result of exposure to new and different perceptions and experiences. Racism is not simply an extreme expression of personal preference for its ubiquitous presence is evident in public as well as private spheres and is noticeable throughout social and political institutions of all types.

It is most definitely related to race, a social construct that was historically mislabeled by Enlightenment thinkers as a biological category. As Clair and Denis note,

> The term race was first used to describe peoples and societies in the way we now understand ethnicity or national identity. Later, in the seventeenth and eighteenth centuries, as Europeans encountered non-European civilizations, Enlightenment scientists and philosophers gave race a biological meaning. They applied the term to plants, animals, and humans as a taxonomic subclassification within a species. As such, race became understood as a biological, or natural, categorization system of the human species. As Western colonialism and slavery expanded, the concept was used to justify and prescribe exploitation, domination, and violence against peoples racialized as non-white. Today, race often maintains its "natural" connotation in folk understandings; yet, the scientific consensus is that race does not exist as a biological category among humans—genetic variation is far greater within than between "racial" groups, common phenotypic markers exist on a continuum, not as discrete categories, and the use and significance of these markers varies across time, place, and even within the same individual. (Clair and Denis, 2015, acknowledging the work of Fiske, 2010)

A recognition that race is a social construct may help to highlight the arbitrary manner in which racial categorization is employed, but it does not detract from its pervasiveness nor its permanence. This is certainly the case when one examines the way in which whiteness has been defined and promoted within Western settings. Theorists have reminded us that whiteness plays multiple, if occasionally contradictory, roles. Whiteness is viewed as both the absence of color and the purest of colors. In the former case, self-identification as part of an ethnic or racial group is viewed as divisive and potentially destructive. The structural policies and practices that maintain and codify white privilege refuse to be acknowledged, and instead, an individualistic, meritocratic view of social and political organization is promoted. Adherents to such a perspective argue that minority group affiliation plays no role in determining one's social position or prospects for future advancement. The very expression of non-white group identity is thus castigated for creating divisiveness and upsetting the natural social order. It is also noteworthy, though, that when they feel victimized or uncertain of their ability to maintain their control of the social order, whites become more willing to explicitly self-identify as whites, and are more willing to assert the primacy of their own group affiliation, in open conflict with non-white racial and ethnic groups. Whiteness visibility increases in response to a perceived threat to the group's superiority (Anderson, 2016).

Viewed in these terms, whiteness (as is true of racism more generally) should not simply be viewed as a social construct but is additionally deeply embedded within various forms of cultural expression. The use of linguistic tools that value white over black and light over dark, along with similar binaries, speaks to the way in which language contributes to the framing of whiteness ideologically. In this vein, Stuart Hall argued that with specific regard to the media, racism could be construed as being overt, whereby the intention to express a racist view against a specific group is made visible and explicit, or inferential, where racist views are shared as being commonsensical, without their assumptions ever being exposed or contested (Hall, 1995, 20). Richard Dyer's analysis of the use of lighting to promote whiteness in film, referenced in Chapter 2, offers further confirmation of the presence of inferential racism in film.

In its most virulent forms, racism legitimizes the demonization of the other to the point where the other is no longer considered to be human. The deliberate effort to erase a group's human existence goes far beyond efforts to maximize privilege or institutionalize discrimination. Its presence is evident in the promotion of slavery and settler colonialism; in our postcolonial world, its existence is present in various iterations of racial capitalism. To be clear, slavery as an historical phenomenon had origins that were independent of European anti-Black racism. In fact, the elimination of the slave trade in the Americas in the nineteenth century actually coincided with the promotion of scientific racism on the part of the Europeans (Drescher, 1990). Nonetheless, the consignment of human beings to the category of property, to be valued only as a source of labor that can be used, commodified, bought, and sold for purposes of acquiring profit and economic advantage, was best rationalized by appealing to racism and racist thinking during the Western European colonization of the Americas.

Orlando Patterson's classic work in this vein, *Slavery and Social Death* (1982), extensively compared historical conditions of slavery on a global basis, and in so doing, he coined the terms "social death" and "natal alienation." By "social death," Patterson refers to the coerced erasure of the enslaved person's status. By "natal alienation," he refers to the forfeiting of one's genealogy and family history, as evidence of having ever been part of human society. As he notes,

> The condition of slavery did not absolve or erase the prospect of death. Slavery was not a pardon; it was, peculiarly, a conditional commutation. The execution was suspended only as long as the slave acquiesced in his powerlessness. The master was essentially a ransomer. What he bought or acquired was the slave's life, and restraints on the master's capacity wantonly to destroy his slave did not undermine his claim on that life. Because the slave had no socially recognized existence outside of his master, he became a social nonperson. This brings us to the second constituent element of the slave relation: the slave's natal alienation. Here we move to the cultural aspect of the relation, to that aspect of it which rests on authority, on the control of symbolic instruments. This is achieved in a unique way in the relation of slavery: the definition of the slave, however recruited, as a socially dead person. Alienated from all "rights" or claims of birth, he ceased to belong in his own right to any legitimate social order. All slaves experienced, at the very least, a secular excommunication. (Patterson, 1982, 5)

Over time, Patterson's thesis has been criticized for the lack of agency he ascribes to the enslaved. But more recently, proponents of Afro-pessimism have reexamined his work and have argued that the concept of social death can be applied to the current set of experiences to which Black people are subjected. Frank Wilderson has specifically argued that for Black people, being enslaved is a permanent condition. Society is dependent upon their labor and their presence in order to survive even as they are continually confronted with social exclusion (Cunningham, 2020; Wilderson, 2020). Although the formal substitution of personhood with property may have ended with the abolition of slavery in the literal sense, the linkages between the two have remained potent. With the transformation of empire into imperial nation-state, the terms through which property could be acquired and protected not only became regulated but became intertwined with notions of citizenship as defined by the state. C. B. McPherson's notion of possessive individualism is especially instructive here, as he argued that seventeenth-century Enlightenment liberalism viewed the social contract between government and the individual as existing for the sole purpose of allowing one the freedom to maximize one's capacity to accumulate property, a desire that could never be fully satisfied and was unending. There was no inherent social obligation or understanding of the common good that defined the contract between government and citizen, and insofar as one's personhood was tied to one's capacity to acquire property, and that there was intense competition to do so, those with less capacity to acquire property were not deserving of social protection (MacPherson, 1962; Little, 2011). Thus, even after the practice of slavery was abolished, racism has been employed as a convenient tool in legitimizing the perpetuation of economic, political, and social inequality.

For scholars such as Cedric Robinson (1983), racism is an intrinsic part of global capitalism and not simply a by-product. He argues that the tendency to divide and create fragmentation between different groups was essential to capitalism's growth because it set the terms for imagining what class division might include. It existed in feudal, precapitalist societies and has become essential to the functioning of the world system. Focusing upon the continuing legacy of institutional racism in the United States, early proponents of critical race theory (CRT) emphasized the ways in which legal precedents that intended to eliminate overt segregation practices actually harmed people of color by failing to confront institutional racism's enduring impact (Delgado and Stefancic, 2017). That conclusion has found particular salience in the aftermath of the George Floyd murder and the growth of the Black Lives Matter Movement into an international phenomenon. There has thus been expanding recognition of the persistence of institutional racism on a global level and of the enduring legacy of settler colonialism and imperialism on peoples of color, raising larger questions not simply about the ways in which institutions and the market continue to collectively perpetuate racism but to the ways in which, under such conditions, personal identity is consigned, shaped, and expressed.

Much of the scholarship we have summarized emphasizes racism's enduring importance. Alexander Weheliye takes this premise a step further, arguing that it is a mistake to identify racism as only one of many unfortunate elements of the liberal individualist state that can be rectified or redressed without challenging the premises upon which the Western notion of "human" is founded. Instead, he argues that we should acknowledge its direct presence within all forms of human expression, for in his view, the suffering that racism produces speaks to the very boundaries of what it means to be human. Indeed, in his view, it is those who are directly forced into experiencing racist suffering who are in the best position to help reconceive of the human for all of humanity (Weheliye, 2014). Paul Gilroy has analyzed issues of race and identity invoking the frame of the Black diaspora, as a way of decoupling the definition of race from the geopolitical markings of the Western European state. In his view, blackness should be viewed as transcending such boundedness, as he views recognition of the Black diaspora as a key to dynamically confronting the whiteness embedded within Western constructions of empire. As he states,

> The diaspora idea invites us to move into the contested spaces between the poles that we can identify roughly as the global and the local. It encourages to proceed in ways that do not privilege the modern nation-state and its institutional order over the sub-national and supra-national networks and patterns of power, communication and conflict that they work to discipline, regulate, and govern. The concept of space is itself transformed when it is seen less through outmoded notion of fixity and place and more in terms of the accidental. . . . Invariably promiscuous and unsystematically profane, diaspora challenges us to apprehend mutable itinerant culture. It suggests the complex, dynamic potency of living memory: more embodied than ascribed. (Gilroy, 1994, 211–12)

Gilroy thus views blackness, when conceived of in transnational and diasporic terms, as offering possibilities for transformation through the construction of identity aided through engagement with varying assemblages, cognizant of the racist oppression that has marked past histories but untethered by it. In analyzing the British anthology film series *Small Axe*, we see a number of Gilroy's views presented, which is not surprising given the fact that he served as a consultant on the project.

Much of the literature cited to date views whiteness and blackness in binary terms, both with regard to the historical and contemporary evidence of majority/minority exploitation, and with respect to the nature of diasporic relationships on a transnational level. The films selected for analysis are also reflective of this perspective. But is such a view overly simplistic, particularly when one examines whiteness and anti-blackness in a global context? In Jemima Pierre's rendering, European colonialism served to combine an indirect rule of African colonies with the imposition of a nativist (and anti-tribalist) mindset that structured white supremacy and set the predicate for contemporary globalized racialism (Pierre, 2013, 11–36). Such racism not only expresses itself through the politics of racial capitalism but manifests itself at the deepest of levels, even with regard to body image, not only in majority/minority societies but within African dominant societies such as Ghana as well (Pierre, 2013, 101–22). As is true of affect theory more generally, with particular regard to assemblage and dis-assemblage processes, highlighting the global dimensions of anti-blackness invokes an acknowledgment of their intersectionality, implicating social, economic, cultural, and political forms of oppression that interact with one another in fluid terms. But does an appreciation for the intersectionality through which whiteness and anti-blackness operate allow us to fully comprehend racism's uniqueness and distinctiveness? The films reviewed here don't explicitly examine whiteness and anti-blackness in global terms, and in many cases, the intersectionality they acknowledge is inferred as much as it is clearly articulated.

The settings they describe are deeply affected by distinctive political and cultural circumstances which serve as powerful identity markers for the characters who are portrayed. Yet when the films are viewed together, they do illustrate different approaches in which racism manifests itself across borders and continents.

Racism and Education

Because the academic literature exploring the relationship between racism and education is as robust as it is diverse, it is impossible to do justice to all of its iterations in a short space. Instead, I offer a few reflections. First, much of the formal academic educational literature, and certainly the comparative and international education literature, views the relationship between education and race in institutional terms. There is a focus upon schooling as a state institution, and as a result, racism is often framed within contours that accept the primacy of the state and institutions beholden to it as enabling or preventing racist policies and behaviors. It is thus not surprising that much of the research has focused upon issues of justice and equity with regard to states' treatment of people of color. Nancy Fraser has noted that there are three aspects of justice that can be interrogated; they involve issues related to the equitable distribution of resources, equity in the procedures and processes of delivering justice to all, and a recognition or respect for the needs of all social groups (Fraser, 2010). The literature addressing the existence of racism within educational institutions speaks to each of these three areas. Examples that speak to the educational settings highlighted in the television series and films reviewed in this section are thus offered as illustrations.

Disparities that minority group communities confront in their efforts to acquire and utilize school resources with respect to teacher training and representation (Tereshchenko, Mills, and Bradbury, 2020; Chisolm, 2019), not to mention facilities, equipment, class size, and curricular options (Kozol, 1991), have regularly been chronicled for decades. Their existence complements discriminatory practices in employment, housing, and health care that of course also afflict minority communities. Thus, the conclusion that the systematic perpetuation of institutional racism is promoted through the use of disparate funding schemes that limit resource allocation and access made available to the schools and similar educational structures located within minority communities, and that there has been a failure to hire teachers of color who are representative of their school communities, are conclusions that have been widely accepted within the academic literature.

With regard to educational process and procedure, there has been considerable documentation regarding the school to prison pipeline in the United States and South Africa whereby students of color who drop out of school become engulfed in the juvenile justice and prison systems (Blitzman, 2021; Ally, Beere, and Moult, 2021), and in the United Kingdom, school "exclusion" or expulsion disproportionately affects Black students (Graham and Robinson, 2004). In examining the mechanisms through which these results come to fruition, there are a number of theories in play. Labeling theory proponents argue that when racist teacher perceptions of students' negative abilities are repeatedly expressed, students internalize their label and learn to play the role to which they have been ascribed (Rist, 1977). Overt racial stereotyping of course also occurs (Gillborn, 1997). Others have commented upon institutional antagonism and/or indifference to minority parents and community members, in ways that make it difficult for parents to advocate on behalf of their children (Calabrese, 1990; Page, Whitting, and McLean, 2007).

The third aspect of injustice that evokes racist practice and policy involves the lack of recognition and/or respect offered to students, parents, and communities of color. The absence of culturally relevant pedagogies and curricula, the whitewashing of the racism embedded in state building and colonialist expansion, the privileging of standard English to the detriment of vernacular languages or dialects taught within schools, and the lack of accommodation for rituals and cultural values in support of religious preference, dress, food, and so on, are all examples of the ways in which schools have been indicted for failing to recognize or affirm the identities of minority students, parents, and community members (Roberts, 2021; Parsons, 2021).

An understanding of the relationship between equality of opportunity and equality of outcome is central to the recognition of the presence of educational racism and its pernicious effects. Those loyal to the conventional notion of equality of opportunity focus upon its tacit embrace of the exercise of individual choice and autonomy as a foundational ethical principle in crafting a just mechanism for distributing economic and social goods. Those who focus upon the importance of equality of outcome argue that there can be no real equality of opportunity when collectively the outcomes of certain policies and practices are so disparately and consistently negative for specific social groups. As Anne Phillips has argued,

> The argument I pursue in this paper is that equality of outcome—measured here not in the ideologically loaded terms of preference satisfaction nor in the narrower metric of income and wealth, but across the broad spectrum of resources, occupations, and roles—has to be taken as a key measure of equality

of opportunity. When differences of outcome are explained retrospectively by reference to differences in personal preference, this assumes what has to be demonstrated: that individuals really did have equal opportunities to thrive. In many cases, moreover, these explanations reproduce ideologically suspect stereotypes about particular social groups: that "women" for example, care more about children than men, or have less of a taste for political power. When outcomes are "different" (read unequal), the better explanation is that the opportunities were themselves unequal. There is room for a stronger argument that presents equality of outcome as itself an intrinsic good, and I note some cases where I believe this to apply. But even if we leave aside this stronger argument, outcome equality cannot be regarded as the crazy alternative to equal opportunities. These are not opposing conceptions of equality, but on the contrary, closely linked. (Phillips, 2004).

Of course, the failure to fully recognize the repercussions of unequal outcomes racial groups experience also speaks to issues involving lack of respect and recognition of the conditions they have been forced to confront. It not only is indicative of the ideology of possessive individualism that has undergirded the liberal state but has been visible in conventional international education development rationales as well, particularly when Global North policies are mechanically applied to racial groups in the developing world without addressing the exploitative conditions that have limited their opportunities from the start. Indeed, the United Nations Sustainability Development Goals for 2030 have been specifically criticized by the UN Special Rapporteur on Contemporary Forms of Racism, Racial Discrimination, Xenophobia, and Related Intolerance, for their inattention to issues of racial injustice (UN News, 2022). The television series and films discussed in this chapter address many of the issues heretofore noted: whiteness, racial capitalism, the African diaspora, possessive individualism, social death, natal alienation, Afro-pessimism, along with varying educational institutional responses, or the lack thereof, in ways that are evocative and dramatic. In so doing, they acknowledge that educational institutions have been complicit in the perpetuation of racism but offer mixed messaging regarding the prospects for viewing education as the primary antidote to combatting racist belief and practice.

The Underground Railroad

The television series *The Underground Railroad* was based upon the Colson Whitehead novel (2016) with the same title that won the National Book Award for fiction in 2016 and the Pulitzer Prize for fiction in 2017. Directed by Academy Award winner Barry Jenkins, the ten-episode miniseries closely follows the plot of the novel with a few notable exceptions. In so doing, it graphically portrays the violence and horror intrinsic to settler colonialism as manifested within the history of the United States. Part of the genius of the novel as well as the miniseries lies in the innovative depiction of time and space as a means of emphasizing the enduring effects of North American slavery upon the entire population. Slavery is thus more than an historical artifact; instead, it is depicted as a conscious effort to subjugate, consume, and destroy the "other" in ways that occur across specific time periods that include contemporary resonances. This is accomplished through the depiction of the "underground railroad" itself. In actuality, the underground railroad was a series of local networks created principally by African-Americans who were either born free or became freed slaves, who attempted to assist fellow African-Americans trying to escape the brutal conditions of slavery. White abolitionists and Native Americans also offered assistance, with abolitionists doing so largely after escapees reached northern states. From a material perspective, the underground railroad included a series of safe shelters and secure locations that housed slaves on their escape routes, escapees using the facilities to surreptitiously hide and then travel to free states in the North and to Canada or to other areas where slavery was outlawed. Slaves tended to travel in small groups and used various means of transportation to aid in their escape including boats, carriages, and in some instances, trains (Foner, 2015).

In the novel and miniseries, the underground railroad is depicted as a literal object, complete with railroad tracks, locomotives, engines, cabin compartments, and so on. Its presence not only allows the author to invoke magic realism as a part of his depiction of an historical narrative, but it encourages the reader and the miniseries audience to view the characters' efforts to escape from the horrors of slavery in ways that are both material and metaphorical. In point of fact, the first passenger railroad in the South, carrying passengers from Atlanta to Chattanooga, was not open to traffic until 1850 (Library of Congress, n.d.). Similarly, high-rise buildings, described as having existed in South Carolina, were not built in the United States until the 1880s. Such intentional anachronisms contribute to the realization that chronological time periods become unimportant when the existence of evil is persistent. Whitehead also makes allegorical references to actual racist events throughout the novel, placing them in different geographical as well as temporal settings. The reader and the viewer are thus confronted with the realization that the enormity of racism's effects transcend time as well as space.

Synopsis

The Underground Railroad focuses upon the life of Cora, born into slavery in the state of Georgia. Left on her own after her mother, Mabel, fled from the horrors of the Randall plantation and allegedly escaped to freedom, Cora is subjected to the systematic and frequent brutality of plantation life. Having felt abandoned by her mother, Cora after being approached by fellow slave Caesar decides to escape with him. During their escape, as they attempt to evade capture, they are intercepted by a white gang, whereupon Cora kills a young white boy and is thus wanted for murder in addition to being a runaway. They are pursued throughout the story line by Arnold Ridgeway, a slave catcher who when contracted to do so was never able to find Mabel, Cora's mother. Capturing Mabel's daughter Cora thus becomes an obsession for him. Together, Caesar and Cora evade escape in Georgia when they find an underground railroad station where they take a train and end up in Griffin, South Carolina.

Griffin, South Carolina, is depicted as a place where, on the surface, African-Americans are treated with more respect than in Georgia. There is no slavery in Griffin, and there is more intermingling between Blacks and whites. Blacks are able to hold their own jobs, although at the behest of the dominant Anglo elites. Caesar finds work in a factory, and Cora works part-time in a museum, where she is part of a diorama displaying plantation life in the South for a curious white audience. Eventually, Cora discovers that the people of Griffin have embraced eugenics as an ideology and have invited doctors and medical personnel to sterilize Black women and to inject patients with poison in the name of scientific experimentation. In this depiction, author Whitehead is making a metaphorical reference to the eugenics movement in the United States, of which we have previously spoken in Chapter 1, and to the Tuskegee syphilis experiment study of 1932, where African-American patients were injected with the disease without any accompanying treatment (Nix, 2020). Ridgeway tracks Caesar and Cora to South Carolina, and before they can flee together, he captures Caesar, who, after being placed in jail, is murdered and dismembered by a white mob allowed to enter the prison. Cora then escapes after finding an underground railroad station and ends up in North Carolina.

For most of her stay in North Carolina, she stays hidden in an attic, protected by a white abolitionist couple in violation of local law. In North Carolina, it had become illegal for any African-Americans to set foot on state territory; those who harbor slaves and captured slaves were summarily hanged. A "freedom trail," graphically displaying the corpses of hanged slaves and others violating the law, figures prominently in the miniseries. The aim was to use immigrants in place of slave labor and in so doing, maintain the economic benefits of a slave system while preserving the whiteness of the state population. The metaphorical reference of this setting involves the history of Oregon, which enacted a series of Black exclusion laws that banned African-Americans from settling in the territory. Even after Oregon was admitted as a state to the United States, it both banned slavery but retained its exclusion law (Nokes, 2022). Returning to the plotline, Cora is eventually outed by the Irish immigrant abolitionist family maid. While abolitionists Martin and Ethel are eventually hanged, slave catcher Ridgeway recaptures Cora, saving her from immanent death, but transporting her with Jasper, another runaway, to Tennessee before returning her to Georgia.

When in Tennessee, the audience learns more about Ridgeway, his upbringing, and his relationship to his father. We also see more of Homer, a young Black youth, freed by Ridgeway, who serves as his clerk, bookkeeper, and secretary. The relationship between the two is one of mutual dependency, with Homer enabling and at times participating in Ridgeway's cruelty. Jasper dies while in Ridgeway's custody. In the novel, Ridgeway shoots him, figuring that the costs of transporting him back to his slave owner are not worth the monetary reward he would receive for doing so. In the miniseries, Jasper starves himself to death, an act of willful resistance to the unjust suffering he experiences. Later, three freedmen suspect that Cora is being kept against her will and rescue her. Their leader, Royal, accompanies her via the underground railroad to a farm in Indiana, where freed African-Americans are allowed a degree of autonomy as long as they don't intermingle with the dominant Anglo population.

Although materially prosperous, the residents of the "Valentine farm" debate whether to leave their residence and move west to more safer grounds, as opposed to continuing to build upon what they have already achieved. In the midst of that open discussion, unprovoked white racists attack the Black population, murdering a number of its inhabitants, burning down its facilities. The depiction evokes parallels with the Wilmington Massacre of 1898, when a white mob, led by a former congressman, torched a newspaper, murdered sixty residents, and deposed a newly elected local government (LaFrance and Newkirk III, 2017). It also shares resonances with the Tulsa Massacre of 1921, when on May 31 and June 1, a white mob looted and burned the Greenwood section of Tulsa, an affluent African-American neighborhood. In addition to destroying 36 city blocks, 800 people were treated for injuries and it is now estimated that over 300 people lost their lives (Tulsa Historical Society and Museum, n.d.).

Royal is murdered during the riot and Cora survives, although she is recaptured by Ridgeway. He commands her to show him the local underground railroad station; she pushes him as he attempts to descend onto the train tracks; in the novel, he dies as a result of the fall, and in the miniseries, she kills him with a gun as he is lying on the ground infirmed. Waking up and ascending from the station, Cora learns that her mother Mabel actually never escaped the Randall plantation but died of a snakebite as she attempted to return to her daughter. The novel and miniseries end with Cora hitching a ride with an African-American male who is going to St. Louis and then to California. Her future is unresolved.

Uses of Affect

It is clear that the themes of social death, racial capitalism, possessive individualism, and Afro-pessimism figure prominently in both the novel and the miniseries. But it is in the miniseries where their impact can be fully appreciated by the viewer, in large part due to its director's use of affect. In the novel, specific slaves are referred to as "it," not deserving of the personal pronoun, nor of the personhood that the personal pronoun identifies, in an effort to demonstrate that they are considered to be and are treated as property. In the miniseries, by contrast, we see the full consequences of that attribution, be it through observing the hanging corpses, methodically lined up along the North Carolina "freedom trail," the horror of seeing bodies deliberately dismembered and burnt or the violence expressed through mass killing in Indiana. As was previously noted by Laura Marks, in Chapter 2, the power of film lies in its appeal to all of its senses, and here, the sense of touch and smell complement the visual images to portray the horror of racism.

The conceit of the novel lies in its depiction of the underground railroad as a material entity. It is the underground railroad that travels through both different time periods and different locations and spaces. It is the glue that enables Cora's journey to proceed, be it through both physical escape and imaginary wandering. In so doing, it is an artistic vehicle for making the connections between historic and contemporary forms of racism visible, permanent, and vibrant. As an invented object, made alive through Cora's dream-like imagination, it is appropriate that the vehicle that promises any hope for escape is situated below ground, in darkened spaces. Although there are instances where Cora imagines an underground station to be opulent, full of light and color, for the most part, the use of minimal lighting to depict the trains and stations as part of the network acknowledges its separation from the reality above ground. It is noteworthy that Ridgeway dies after "entering" the underground railroad station in Indiana; it is a space that he has transgressed and can't be allowed to remain. It is also noteworthy that when Cora leaves Indiana, hitching a wagon ride with a freedman traveling first to St. Louis and then to the West, in search of freedom from the oppression that has marked her life, the underground railroad is no longer useful. Of course, the nature of the ending of the journey she is pursuing is unknown and unresolved, as is true of contemporary social relations where racism continues to be predominant.

Precarity is only one of the attributes of affect, previously noted in this volume, that holds resonance for *The Underground Railroad*. Its graphic display of violence and systematic depiction of cruelty evoke an intensity of encounter that is unsparing in its message that the injustice perpetuated by slavery has had lasting consequences and that the racism that has continued in its aftermath cannot be separated from its historical origins. Such a message holds special significance in the post-George Floyd/ Black Lives Matter era, where efforts to fully confront historical and contemporary injustice have been met with reflexive racist reactions on the part of white nationalists. Cora's strength as a character lies in her desire to find meaning in a world devoid of ethical accountability on the part of those perpetuating white supremacy. This is also the case for other characters such as Caesar, Royal, Jasper, and Mabel, all of whom confront the conundrum of searching for meaning in circumstances devoid of its presence. Such negotiations, of course, deeply involve assemblage. The potential power of assemblage is recognized in the efforts of white elites to disrupt its formation, be it within the Randall slave plantation in Georgia, the eugenics movement in South Carolina, the elimination of the Black population in North Carolina, or the destruction of the self-sufficient farm in Indiana. One of the major themes of *The Underground Railroad* thus involves dis-assemblage as much as it includes assemblage. Cora's individual journey to the West, in the aftermath of the Indiana mass atrocity and Ridgeway's death, further confirms that the solidarity envisioned through engaging in acts of assemblage can be as ephemeral as it is unstable.

Education and Racism

Education is treated with a strong degree of ambivalence in *The Underground Railroad*. On the one hand, the novel and miniseries both emphasize how important receiving an education was to those who were denied formal access to it. Its significance in promoting independent thinking and autonomy was widely understood, which is why anti-literacy laws in the antebellum South were so draconian. When literacy was countenanced by white slave owners, biblical literacy was emphasized as it was believed to assist in keeping slaves dependent and accepting of the conditions around them. While learning how to read may have occasionally been tolerated, writing was strictly prohibited. Nonetheless, slaves attempted to learn how to read and write in spite of the severe prohibitions to do so, facing consequences that included digital amputation. They did learn basic reading and writing skills surreptitiously, "stealing an education," often learning from white children who were engaged in formal schooling. Slaves who learned to read tended to either reside in urban areas or fulfilled domestic responsibilities within the plantation household, where literacy was closely associated with domesticity and the performance of domestic chores (Cornelius, 1983). Under such conditions, it is estimated that 10 percent of slaves and freed slaves were able to read by the outset of the Civil War (Schweiger, 2013). It is thus significant that Caesar and Royal, in particular, as strong, freedom-seeking male characters, are depicted as being literate individuals who affirm the value of being educated. Caesar, in particular, cherishes his version of *Gulliver's Travels*, which he keeps with him, while Cora's persistence in attempting to rectify her own illiteracy is indicative of her own inner strength and resolve.

However, there is much more ambivalence expressed with regard to educational function when associated with the character of Homer. Homer, the slave bought by Ridgeway and then freed, who became his apprentice clerk, secretary, bookkeeper, and confidant, became literate as a slave and after he freed him, Ridgeway found him useful because of the level of education he achieved. Indeed, Homer is complicit in all of Ridgeway's cruelty and at one point, takes it upon himself to commit murder when he shoots Ridgeway's childhood acquaintance, Mack. In Whitehead and Jenkins's worldview, one's education can be manipulated to enable the worst forms of racism, as embodied within the Homer character. The Homer/Ridgeway relationship is not simply one of manipulation, though; it is also one born of dependency. Far from offering Homer a sense of personal autonomy or freedom, his education perpetuates his dependency upon his former master and later father figure to the point where he becomes comfortable living under unjust racist conditions, unable to conceive of a possible alternative. The notion that some literate Blacks failed to use their educational opportunities to confront the racial injustice broadly afflicting their community members was further expressed during the debates on the Black-owned farmland in Indiana. Not wanting to jeopardize their fragile autonomy by alienating white elites, some members of the community expressed reluctance in assisting those arriving at the farm who had attempted to flee from the oppressive conditions of enslavement to which they had been subjected.

In *The Underground Railroad*, education was viewed as not only enabling racist oppression, but it was instrumental in actively perpetuating it. It was implicated in legitimizing eugenics and unethical scientific experimentation upon African-Americans, as referenced in the description of South Carolinian living conditions in the novel and miniseries. It is noteworthy that although somewhat less viscerally shocking, Cora was also forced into "playing" the role of the slave in an artificially constructed diorama in this episode, supposedly for the educational benefit and entertainment of white school children and tourists, curious about plantation life in the Deep South. The educational presence in this episode was thus viewed as being complicit in fostering racist stereotyping and cultural erasure as much as it was foundational in promoting physical genocide. Alternative views that hold that the realization of educational opportunity provides the best panacea for confronting the existence of racism thus seem broadly naïve, if not completely self-serving, in this treatment of the historical record. Thus, while not entirely dismissive of the power and importance of education under conditions of racist oppression, Whitehead and Jenkins are much more circumspect in assessing its relevance while being cognizant of its potential harm.

Small Axe

A significant portion of post-Second World War British history involves the intersection of race, immigration, and empire, themes that receive visual representation in Steve McQueen's five-film series, *Small Axe*. Together, the films highlight many of the negative experiences members of the West Indian communities confronted in the UK during the latter part of the twentieth century. Often, the films serve as commentaries on actual historical events; on some occasions, they are reflective of the director's personal experiences as the child of West Indian immigrant parents. Together, they paint a picture of a diasporic community attempting to assert its identity within a larger climate infused with racism.

In 1948, the passage of the British Nationality Act incentivized greater immigration to the UK from those residing in British colonies. Part II of the act explicitly stated that any individual born in the UK or its colonies after passage of the act, or any person whose father was a citizen of the UK or the colonies at the time of one's birth would receive UK citizenship status. Given postwar labor shortages, the passage of the BNA was designed to offer significant benefits to a British economy, still experiencing significant challenges after the war. The Nationalities Act thus encouraged a significant degree of immigration from the colonies, particularly from Caribbean countries. Those who came to the UK between 1948 and 1971 from this region were labeled the Windrush Generation, named for the ship *MV Windrush*, that brought 492 workers and some children from Jamaica, Trinidad, Tobago, and other areas of the region to the UK, docking in the city of Tilbury on June 22, 1948. Although they were subject to racism from the time that they entered the UK, immigration first became more restrictive in 1962, after the Commonwealth Immigrants Act was enacted. Under its terms, more specific eligibility rules determining who could immigrate were established, so that there would be a way of limiting the additional number of people of color who could enter the country (Slaven, 2021; Wardle and Obermuller, 2019). Subsequent immigration acts continued to not only constrain future immigration but also disrupt the daily lives of those who had settled in the UK. With the passage of the Immigration Act of 1971, which took effect in 1973, immigrants not only had to confront increased monitoring on an individual basis (Slavin, 2021), but were subject to significant harassment as well, often being forced to provide documentation of their residency status even when it did not exist while being denied basic social services to which they were entitled. As Wardle and Obermuller note,

> Family members born at one time, or who entered Britain at a certain moment, could find their legal status was fundamentally distinct from others who had moved or stayed under a different set of rules. Return to the Caribbean often meant the removal of naturalization rights that should have come with having lived in Britain and the established presence of other family members there. The inherent historical complexity of the legal status of many migrants with a Caribbean background meant that enforcement of "hostile environment" policies inevitably caused chaos. A key feature of the "hostile environment" was that the people targeted would be forced to evidence something for which the evidence did not exist. Migrants must now demonstrate that they or their parents have been in the UK continually since 1 January 1973. Leaving the country for more than two years results in a loss of rights connected to "continuous residency." For many, the Home Office's failure to maintain the records of the people to whom it granted indefinite leave to remain in the 1970s have made "continuous residency" impossible to demonstrate. (Wardle and Obermuller, 2019, 83)

Clearly, making life uncomfortable for those who had settled in the UK was viewed as a mechanism for deterring future immigration. In 2018, the treatment of the Windrush Generation was labeled a scandal, as exposés examining government policies and actions from the 1970s onward were published, and as documentation attesting to the illegal deportation of British citizens who were part of the Afro-Caribbean community was collected and circulated. In reacting to popular outrage, the Home Office reviewed the cases of 11,800 individuals who were detained and/or removed from the UK and specifically examined the cases of 2,000 Caribbean individuals who arrived before 1973 but were not given sufficient documentation attesting to their official status after their arrival. Almost 164 of these individuals were detained or removed from the UK since 2002, 18 of whom were wrongly denied their right to live in the UK, although the total number of people adversely affected by these policies is probably much larger (Williams, 2020, 24). As Williams notes,

> The scandal has affected hundreds, and possibly thousands, of people, directly or indirectly, turning lives upside down and doing sometimes irreparable damage. They were essentially denied their rights: the right to live and work in the UK, to receive healthcare, to have a pension, claim state benefits and to re-enter the UK. At its most extreme, they were deprived of their liberty and ability to live in the UK, splitting families. (Williams, 2020, 25)

Synopses

Small Axe documents the racism the Afro-Caribbean community confronted in the 1980s in graphic terms. Each of the five films that is part of the series portrays an actual set of historical events, the biographical experiences of noted individuals, or the daily struggles of community members confronting racist practices. The first film in the series, *Mangrove*, faithfully recalls the historical events leading to the Mangrove 9 protest and subsequent trial. The *Mangrove*, a restaurant serving Trinidadian cuisine, was founded by Frank Crichlow in the Notting Hill London neighborhood in 1968. The restaurant quickly became a vibrant social and cultural resource for the Afro-Caribbean community and was even occasionally frequented by international celebrities, but its patrons were constantly harassed by police and its owner was repeatedly threatened with license suspension and closure. Constable Frank Pulley, who expressed avowed racist sentiments, led periodic raids on the restaurant, and on August 9, 1970, 150 people gathered for a protest, led by members of the British Black Panther Movement. Over 200 police were dispatched and many protesters were subsequently assaulted. Nine protest leaders were arrested and charged with inciting a riot. Two of the leaders of the demonstration, Altheia Jones and Darcus Howe, represented themselves in the trial and eventually all of the defendants were acquitted of the most serious charges against them. The trial was also noteworthy for while the presiding magistrate stated that the trial showed evidence of racism on both sides, the admission for the first time that racism within the police department existed was significant (Pahwa, 2020; National Archives, n.d.). The film dramatizes these events, emphasizing the role of the restaurant as a safe space that allowed members of the Afro-Caribbean community to express a shared sense of cultural identity while also focusing upon the trial and the importance of community leaders (especially Darcus Howe) publicly and actively defending themselves as part of the judicial proceedings.

The second film in the *Small Axe* anthology is titled *Lovers Rock*, named for a musical genre that was an offspring of reggae. Set in 1980, much of the film takes place in a house party, commonly frequented by Afro-Caribbean youth at the time, since they were often refused entry into white clubs. As was true of the *Mangrove* restaurant, the house party represents a safe space allowing youth the opportunity to freely interact with one another away from the daily pressures that they are forced to regularly confront. The safety preserved within the house party is always precarious, though. The emasculation young men feel as second-class citizens in an Anglo-dominated environment leads in one case to a performative masculinity that condones sexual violence; in another case, feelings of agency and autonomy, encouraged by the house party milieu, evaporate as the subsequent realities of racist employment practices become visible.

The third film in the anthology, titled *Red, White, and Blue*, tells the true story of Leroy Logan, a trained forensic scientist who joined the police force at the age of twenty-six, to later become the first chair of the National Black Police Association in 1998, and received a Member of the British Empire Award from Queen Elizabeth in 2000 (Haynes, 2020a). The film chronicles Logan's struggles both within a deeply racist police force and with his family and friends, who were skeptical of his decision to give up a promising career and work for the "establishment" police. His own father having been the victim of police misconduct, Logan was well aware of the resistance he would confront from family, friends, and community members in trying to reform the police from within the institution but thought it a necessary and worthy cause that had to be pursued. In addition, he had to confront overt hostility within the police department and survive in an environment where he was often given only nominally important assignments or was placed in dangerous situations without necessary peer protection and support, being set up to fail.

In both *Mangrove* and *Red, White, and Blue*, Afro-Caribbean protagonists work within white establishment institutions in order to make them more just, and they do so without compromising their racial and ethnic identities. In McQueen's fourth film in the anthology, Alex Wheatle, the protagonist, finds himself in prison which is where, with the help of an older Rastafarian inmate mentor (Simeone), he confronts questions of personal identity while finding his voice as an author. Wheatle, born to Jamaican parents, grew up in a notorious children's home, *Shirley Oaks*, in Croyden, where children were systematically subjected to racial, physical, emotional, and sexual abuse. Alex himself was beaten and sexually assaulted there, and in 2020, it was reported that over many decades, pedophiles systematically targeted children placed in the home, even though contemporaneous allegations of abuse were never investigated (BBC News, 2020). At the age of fifteen, Alex left the home and moved to Brixton, where he lived in a youth hostel. The film spends time showing how having been raised in ignorance of his cultural heritage, he had to learn what his heritage entailed and what kinds of cultural norms, with regard to dress, musical taste, and movement, were expected. He did so through befriending other youth, including a particularly close friendship with fellow youth Dennis Isaac. As he becomes more involved with the Brixton community, Wheatle becomes more politically aware and radicalized, to the point whereby he participates in the Brexton uprising in April 1981. After repeated police harassment, growing mistrust over the failure to fully investigate a suspicious fire causing the deaths of thirteen youth, and the death of a youth who, after having been stabbed, was perceived to have been a victim of police misconduct, riots ensue, and Wheatle is one of many who is arrested. He serves a prison sentence of six months, where mentor Simeone encourages him to read *The Black Jacobins*, C. L. R. James's historical account of the Haitian Revolution. Eventually Wheatle becomes an award-winning author, publishing his first novel, *Brixton Rock*, in 1999 (Haynes, 2020b).

In *Mangrove, Red, White, and Blue*, and *Alex Wheatle*, the role of education as a positive tool for confronting racism is repeatedly acknowledged. Prominent protagonists such as Darcus Howe, Leroy Logan, and Alex Wheatle are successful in spite of the institutional racism inherent in the judicial, police, social welfare, and prison systems, in large part because their educational success gives them the tools to effectively confront these bureaucracies. They certainly possess other qualities that make them successful, including personal charisma and a sense of responsibility to their community, but there is little skepticism expressed regarding the power and importance of formal educational access in combatting racist policies and practices. The final film in the anthology, *Education*, serves as a coda for this theme.

Education, loosely based upon Steve McQueen's own educational experiences as a child and youth, focuses upon Kingsley, a twelve-year-old who is obviously intelligent, professing interests in rocket ships and astronauts, but who not only is intellectually unchallenged in school but also has a reading disability that he covers up. Upon unfairly labeled as a trouble-maker and viewed as intellectually inferior due to his performance on a standardized test, Kingsley is sent to a special school, one of a number of institutions designated as "schools for the educationally subnormal." Kingsley's mother, heretofore unaware of his academic difficulties, does not possess the cultural capital necessary to contest the placement, which is of course couched in language that speaks of addressing the child's best interests (Brissett and Bailey, 2021). The placement turns out to be a disaster, as students in the school are left unattended without adequate supervision, no authentic program of instruction is offered, teachers are unqualified, demonstrating little concern for student welfare, and then they regularly quit unexpectedly. Guided by a community activist, Kingsley's mother realizes that her son's educational future is bleak, and as she becomes more politically aware, she enrolls Kingsley in an independent supplementary school, staffed by community teachers and leaders. With the encouragement of his mother and teachers at the supplementary school, Kingsley shows progress in learning how to read as the film ends.

Although these events may reflect some of McQueen's own experiences, they also accurately depict a historical record of educational racism that affected many children of the Windrush Generation. In 1969, the Education Committee of the London Borough of Haringey produced two reports advocating the adoption of "banding" or streaming policies that would separate students in classes supposedly according to academic ability, with a significant student population being of Afro-Caribbean descent. One of the reports, titled the "Doulton Report," stated explicitly that "On a rough calculation about half the immigrants will be West Indians at 7 of the 11 schools, the significance of this being the general recognition that their I.Q.s work out below their English contemporaries. Thus academic standards will be lower in schools where they form a large group" (George Padmore Institute, n.d.). Although the banding proposal was eventually withdrawn, the channeling of Afro-Caribbean students into subnormal schools continued in an unabated fashion but was drawn to widespread public attention with the publication of Bernard Coard's book, *How the West Indian Child Is Made Educationally Sub-Normal in the British School System*, in 1971 (Coard, 1971; George Padmore Institute, n.d.).

Many of the resistance strategies chronicled in the film actually took place as part of the Black Education Movement and the Black Supplementary Schools Movement. As was depicted in the film, teachers and community activists went to "subnormal schools," sometimes surreptitiously, to gather evidence about the unprofessional and unacceptable practices that were regularly occurring. Members of the Black Supplementary Schools Movement created supplementary schools such as the one Kingsley attended, staffed by teachers and professional volunteers, emphasizing the teaching of Pan African history and culture, English, mathematics, and geography. Initially developed by members of the British Black Panther Movement, the schools operated during certain weekday afternoons and on Saturdays, with at least one of the schools continuing to operate into the 1990s (George Padmore Institute, n.d.).

Analysis

The title of the *Small Axe* anthology comes from the Bob Marley and the Wailers 1973 song of the same name. Not surprisingly, the themes of resiliency and resolve in the fight against racist oppression, themes that are implied in the song, reverberate throughout the film anthology. Although the desire to create the anthology had been present for a decade, the films were released in 2020, when the Black Lives Matter Movement gained international attention, while the repercussions of the Windrush scandal were being processed in the aftermath of the Brexit decision. Thus, their significance lay not only in their faithful chronicling of the historical record but in their ability to draw attention to the fact that contemporary racist attitudes and practices were as long-standing as were the efforts to combat their pernicious effects. The strategies employed in the struggle against UK racism involved both affirmation of group identity as Afro-Caribbeans and fighting for social justice by demanding institutional reform. It is clear that three aspects of social injustice that Nancy Fraser identified—resource disparity, procedural inequity, and lack of recognition—were all addressed in the Afro-Caribbean struggles noted in the film series. The inadequate resources allocated to the "subnormal school" Kingsley attended and the deplorable conditions at the Shirley Oaks children's home that Alex Wheatle was forced to confront offered evidence for an unjust allocation of institutional resources that perpetuated racism against the Afro-Caribbean community. Numerous procedural violations including unmitigated police harassment against members of the community, a judicial system that condoned police racism, and the placement of large numbers of Afro-Caribbean students in subnormal schools on the basis of racial stereotyping all offered evidence of deeply embedded institutional racism that was facilitated by procedural inequity. And, whether it be the lack of culturally responsive curricula in the schools, the periodic attempts to close the Mangrove restaurant, or the restrictive practices that forced youth into creating their own safe social spaces by organizing private house parties, the lack of recognition of and appreciation for this community's cultural uniqueness demonstrated a level of disrespect characteristic of racism and social injustice.

Much of the academic literature that we previously noted also resonated in the fifth and final film in the *Small Axe* anthology, *Education*. Here we see the racism inherent in labeling theory (Kingsley mistakenly labeled to be incorrigible and intellectually challenged), the misuse of standardized testing to rationalize the placement of children of color in poor serving schools, the disparity of teacher quality in schools serving a minority population, and so on. It is also clear that absent parental intervention, the social reproduction function of schools is affirmed here; we know that Kingsley's future as well as that of his peers within the Afro-Caribbean community will be largely determined by the lack of attention to his reading difficulty and his unfair placement in a substandard school.

With the possible exception of the second film in the anthology, *Lovers Rock*, the tone of the *Small Axe* films is positive and affirming. The heroes of the anthology receive audience admiration for their successes in fighting against institutional racism. One can honestly question the extent to which their achievements can be generalized and whether they are notable exceptions, unrepresentative of the millions who have not been so fortunate in overcoming the consequences of racist practice in the UK. But such optimism should be viewed as affirming a diasporic framing of race that is quite different from the Afro-pessimism that frames Colson Whitehead and Barry Jenkins's perspective in *The Underground Railroad*. To craft such an identity requires one to reimagine one's identity that is not fixated according to conventional spatial terms. Disaporic identity involves displacement but it also affirms reinvention, which, it is argued, can be accomplished without jettisoning one's past. It is for this reason that preserving Afro-Caribbean cultural attributes, as expressed through food, dance, and music, is a necessary element that complements the fight to make UK institutions more just. The struggle for the latter is always ongoing. But the anthology leaves the audience with little doubt that outcomes of such a struggle are not predetermined and hold the possibility of success.

Not surprisingly, the various aspects of affect that we have previously identified are also expressed within the diasporic frame throughout the anthology. Intensity of encounter is present with regard to protagonists' interactions with racist institutions, within family settings, in social spaces, and through public protest. Meaning-making is also expressed through the struggle to assert an independent Afro-Caribbean identity while living within an Anglo-dominated nation. It is further evident in the various efforts to understand the institutional logics that encourage racism and the strategies employed to combat it. Assemblage is itself acknowledged as being crucial to the assertion of diasporic identity through family interactions, within public and private social spaces, and through political protest. Somewhat surprisingly, precarity is most heavily emphasized in the second film in the anthology, *Lovers Rock*, where the safety and freedom youth discover in their house party is ephemeral, subject to externally imposed limitations of whiteness and prevalent racist attitudes toward the youth and their community. Indeed, the optimism depicted in the other four films leaves little ambiguity with regard to the favorable results that arise when the Afro-Caribbean community fights against racial injustice. The audience is left aware that racial injustice remains, but is comforted in the retelling of the success stories. Unlike *The Underground Railroad*, where an unresolved ending highlights the persistence of racism, its inevitability, and its ability to morph into different forms, here, the modernism implicit in educational and social reform efforts is comforting, even if the larger implications of continued racial oppression and its affirmation of whiteness remain unchallenged.

Tsotsi

The word "tsotsi," common in many South African languages, connotes the notion of street thug or hoodlum. It has been associated with Black township youth for many generations, and its lexical origins trace back to the term "zoot suit," made popular in the United States by African-American entertainer Cab Calloway, whose films were seen in South Africa in the 1940s. As Rosalind Morris notes, its association with jazz and the musical shifted over time to that of gangster movies and film noir, where it eventually morphed into an identifier of urban youth as purveyors of violence and criminality (Morris, 2010). The film

Tsotsi was an updated version of the novel of the same name by acclaimed South African author Athol Fugard (published in 1980 but written around 1960) and was directed by Gavin Hood. Released in 2005, it received the Academy Award for best foreign language film in 2006. Set in post-apartheid South Africa, the film depicts the lingering effects of the apartheid system with its focus upon poverty and violence in the economically deprived township, contraposed with the affluence of a Johannesburg suburb.

The main character in the film, an African teenage boy, is referred to as Tsotsi, his real name (David) unknown for much of the story line. Tsotsi is a part of a violent criminal gang that includes three other members, Butcher, Aap, and Boston. We first see the gang accost a man in a subway, knife him, and steal his wallet. The victim is stabbed by Butcher and is dead before the gang leaves the subway car. Afterwards, while hanging out in a local bar, Boston asks Tsotsi sensitive questions regarding his embrace of brutality, inability to feel emotion, and what it was in his background that influenced his current disposition. Tsotsi erupts in a rage and beats Boston severely before leaving the bar. After doing so, he wanders into a middle-class suburb where an African woman has gotten out of her car, attempting to open the locked gate to her residence. At gunpoint, he gets in the car and when she tries to stop him, he shoots her in the lower body area and drives off. We later learn that she has become paralyzed from the waist down. Soon he recognizes that there is a baby in the back of the car, and he takes the baby to his house.

Initially, Tsotsi attempts to take care of the baby himself, feeding the child with some milk. When his gang mates come to the door, he agrees to meet them at a subway station a bit later. On the way, he meets a disabled man, Morris, whom he mocks because of his inability to walk. We learn that Morris broke his back while working in the mines, and contrary to Tsotsi's suspicion, he was not faking his infirmity. Upon returning to his home, Tsotsi sees that he cannot care for the baby on his own, so he takes the baby to a woman (Miriam), whom he forces at gunpoint to breast feed. Miriam is a widow, her husband having died as a result of gang violence, and Tsotsi begins to regularly count on her for assistance in caring for the baby. At the same time, he is adamant that the baby is his property.

While surreptitiously caring for the baby at his home, Tsotsi also agrees to take care of Boston, his fellow gang member whom he assaulted at the beginning of the film, and brings him to his home. He and his fellow gang members decide to rob the residence of the baby's parents in order to retrieve items that will assist in the baby's care. They tie up the baby's father, John, and when he attempts to contact the police, one of the gang members, Butcher, finds a gun and attempts to shoot John.

Tsotsi then himself shoots Butcher before John is harmed. After their escape, one of his remaining gang mates, Aap, leaves, not understanding the reason for Tsotsi's violence, noting that he had already assaulted Boston and killed Butcher.

Upon returning home, he sees Miriam who tells him that he must return the baby to its legal parents. He apologizes to Boston for his assault and then takes the baby with him. At the subway station, he once again sees Morris, the disabled person whom he previously mocked, and in another redemptive act, offers him money. He then goes to return the baby to its home, is noticed by the police, who, at the intervention of the baby's father, tells them not to shoot. Tsotsi gives up the baby in front of its home and raises his hands, waiting to be arrested (IMDb, n.d.).

Analysis

Based upon a novel written by a white South African, with a screenplay rewritten and directed by a second white South African of another generation, *Tsotsi* defines blackness in terms of the main character's toxic masculinity and embrace of violence. While the major theme in both the novel and film focuses upon the main character's personal search for redemption, that theme is problematic for a number of reasons. Although more muted in the film, there is explicit Christian messaging in both the novel and the film that is associated with his redemptive journey. Ultimately, it is his bonding with the innocent baby he has unintentionally kidnapped who helps him begin to trust others and discover his inner humanity, and at the end of the film, he makes the personal sacrifice of returning the baby to its parents knowingly facing incarceration or worse. But what of the violent, remorseless youth to whom we are first introduced in the film? Why is it that he has to be "redeemed" in order that his basic personhood be acknowledged? As soon as we are introduced to his character, we are presented with an individual who shows no remorse for the injury he commits to others. A violent criminal, devoid of conscience, he has to discover an inner moral compass that values the protection of the innocent in order to gain audience sympathy. He generates little such sympathy during the first part of the film, where there is little to no historical context that is presented to explain the causes for the poverty, violence, and gang activity that characterize Tsotsi's township, in dire contrast to the affluent Johannesburg suburb where the carjacking occurs. Instead, this Black youth is presented as an object worthy of being feared and reviled. As no mention is ever made of apartheid, its lasting social ramifications after its official demise are never fully explored.

Instead, Tsotsi's personal circumstances are emphasized in order to better understand his motivations and behavior. We learn, later in the film, for example, that Tsotsi's mother died of HIV/AIDS and his father was quite violent and abusive, causing him to leave home surviving by living in construction pipes. His association with the baby causes him to recall the circumstances that robbed him of his own childhood; through trying to care for the baby, he begins his struggle for redemption. We see the fruits of the journey in the eventual empathy he demonstrates toward Morris, the paraplegic man he sees in the subway station, in trying to take care of Boston, his gang mate whom he previously assaulted, and in his bonding with Miriam, the woman who helps him care for the baby. In each of these instances, his initial mistrust of the other gives way to acts of tolerance and empathy. They crystalize in his decision to save the life of the baby's father (John) and in his ultimate decision to return the baby to its rightful parents.

Lindiwe Dovey has persuasively argued that in Gavin Hood's rendering, *Tsotsi* offers a neoliberal perspective on post-apartheid South African society. In his view, Tsotsi's path toward personal redemption is intertwined with the conceit that offers the possibility that such a journey can be successfully achieved without significantly addressing broader political and economic inequality fostered by South Africa's racist past. This allows the audience to feel not only complacent about the real lack of social progress evident in early twenty-first-century South Africa but also dismissive of the need for systematic social reform (Dovey, 2007). A second, somewhat related, issue involves the film's affirmation of whiteness as the placeholder for normalcy as well as purity. The only Anglo characters depicted in the film are police officers, who fulfill their duties by combatting lawlessness and apprehending Black criminals and gang members in the township. They thus set the terms and create the conditions under which the success of Tsotsi's struggle for redemption can be judged. Indeed, there is little intrinsic to township life that is positive. One of course sees the material deprivation that manifests itself through abject poverty, the fragility of shack dwelling, and the volatility of gang violence, which make stable interpersonal interaction nearly impossible. The solution posed in the film and then the novel is not one of affirming solidarity or cohesiveness within the Black community but seeking to purify oneself as the only way of transcending such conditions: in other words, becoming white (at least in the metaphorical sense).

It is thus not surprising that educational provision plays a very minor role in the film. Boston is the most formally educated member of Tsotsi's gang, having attended a university and studying to become a teacher before leaving. He is the one gang member who is most reflective and critical of the violence the gang perpetuates. But in himself becoming a victim to the violence, he ends up dependent upon Tsotsi for care and protection. His education may have enhanced his social awareness and moral compass but has done little to help him escape from a disappointing fortune. In reality, there are few educational opportunities for the inhabitants of the township, but there is little evidence to suggest that even if present, they would be transformative, in the same way that Tsotsi is able to independently will his own personal transformation.

Aesthetically, the film graphically portrays the squalor of township life as well as the violence that marks Tsotsi's existence as well as that of his fellow gang members. The use of nonprofessional actors in major roles creates a sense of authenticity to which audiences can easily relate. However, when we think of which of the principles of affect are utilized within the film, the message is more mixed. Certainly, intensity of encounter is highlighted throughout the film, be it with the interactions among the gang members and their dealings with their victims, and through Tsotsi's relationships to the baby he has kidnapped and adopted, as well as with Miriam, Morris, Boston, and others. As we have noted, while initially averse to engaging in meaning-making, retrospection and reflection being too painful for him to pursue, much of the film focuses upon Tsotsi's attempt to find meaning through caring for the baby he has kidnapped while finding his moral compass. The fact that his journey is largely solitary and individualistic speaks to the lack of emphasis on assemblage in the film and the novel. Alliances with fellow gang members are fragile and transitory as are other relationships within the township. The rugged individualism that at its core frames his growing ethical awareness is thus striking (Dovey, 2007). Finally, while his material future is uncertain, once having returned the baby to safety, his journey toward redemption is complete. The certainty of that act allows the audience to empathize with the character without being forced to fully contemplate the precariousness of his or others' material circumstances.

Conclusion

It is fascinating to note the ways in which the films discussed in this chapter reflect many of the prevalent themes that are apparent in the academic discourse involving race and racism. As has been noted, *The Underground Railroad* is reflective of the discussions of social death, racial capitalism, and Afro-pessimism that attempt to explain why historic patterns of racism remain so persistent in contemporary life. The films in the *Small Axe* anthology reiterate an optimistic cosmopolitanism that is reflective of the Afro-Caribbean diasporic experience. In so doing, they emphasize the generic hybridity of that experience, illustrating the importance of fostering community solidarity through encouraging the preservation of shared cultural practices while engaging in political activism so as to demand an end to social injustice. And, in *Tsotsi*, we see an affirmation of whiteness, even as the violence and suffering in post-apartheid township life is dramatically portrayed. We began this chapter with the assertion that the concept of race has always been a social construction, and its various attributions in these films offer further evidence for its various permutations.

We also commented upon the diversity of viewpoint regarding the connection between education and racism in the academic literature. Particularly with regard to its institutional iteration, education has been viewed as a perpetuator, enabler, or antidote to racist attitude and practice, and here too, the films in question reiterate this eclecticism of perspective. In *The Underground Railroad*, education is directly tied to racism through its referencing of eugenics and scientific experimentation inflicted upon African-Americans; it at times enhances resistance to racist practice and is thought of as a threat to slavery by promoting independent thought; its heroes largely embrace the autonomy that literacy in particular promises. At other times, though, and particularly in the character of Homer, its presence rationalizes subservience and contributes to dependency. The films within the *Small Axe* series, and the film *Education* in particular, are also reflective of the academic literature examining the relationship between education and race. Issues involving resource disparity, procedural inequity, negative stereotyping and labeling, and indifference to cultural and ethnic diversity are all mentioned as factors contributing to institutional racism. At the same time, the series includes many examples of those who through educational achievement became empowered, with the portrayal of the community-based supplemental school serving as an exemplar for how alternative educational provision was used to successfully respond to social injustice. Not surprisingly, *Tsotsi* says little about the nature of education and institutional racism, given the lack of educational opportunity in post-apartheid township life and the film's general effort to frame responses to social injustice in terms of individual aspiration and spiritual affirmation.

From an affective perspective, the films are interesting in the differing ways in which they address the nature of time and space. In *The Underground Railroad*, the associations with different historical events that appear outside of their original time frames evoke a sense of racism's timelessness and its persistent endurance. Its ambiguous ending offers further evidence for the contention that efforts to successfully eliminate its presence will always be precarious. In terms of spatial representation, the accuracy of the geographical positioning of depicted historical events is less important than the events themselves, leading credence to the contention that the pervasive nature of racism cannot be contained within discrete spaces. In *Small Axe*, time is portrayed in a more conventional sense. Offering a faithful rendering of actual historical events occurring in the 1980s, one of the purposes of the miniseries is to remind viewers of a past that, for the Anglo majority, has been forgotten or marginalized. In a spatial sense, the setting is also fixed, with a focus upon those areas of London where the Afro-Caribbean community congregates. The assertion that these UK residents fought to assert their legitimate rights is important, as it reiterates the boundaries which define the nature of their diaspora. In *Tsotsi*, the story of one's personal journey toward redemption is itself timeless, with the lack of reference to the historic racism that has caused the poverty and violence present in contemporary township life being especially telling. Spatially, though, the depiction of the slum and suburban contrast is fixed, evoking the presence of discrete spaces that will not be easily transgressed.

Although the cinematic techniques employed in these films are conventional, their directors rely upon a number of choices that highlight affect, be it through the graphic depiction of violence in *The Underground Railroad* and *Tsotsi*, to the use of close-ups and intimate spacing to evoke a sense of community in *Small Axe*, or the wide-scale lens to illustrate the depth of poverty in the Johannesburg slum in *Tsotsi*. Both *The Underground Railroad* and *Tsotsi* are based upon novels. Although the interiority that allows for a greater appreciation of characters' consciousness with regard to their attitudes and dispositions cannot be easily reproduced within the cinematic medium, these films offer an affective connection to the characters that, on its own terms, is especially direct and compelling.

6

Indigeneity/Colonialism
Cultural Elimination and Resistance

Many of the themes salient to our previous discussions of globalization and racism reappear in the three films that have been selected to highlight the relationship between education, indigeneity, and colonialism. The aim of this chapter, rather than serving as a coda for those discussions, is to extend those conversations. Two of the films that are highlighted, *The Pearl Button* (*El botón de nácar*) and *We Were Children*, are acclaimed documentaries from Chile and Canada. *Rabbit Proof Fence*, although a commercial venture, is directly based upon the experiences of Molly Kelly, a member of Australia's stolen generations, as memorialized by her daughter, Doris Pilkington Garimara, in her book *Follow the Rabbit Proof Fence*. Together, they highlight the challenges of accurately representing indigeneity before largely non-Indigenous audiences as well as defining what decoloniality might mean. Such challenges are of course also evident within the academic literature, and, as has been noted, they are especially present when considering the historic role of education in perpetuating power and privilege in the service of modernism.

Webster's dictionary defines Indigenous as "of or relating to the earliest known inhabitants of a place and especially of a place that was colonized by a now-dominant group." The United Nations elaborates, stating:

> Indigenous Peoples are inheritors and practitioners of unique cultures and ways of relating to people and the environment. They have retained social, cultural, economic and political characteristics that are distinct from those of the dominant societies in which they live. Despite their cultural differences, Indigenous Peoples from around the world share common problems related to the protection of their rights as distinct peoples.
>
> Indigenous Peoples have sought recognition of their identities, way of life and their right to traditional lands, territories and natural resources for years, yet throughout history, their rights have always been violated. Indigenous Peoples

today, are arguably among the most disadvantaged and vulnerable groups of people in the world. The international community now recognizes that special measures are required to protect their rights and maintain their distinct cultures and way of life. (United Nations Department of Economic and Social Affairs, n.d.).

Amnesty International has identified more than 476 million Indigenous People in the world, living in over 90 countries, the majority of which are in Asia. They speak over 4,000 languages, constitute 5 percent of the global population, and make up 15 percent of the world's extreme poor. They note that Indigenous Peoples

- self-identify as Indigenous Peoples.
- have a historical link with those who inhabited a country or region at the time when people of different cultures or ethnic origins arrived.
- have a strong link to territories and surrounding natural resources.
- have distinct social, economic, or political systems.
- have a distinct language, culture, and beliefs.
- are marginalized and discriminated against by the state.
- maintain and develop their ancestral environments and systems as distinct peoples. (Amnesty International, n.d.)

Ian Baird (2020) has argued that indigeneity as a concept is grounded in notions of time and space. With regard to time, the relationship Indigenous People have with the land where they originally settled has not only stood the test of time but is current and continuous. With regard to space, it is their interaction with unique spaces that form the basis for identity construction with regard to language, culture, religion, and daily practice. Time is certainly implicated in the historical record of oppression, fostered by settler colonialism, and in more modern iterations, capitalism and racism. The spatial nature of indigeneity is also highlighted through the repeated efforts to dispossess Indigenous Peoples of the lands they have claimed to be their own. However, conceiving of time and space with respect to indigeneity in fixed terms poses a set of dilemmas that are worth noting.

Baird notes, for example, that settler colonialism was less prominent in Southeast Asia than in other regions, even though large numbers of groups not directly subject to the effects of settler colonialism claim Indigenous status (Baird, 2020). Indeed, as Indigenous status has achieved global recognition, there are many groups that claim such status even though they have become physically far removed from the place of origin. Notions of time, with regard to origin of settlement, can also be problematic. At what point does one's inhabitance of specific space become permanent? How are conflicting historical accounts of origin of settlement among native peoples equitably resolved? And, as the concept of indigeneity has become globalized, how does one resolve the tendency to universalize experience that is rooted in interactions with specific and unique physical environments? The articulation of such questions does not fundamentally challenge our understanding of indigeneity as an operational concept, but it does highlight the importance of appreciating its expansive as well as fluid nature.

The rights-based language that forms the basis of the United Nations Declaration of the Rights of Indigenous Peoples and the Amnesty International statement that has been mentioned above emphasize the fact that the repression Indigenous Peoples have and continue to confront is unique in terms of its longevity and impact. The treatment of Indigenous Peoples thus cannot be considered to be simply one of any number of types of racism because their very existence has been viewed as a fundamental threat to the sovereignty of the modern state. In his classic work, Benedict Anderson argued that the construction of "imagined communities," created through the use of print media, served as a basis for legitimizing the state as protector and guarantor of national sovereignty (Anderson, 1983). But as Arathi Sriprakash, Sophie Rudolph, and Jessica Gerrard note in their important book *Learning Whiteness* (2022), it is the instability inherent in the construction of the modern state that makes whiteness and its accompanying practices of settler colonialism and capitalism so virulent. This is the case because, unlike their Anglo counterparts, Indigenous communities are not "imagined" nor socially constructed. Their presence is acknowledged as being substantial rather than ephemeral; their communities didn't need to be imagined or mythologically constructed. As a result, the imperative to complete their eradication is clearly understood, in order for the modern state to assert its legitimacy. As was noted in Chapter 5, the "possessive individualism" that has fueled the drive for settler colonialism and then capitalism is so intrinsic to the formation of the modern state that it can't be separated from it, even though the forces it encourages are perpetually as disruptive as they are insatiable. Under such terms, the contradiction of a nation-state global system asserting its commitment to defend the rights of Indigenous Peoples through the discourse of international human rights instruments seems particularly egregious. And yet, as we have noted throughout this volume and particularly in Chapter 3, the nation-state as a modernist construction continues to assert its prominence within a world system that has become increasingly impacted by globalization forces.

It is a recognition of the continued power of the modernist state that has fueled the decoloniality movement, whose proponents aim to make visible the contemporary practices that encourage colonial thinking. In so doing, they recognize that efforts to erase Indigenous identity are not restricted to the historic practices of land confiscation along with ensuing attempts to eradicate native populations. Such eradication has also involved eliminating native languages, traditional cultural practices, and Indigenous knowledge. If recognition of the existence of authentic preexisting communities threatened those seeking a rationale for the construction and perpetuation of the nation-state, so have the Indigenous forms of knowledge and practice that reject Western norms.

As Aníbal Quijano notes,

> in spite of the fact that political colonialism has been eliminated, the relationship between the European also called "Western" culture, and the others, continues to be one of colonial domination. It is not only a matter of the subordination of the other cultures to the European, in an external relation; we have also to do with a colonization of the other cultures, albeit in differing intensities and depths. This relationship consists, in the first place, of a colonization of the imagination of the dominated; that is, it acts in the interior of that imagination, in a sense, it is a part of it. (Quijano, 2007, 169)

In echoing the criticisms espoused by the affect theorists noted in this volume, Quijano views the Western epistemological turn that conceived of rationality in terms of individual autonomy as a key factor in constructing relations between colonizer and the colonized. Through conceiving of knowledge as a product of the Western subject's autonomous thought processes, eschewing its intersubjective essence, Western Europeans viewed knowledge production as a form of property; the act of knowing meant creating objects that were inherently separated from their individual subjects. The subject, in the exercise of one's rationality, was thus able to control and dominate the natural world with knowledge produced in the service of that aim. As a result, all knowledge traditions that failed to reify the rationality constructed by the individual subject were dismissed as being primitive. Perceived as beholden to the natural world as opposed to human rationality, non-Western peoples were further denied access to the very forms of scientific inquiry Westerners proclaimed as being universally applicable (Quijano, 2007, 172–6). Criticism of the Western fixation upon the construction of the autonomous, rational subject has been widespread, and in the comparative and education literature, its assumptions are most systematically deconstructed in Stephen Carney and Ulla Madsen's work, *Education in Radical Uncertainty* (2021). However, Quijano was one of the first scholars to directly link such assumptions with the political, economic, and social agendas that colonialism and, in contemporary times, coloniality have perpetuated.

There are additional theological implications involving the construction of the autonomous, rational Western subject that have been intensively analyzed by literary and social theorist, Sylvia Wynter. Wynter reminds us that with the growth of Western humanism, the notion of what it meant to be human was profoundly challenged. The traditional Christian view defined human in terms of Original Sin; one's relationship to God was based upon subservience to the spiritual, a dependency recognizing God's omnipotence in contrast to human weakness. Under such terms, there was no need to differentiate between types of human beings as they were all defined by their inability to reach a spiritual state. By merging Christian principles with Platonic concepts, Western humanists redefined the relationship between human beings and God, arguing that the ability to engage in rational thought was evidence of the close nature of that relationship, reason being a precious gift that could only have been actualized as a result of God's benevolence. The relationship between humans and God was thus conceived of in closer terms, with humans taking on responsibility of exercising their rational faculties in this world at the insistence and with the encouragement of God. Under such terms, what traditionally was applauded as an exercise of spiritual commitment became denigrated as both nonrational and therefore nonhuman. The Western embrace of autonomous rationality further demanded a degree of classification unnecessary in the traditional Christian worldview. Those who were viewed as nonrational were deemed nonhuman, establishing a predicate for colonialist exploitation, as the modern state replaced the church as a source of political authority (Wynter, 2003).

As a form of social protest, decoloniality advocates have exerted pressure for a broader reckoning of the legacy of colonial oppression, and within the higher education field in particular, have lobbied for policy changes that eliminate its vestiges and offer the possibility for a more concerted effort to address Indigenous Peoples' needs. One of the most successful examples of social protest that evoked decoloniality principles was the Rhodes Must Fall Movement, where in October 2015, South African students at the University of Cape Town called for the removal of the statue of Cecil Rhodes, avowed racist and British colonialist leader. The movement was successful, not only because the statue was removed in April but because it led to wider protests involving persistent institutional racism among South African higher education colleges and universities. Thus, a Fees Must Fall protest grew out of the initial demonstrations, as government efforts to dramatically raise tuition at state-sponsored universities inspired such wide protest that forced the government, for a time, to back down. The awareness that decoloniality implies interrogating institutional policies of all types and not simply the cultural symbols of named statues and buildings was particularly significant. Of additional significance was the global impact of the Rhodes Must Fall Movement, which ignited demonstrations in the United Kingdom and the United States, although whether such efforts have comprehensively addressed continuing issues of institutional racism remains an open question. Riyad Shajahan, Annabelle Estera, Kristen Surla, and Kirsten Edwards, surveying much of the literature related to education and decoloniality, have concluded that how decoloniality is perceived and what policy choices arise from those perceptions are often context-specific, with curricular reform efforts somewhat easier to implement rather than other forms of institutional equity redress (Shajahan, Estera, Surla, and Edwards, 2022). Certainly, the alternative university initiatives mentioned in Chapter 1 as part of the Ecoversities Alliance and the Global Tapestry of Alternatives represent sincere efforts to holistically confront the challenges a commitment to decoloniality demands. However, for many Indigenous scholars, decolonial voices emanating from the Global North continue to engage in a form of academic navel-gazing, speaking to predominantly Global North audiences, rather than directly incorporating Indigenous voices into discussions and deliberations (Huaman, 2022). Some may draw similar conclusions from the films under discussion in this chapter.

Rabbit Proof Fence

In 1869, the Australian state of Victoria passed the Aboriginal Protection Act, allowing government authorities to forcibly remove Aboriginal and Torres Strait Islander children from their parents. Subsequent legislation in the other Australian states followed suit, with "Aboriginal Protectors," designated by the state, exercising control over these children's lives. Many were placed in institutions with Christian denominational affiliations; some were placed in government facilities; others were given over to foster care. Such policies remained in place from the late nineteenth century until 1969, although in some cases, they continued into the early 1970s with up to one in three children having been taken between 1910 and the 1970s (Healing Foundation, n.d.). One of the primary motivations for implementing this policy was to "whiten" the Aboriginal and Torre Strait Islander population by forcing them to learn Anglo values and practices. Biracial children or children of "mixed" heritage, where one of their parents was Anglo, were particularly targeted as it was believed that they would be easier to transform. Girls were also disproportionately forced into the system (Wikipedia, n.d.). It should be noted that the consequences of these policies extended beyond immediate family separation and dislocation. Aboriginal and Torres Strait Islander children were considered vital members of their communities. Their education was geared toward their participation in the community within the practical and spiritual realms, and such participation occurred early in their upbringing. Their forced removal thus was intentionally intended to exterminate these communities as much as it was an effort to "save" the children so that they would learn to better function in an Anglo-dominated world. With regard to the children themselves, the Healing Foundation reports that as of 2018, there were 17,150 Stolen Generation survivors living across Australia with one in seven survivors living with a significant disability, and 33 percent having had difficulty accessing government services (Healing Foundation, n.d.).

Rabbit Proof Fence is a dramatization of the early life of Molly Kelly, whose entire life story was told by her daughter, Doris Pilkington Garamara, in the book *Follow the Rabbit Proof Fence*, published in 1996. Molly was fourteen when in 1931, she, her younger sister Daisy, and cousin Gracie were kidnapped and transported to the Moore River Settlement, over a thousand miles from her home in Jinglong, a small town in Western Australia. Immediately after she arrived, Molly was determined to escape and reunite with her mother and soon did so, taking with her sister and cousin. Unfamiliar with the immediate environment and local landscape, she used the fencing that had been constructed to keep rabbits apart from farms as a guide to help track her way back to Jinglong. At the same time, she used the Indigenous knowledge she had already acquired to navigate the hardships of the return journey. Local farmers offered the girls some food along the way, but they were also forced into repeatedly fending for themselves. Molly's cousin Gracie was captured during the girls' return journey and became permanently separated from the family, but eventually Molly and her sister successfully negotiated the 1000-mile trek and returned home.

Although this is where the film narrative ends, it is not the end of Molly's story. In 1941, Molly was taken to Perth and hospitalized with appendicitis. Her two daughters, under the orders of A. O. Neville, who had been placed in the position, "Chief Protector of Aborigines," in 1915 and was responsible for

Molly's, Daisy's, and Gracie's original kidnapping, ordered that Molly's daughters be sent to the same Moore River Settlement, where Molly was also returned after recovering from her operation. After a year, Molly escaped again, taking her eighteen-month-old daughter, Anna, with her, but leaving her four-year-old daughter, Doris, in the care of sister Daisy, who earlier had also been forcibly returned to the institution. Eventually, Doris was moved to a farm run by missionaries, and Anna was recaptured and grew up in a different settlement, housing Indigenous Peoples with lighter skin. In adult life, Doris became a community health worker, and later a journalist, and was able to reconnect and reconcile with her mother, whom she had mistakenly believed had voluntarily given her away to the Anglo authorities (Woo, 2014; Olsen, 2004).

The film is especially insightful in its depictions of the contradictions within the settler-colonialist/Indigenous Peoples relationship. It is noteworthy, for example, that Molly relies not simply upon her acquired Indigenous knowledge that allows her to navigate the natural environment around her as she completes her escape, but also is able to facilitate the escape from the Moore River Settlement by following the outer boundaries of the colonizer constructed fence in successfully returning to Jinglong. Although victimized by such affectations of colonial modernism, she is still able to manipulate them to her advantage because of her understanding of their functioning. The Indigenous knowledge she possesses does not prevent her from exercising such resiliency; it in fact contributes to her ability to understand and adapt to a series of crises that are externally imposed upon her. The same cannot be said for her colonial oppressors. Not only do they need to rely upon a coerced Indigenous tracker to trace the movements of Molly, Daisy, and Gracie, as they would also do so for other escapees, but they initially couldn't conceive of the possibility that Molly could logically plan a return to her home through utilizing the directional space chartered by the fence. As portrayed in the film, A. O. Neville and his staff are, by comparison, clueless regarding the nature of the environment and the exigencies it presents to its inhabitants.

A second contradiction involves the "whitening" ideology Neville promoted. As portrayed in the film and reflective of some of his actual writings, Neville asserted that his policies of kidnapping, forced separation and relocation, and inculcation of English language and lower level skill development upon innocent Indigenous children were part of a moral crusade, rather than being simply part of a plan to extract economic benefit for the settler class. Indeed, he confronted resistance to his efforts on the part of government security officials who recoiled at the expense of tracking runaway children such as Molly, Daisy, and Gracie. But the locus of his "moral" perspective was unclear. On the one hand, he argued that the forced kidnapping and subsequent training of Indigenous children so that they would engage in low-skilled domestic work was meant to "save them" so that they would be better able to survive in a settler-colonial state. On the other hand, the fixation with capturing and training biracial children, many of whom tended to be girls, served another, even more nefarious purpose. It was expected that as these children would continue to intermarry, the entire population would become "whitened," eliminating previous traces of Indigenous identity. But if this was indeed the ultimate goal of the project, why bother to offer any provision to the children at all? Imbedded within such racist sentiment was a deep fear of the power of Indigenous identity and Indigenous knowledge, and in conceding such fear, the Australian colonizer class admitted that it would always feel threatened unless indigeneity was erased through biological reproduction. In coming to such a conclusion, however, the logic of providing and caring for Indigenous children under any circumstance was compromised.

It is noteworthy that *Rabbit Proof Fence* chronicles only part of Molly's story. At the end of the film, brief reference is made to the tragic aspects of her life after she found her way back to her home in Jinglong at the age of fourteen, but this is not part of the film's focus. Although the feat of navigating over 1,000 miles of terrain on one's own, in support of her younger sister and cousin, was indeed remarkable, the film's emphasis is one that accentuates her personal fortitude and resiliency. It thus is somewhat like the South African film *Tsotsi*, reviewed in Chapter 5, insofar as a predominantly Anglo audience is encouraged to express empathy for the main character without fully confronting the meaning and legacy of the systematic oppression to which that character was subjected throughout her life. Audience members are thus asked to appreciate the power of Indigenous knowledge, practice, and identity expression without being forced to address the consequences of its marginalization.

We Were Children

In 2015, the Truth and Reconciliation Commission of Canada issued its final report detailing the abuses and harms inflicted upon Indigenous children through their forced participation in the country's residential school system, separating them from their parents and guardians. These schools were in existence for over 130 years and were finally disbanded in 1996. The report determined that the practices associated with the residential education system amounted to the promotion of cultural genocide and detailed the abusive conditions to which the children were subjected.

> The Canadian government pursued this policy of cultural genocide because it wished to divest itself of its legal and financial obligations to Aboriginal people and gain control over their land and resources. If every Aboriginal person had been "absorbed into the body politic," there would be no reserves, no Treaties, and no Aboriginal rights. Residential schooling quickly became a central element in the federal government's Aboriginal policy. When Canada was created as a country in 1867, Canadian churches were already operating a small number of boarding schools for Aboriginal people. As settlement moved westward in the 1870s, Roman Catholic and Protestant missionaries established missions and small boarding schools across the Prairies, in the North, and in British Columbia. Most of these schools received small, per-student grants from the federal government. In 1883, the federal government moved to establish three, large, residential schools for First Nation children in western Canada. In the following years, the system grew dramatically. According to the Indian Affairs annual report for 1930, there were eighty residential schools in operation across the country. The Indian Residential Schools Settlement Agreement provided compensation to students who attended 139 residential schools and residences. The federal government has estimated that at least 150,000 First Nation, Métis, and Inuit students passed through the system. Roman Catholic, Anglican, United, Methodist, and Presbyterian churches were the major denominations involved in the administration of the residential school system. The government's partnership with the churches remained in place until 1969, and, although most of the schools had closed by the 1980s, the last federally supported residential schools remained in operation until the late 1990s. For children, life in these schools was lonely and alien. Buildings were poorly located, poorly built, and poorly maintained. The staff was limited in numbers, often poorly trained, and not adequately supervised. Many schools were poorly heated and poorly ventilated, and the diet was meagre and of poor quality. Discipline was harsh, and daily life was highly regimented. Aboriginal languages and cultures were denigrated and suppressed. The educational goals of the schools were limited and confused, and usually reflected a low regard for the intellectual capabilities of Aboriginal people. For the students, education and technical training too often gave way to the drudgery of doing the chores necessary to make the schools self-sustaining. Child neglect was institutionalized, and the lack of supervision created situations where students were prey to sexual and physical abusers. (The Truth and Reconciliation Commission of Canada, 2015, 3–4)

In 2021, with the use of ground radar technology, evidence of children's unmarked graves was uncovered containing the remains of 215 students from the Kanloops Residential School in British Columbia. This discovery led to the uncovering of other remains at school sites across Canada, and it is now believed that over 10,000 children vanished without ever being accounted for (Austen, 2021, 2023). As a result, the Canadian government, in response to a number of lawsuits, has agreed to pay over two billion Canadian dollars in compensation to victims' families and relatives, the fifth legal settlement since 2006 related to the abusive and deadly practices perpetuated by the residential school system (Austen, 2023). *We Were Children* (2012) is a documentary that chronicles, through reenactment, the experiences of two of the survivors of the system, Lyna Hart and Glen Anaquod, who, as narrators, retell their own stories.

Lyna was three years old when she was sent to a Christian boarding school, where upon arrival, she was immediately forced to undress, shower, wear bug powder for twenty-four hours, and given a haircut. Children were forced to speak English and go to church and offer prayers regularly. Corporal punishment was invoked upon those who refused to speak English. Compelled to eat institutional food which she could not tolerate, Lyna was sent to the institution infirmary after fainting in her classroom, where she witnesses a priest raping one of the young boys. After eventually confiding in a nurse as to what she saw, Lyna herself was sexually assaulted by a priest. She stayed at the school until she was released at the age of eighteen.

When we see Glen as a young child, he expresses a desire to return to his home for a visit. A priest acts as if he will take Glen home but instead takes him to a house where other priests congregate and leads him to a basement room where he is locked up in the dark. There he sees another girl being held captive against her will, crying as priests enter her room. Eventually, Glen is eventually rescued but the girl is not found, and the sister who rescues Glen is sent away. The priest who initially kidnapped Glen also departs but is sent to another school. A story is also told of two boys, who escape from the school and return to an aunt's house, but she then calls authorities who return the boys to the institution. Glen, as an orphan, leaves the school without the support of living relatives battles alcoholism and suicidal tendencies for much of his adult life, as he speaks directly of his challenges during the latter part of the film (IMDb, n.d.).

Through depicting the horrors of their upbringing in their own words, Lyna and Glen are able to frame the systematic abuses Indigenous children confronted in personal terms. The audience is able to not only empathize with the pain they have endured but also becomes aware of its permanent effects upon their lives. Through their own testimonies, Lyna and Glen give further voice to the demands for collective reparations that, over ten years after the making of the film, are making their way through the Canadian legal system and within its political space. However, the cruelty that they were forced to confront raises a number of important issues regarding the nature of indigeneity and coloniality that offer specific resonance. On the one hand, the similarities between the stories told in *Rabbit Proof Fence* and *We Were Children* are striking. The forced removal of Indigenous children from their parents and family members, the sanctions enacted for their refusal to speak English as opposed to their native languages, the use of coercive disciplinary policies to instill institutional loyalty and obedience were true not only of the practices directed toward Indigenous children in Australia and Canada but were commonly employed in numerous countries that created residential institutions for Indigenous children. Yet the tone of these two films is quite different; the theme of personal resiliency so evident in *Rabbit Proof Fence* is contrasted with the enduring effects of abuse and mistreatment, creating lifelong consequences for those portrayed in *We Were Children*. From a decoloniality perspective, *We Were Children* offers a more truthful accounting, insofar as the legacy of injustice that it chronicles remains unresolved.

The importance of the church, while evident in both films, is even more apparent in *We Were Children* than in *Rabbit Proof Fence*, where the institution of record was under direct state control. Certainly, the impetus to purify these Anglo-dominated settler-colonial societies evokes the Christian-related themes that Sylvia Wynter has extensively analyzed. However, in *We Were Children*, we see that the efforts to inflict cultural genocide upon Indigenous People were intimately related to the attempts to physically harm and, yes, destroy Indigenous children. Some of the most disturbing scenes in the film recount the experiences of sexual assault that Lyna witnessed and personally experienced. And while the sexual misconduct of priests and church clergy has been well documented as an international phenomenon, the impunity with which residential school staff assaulted and mistreated Indigenous children was in itself somewhat unique and especially striking in the film. Such cruelty went far beyond racist-based efforts to "altruistically" reform the children but speaks instead to their categorization as "savage" and "inhuman," undeserving of the protection commonly afforded human beings, let alone children.

The Pearl Button (El botón de nácar)

Patricio Guzman is one of Chile's most acclaimed documentary filmmakers. Initially known for his films *The Battle of Chile* and *Salvador Allende*, over the last decade and a half, he has directed three award-winning films, *Nostalgia for the Light* (*Nostalgia de la luz*) in 2010, *The Pearl Button* (*El botón de nácar*) in 2015, and *The Cordillera of Dreams* (*La cordillera de los sueños*) in 2019. The trilogy differs from his earlier work in that each film shows spectacular images of Chile's diverse natural environment while offering poetic meditations about the country's historical past and conflicted present. All three films have been honored with international recognition, *The Pearl Button* having received the Silver Bear Award for best script at the 65th Berlin International Film Festival in 2015 and the Lumières Award for best documentary at the 21st Lumières ceremony in 2016.

Guzman's focus in *The Pearl Button* is on the importance of water and its impact upon Chile's history. At the very beginning of the film, Chilean poet Raul Zarita's words set the tone for Guzman's cinematic meditation, as he is quoted, "Todos somos arroyos de una sola agua (We are all streams from one water)." We first see a large cube of quartz, taken from Chile's Atacama Desert, the driest part of the earth, and within the cube, the camera focuses upon a single water drop. The image is juxtaposed with that of radio telescopes, pointed to the stars, and we are reminded that water's presence is ubiquitous, existing throughout the universe and it is, of course, essential for life to exist. Guzman himself grew up in the south of Chile, and as we see both the snow-capped Andes and the rainy environment of the Chilean archipelago, he notes that the sound of rain on the household roof has followed him through his entire life. This being said, he notes later that modern Chileans have lost a sense of intimacy with the sea.

This was not true of the native peoples of Patagonia, who arrived over 10,000 years ago, felt in communion with the cosmos through their association with water, traveling by water, living around water, and surviving through employing a maritime-based daily diet. In relating the Indigenous wisdom, the Kawesqar, Selk'nam, Aoniken, Hausch, and Yamana peoples employed as water nomads, creating a lifestyle that was entirely sea-based, Guzman's own cosmological insights resonate with the traditional understandings of these people. We thus hear from Martin Calderón, who traveled with his father at the age of twelve in a small canoe from Cape Horn to Punta Arenas but can no longer do so because of government restrictions. We also listen to Gabriela's story, who as a child paddled over a thousand kilometers from an island to the Gulf of Penas, and hear from anthropologist Claudio Mercado, who learned from Indigenous Peoples the language of water and replicates for the film audience the music and sounds that emanate from rivers and the sea. Although once numbering around 8,000, there are now about twenty direct descendants of these peoples, and those interviewed in the film translate words into their native language, struggling to maintain an ancestral and spiritual understanding of the world that is quickly disappearing.

Disappearance is an important theme in the film. Guzman, in an example of foreshadowing, informs the audience that he has lived with personal loss, and one of his childhood friends was lost at sea when he was a young boy. The history of the Indigenous Peoples he interviews and focuses upon is one that is replete with violence, injustice, and death, leading to their permanent disappearance in the not too distant future. Guzman thus chronicles how in 1883, colonial settlers including gold hunters and cattle farmers, supported by the military, police, and Catholic missionaries, declared that these Indigenous Peoples were barbaric and corrupt. Many ended up on Dawson Island in the Strait of Magellan with their beliefs, language, and canoes taken from them. They were given old clothes contaminated with disease, and most died within fifty years after having been captured. Others were hunted down, and as the film narration notes, atrocities were systematically encouraged as farmers paid one pound for the retrieval of a male testicle, one pound for a women's breast, and ten shillings for a child's ear.

Of course, colonial settler views of Indigenous Peoples as being less than human did not begin in 1883; they were present during Chile's Spanish initial colonization in the sixteenth century. Hence, as Guzman notes, Indigenous People were viewed as monsters, the term "Patagonia" being derived from the settlers' labeling of Indigenous Peoples, "Patagones," because of their "abnormally" long feet. Guzman's most striking example of settler/colonialist disrespect involves the story of Jemmy Button, a member of the Fuegan people, who, along with three others residing in the Tierra del Fuego area, was sold to British captain Robert Fitzroy in 1830 for a pearl button and sent to England, ostensibly for the purposes of becoming "civilized." After a year or so, he returned to Patagonia, speaking half in English and half in his native language but was shunned by his own people. As Guzman narrates, he "traveled thousands of years into the future, and then back into the past, from the Stone Age, to the Industrial Revolution, and back." He tried to let his hair grow long but was never the same person, ultimately becoming exiled in his own land.

Until this point, Guzman has categorized disappearance in terms of the loss of language, of practical and spiritual knowledge, of identity, and in the case of his childhood friend, the loss of life, ruminating about the life and death polarities that characterize a country defined in part by its relationship to water. But the film takes an important turn when Guzman briefly notes the

Allende government's effort to begin to redress injustices inflicted upon Chile's Indigenous Peoples, and then focuses upon the atrocities that occurred during the Pinochet dictatorship. His ability to note similarities in the cruelty inflicted upon political opponents of Pinochet with the treatment of Southern Patagonia Indigenous Peoples by settler colonialists makes *The Pearl Button* a unique and compelling artistic statement.

Guzman notes, for example, that the same Dawson Island that served as a holding site to where Indigenous Peoples were transported in the late nineteenth century was also used as a prison and concentration camp for officials in the Allende government as well as Allende supporters who lived in the city, Punta Arenas. The camera at one point focuses upon survivors, who recount the time spent on Dawson Island and the cruelties which they were forced to endure. The narrative includes an enumeration of the many forms of torture that were inflicted upon victims: prisoners hung from the ceiling, burned by acid and cigarettes, and subjected to electrical current, women raped in front of their husbands and children, throats slit, confinement in boxes about one meter in length, width, and height, and the commentary is accompanied by graphic images of the technologies used to implement the torture along with photographs of the victims themselves.

From 1,200 to 1,400 Chileans were forcibly "disappeared" by Pinochet's army, in many cases injected with cyanide or sodium Pentothal, tied up with wire to wooden railway planks, covered with cellophane and cloth bags, and then dropped into the ocean from airplanes and helicopters. The body of one of the victims, Marta Agarte, with eyes wide open, washed up on the coast not far from where Patricio Guzman's childhood friend disappeared. We learn that her execution was botched and she survived initial efforts to kill her, hence her eyes left opened after her death and her body left intact. The audience also is introduced to a civilian who recounts the process of dumping bodies into the ocean, and we see a reenactment of the act of disposing the bodies into the sea. In addition, we hear the testimony of Paul Veas, a diver who repeatedly helped to find the remains of the disappeared, bringing rail planks stuck in the bottom of the ocean for over thirty years to the surface. One of those rails included a pearl button, the surviving remnant of clothing belonging to a disappeared person. In viewing the pearl button, and in associating it with the similar artifact sold to deprive Jemmy Button of his identity, the connection between the historical extermination of Indigenous Peoples and the contemporary elimination of political opposition to the dictatorship is made explicit.

The power of *The Pearl Button* lies not only in its compelling narrative, with its poetic and metaphoric associations, but with its imagery as well. The scenes of the Chilean coast, the snow-capped Andes, the Atacama Desert, the Chilean night time star-infested sky, not only illustrate the natural beauty of a universe for which water is an essential component, but they compel us to reevaluate our own place and presence in the universe along with our relationships to it and to one another. In so doing, as has been true of many of the other films discussed throughout this project, they tap not only into our visual sensations but evoke haptic responses as well. The power of the pearl button, the railroad plank, the small canoe Southern Patagonian Indigenous People's used to navigate the Chilean archipelago, and indeed of water itself, lies in the memories they evoke through physical touch and feel. In addition, the film addresses all of the other aspects of affect that have been previously discussed. There is intensity of encounter when one is asked to reflect upon our relationships with the natural world and with one another, as we are made aware of how those relationships are interconnected. For example, Guzman makes a point of noting that one of the largest supernovas ever recorded occurred at the time of the Pinochet coup, its presence prominently displayed on screen. Assemblage and dis-assemblage, be it through conflict, conquest, appearance, and disappearance, is an obvious theme in this work, as is the attempt to make meaning of our understanding of the natural world and our relations with one another. It is a particular strength of the film that it applauds the wisdom of Indigenous knowledge while connecting it to contemporary self-reflection. Contingency is also an important element of this work. At one point within the narration, Guzman asks when reflecting upon the horrors of settler colonialism, whether the same thing has happened on other planets, and whether, thinking of the universe in its totality, the strongest people always dominate everywhere. The inability to answer such questions speaks to the contingency that characterizes all efforts to understand our humanity and is certainly a central focus of the film.

Conclusion

In reviewing the theoretical literature that speaks to issues of indigeneity, it was noted that the experiences of Indigenous Peoples differed from those of other historically oppressed groups with regard to the extreme degree of violence inflicted upon them that has led to their elimination in some spheres and potential extinction in others. Their very existence threatens the settler-colonial state because they categorically reject the possessive individualism that legitimizes that state's presence. In constructing an identity based upon reverence for the natural world rather than viewing the earth as a form of property subject to human control and exploitation, Indigenous Peoples embrace a worldview that can never be reconciled with settler colonialism. In viewing knowledge and wisdom as being derived from the interaction between humans and other living and nonliving entities within not only the planet but the universe, they reject modernist views of knowledge as objects worthy of accumulation, possession, and consumption. And, in infusing their daily practices with a spiritualism that assumed a connection with their ancestors, their beliefs have posed a direct threat to foundational elements of Christian humanism.

It is therefore unsurprising that educational efforts to engage in decoloniality have been difficult to achieve. Modern schools are institutions designed to serve the interests of the state; the historical record has been one of where they have been used as effective instruments in the perpetuation of cultural genocide against Indigenous Peoples in a variety of colonial settler state environments. While participants within the decoloniality movement have given voice to that historical record, and have pressed for curricular reforms that address some of those outcomes, it is difficult to conceive of Indigenous Peoples receiving full and appropriate educational redress given the continuing ties to the colonial state that most contemporary educational institutions maintain.

The films reviewed in this chapter are illustrative of a similar dilemma. In speaking for the most part to non-Indigenous audiences, they present a compelling historical record of abuse and atrocity committed against Indigenous Peoples, but they only challenge the neoliberal structures that gird contemporary settler states infrequently. In both *Rabbit Proof Fence* and *We Were Children*, state-sponsored institutions with supposed educational missions are accurately depicted as engaging in both physical violence and cultural genocide in their abominable treatment of Indigenous children. But in *Rabbit Proof Fence*, the message of individual resiliency, as expressed in the telling of Molly's heroic struggle to return to her own community, overshadows the long-term harmful consequences of the Australian colonial settler state's efforts to eradicate its Indigenous Peoples. In *We Were Children*, the lasting effects of the institutionally directed violence and abuse perpetrated upon innocent Indigenous children are made clear, adding support for contemporary calls for reparations. It additionally places the Christian church as a significant force that assaulted their bodies and their dignity. The film offers a compelling case regarding the enduring effects of monstrous behavior that creates enduring personal tragedy. Its emphasis upon the horrific physical and sexual abuse inflicted upon Indigenous children, however, somewhat eclipses the effects of the destruction of their cultural identity, insofar as the centrality of Indigenous knowledge and cultural expression to their well-being is never fully explored.

This is less so the case in *The Pearl Button*, where reverence for Indigenous knowledge is made explicit and its universal relevance to our humanity is reiterated on a regular basis throughout the film. Unlike its counterparts, *The Pearl Button* expands our focus beyond a reckoning of state-sponsored educational institutional violence, viewing the essence of colonialism as being so fundamental to the state that its presence exceeds institutional boundaries. The film's genius lies not only in connecting examples of historical and contemporary atrocity to one another but in arguing that looking at the world and ourselves from an Indigenous perspective need not be an alien exercise, but instead has universal value ethically and aesthetically. At the same time, the film offers no solutions to the barbarity it chronicles; one leaves the film resigned to accepting human cruelty as a constant and continuing component of human behavior without conceiving of the possibility of plausible alternatives ever arising. However, it should be emphasized that regardless of their conceptual limitations, all three films present their audiences the plight of Indigenous Peoples through the use of affect, and in so doing, they make it more difficult to ignore and dismiss the injustices to which they have been and continue to be repeatedly subjected.

7

Environmental Consciousness

Exploiting, Understanding, Respecting the Natural World

There is no doubt that the global climate crisis presents an existential threat to planetary survival, a threat that has been made more palpable as we have experienced increasingly more extreme weather events over the past few decades. The implications of those events have compelled us to address our relationships to one another, our obligations to future generations, and our responsibilities to other living and nonliving entities, along with our evolving understandings of what it means to be human. It is thus unsurprising that such concerns have played a significant role in both educational and cinematic settings.

Environmental studies, as an academic field, became established in the late 1960s and early 1970s in the Global North. The publication of Rachel Carson's *Silent Spring* in 1962, followed by a television documentary about the book in 1964, raised public consciousness in the United States regarding the harms of the pesticide DDT and its effects upon both human life and the natural environment (National Resources Defense Council, 2015). In so doing, it established the predicate for the creation of the Environmental Protection Agency in 1970. In the UK, it is generally acknowledged that the beginnings of the environmental movement can be traced to the creation of *The Ecologist* magazine in 1970, the British section of the Friends of the Earth organization in 1971, and even beforehand, to the Conservation Society in 1966 (Prendiville, 2014). In both countries, there was a growing recognition that scientific perspectives addressing human relationships to the natural environment had to be broadened in order to adequately address the complexity of such interactions. Echoing such sentiments, UNESCO established the Man and the Biosphere Programme in 1971, whose aim has been "to establish a scientific basis for enhancing the relationship between people and their environments. It combines the natural and social sciences with a view to improving human livelihoods and safeguarding natural and managed ecosystems, thus promoting innovative approaches to economic development that are socially and culturally appropriate and environmentally sustainable" (UNESCO, n.d.).

From an academic perspective, the embrace of an ecological approach to the exploration of environmental issues acknowledged the importance of addressing such questions systematically. Understandings gleaned from a multiplicity of disciplinary perspectives thus offered the best opportunity to address problems whose generic complexity belied relying upon narrowly focused solutions. Thus, since their inception, environmental studies and environmental science programs at the university level embraced a multidisciplinary approach, including course work from traditional science and some social science disciplines. Of course, an embrace of multidisciplinarity is not the same as affirming the importance of interdisciplinarity, as the latter assumes a degree of collaboration and integration not present in the former. Thus, while complex investigations may inexorably lead to the utilization of interdisciplinarity, where concepts from the traditional disciplines are used in ways that strengthen one another in the service of problem-solving, there has been some resistance in academic circles to such an approach on a regular basis. The possibility of creating trans-disciplines unbeholden to conventional boundaries, which would require even greater collaborative effort, remains largely aspirational within academic research and curricular settings (Stock and Burton, 2011).

Therefore, it is not coincidental that there have been tensions in the construction of the environmental studies field based upon the carving out of disciplinary territoriality, the degree of emphasis afforded science as opposed to social science disciplines, and the extent to which issues of environmental justice as opposed to a narrower focus upon environmental sustainability are addressed. Such tensions clearly were evident more broadly in the evolution of environmentalism in the United States. The US Environmental Protection Agency defines environmental justice as

> the fair treatment and meaningful involvement of all people regardless of race, color, national origin, or income, with respect to the development, implementation, and enforcement of environmental laws, regulations, and policies. This goal will be achieved when everyone enjoys the same degree of protection from environmental and health hazards, and equal access to the decision-making process to have a healthy environment in which to live, learn, and work. (EPA, n.d.)

Originating as a result of the efforts of grassroots organizers and activists with deep ties to the US Civil Rights Movement, environmental justice concerns began to be articulated within the academy in the 1990s. Robert Bullard's *Dumping in Dixie*, published in 1990, has been recognized as the first book in the United States to document the efforts of communities of color to fight for safer living environments, while the Deep South Center for Environmental Justice was established at Xavier University in Louisiana in 1991, the first of its type to be situated within a HBCU (Historically Black College and University). The first environmental justice program for university undergraduate and graduate students was created in 1992 at the University of Michigan (EPA, n.d.). All this being said, historically, there was tension among early proponents of sustainability and those who aligned with the environmental justice movement.

The existence of such tension is understandable when one examines the historical record, where major US leaders of the Conservation Movement in the late nineteenth and early twentieth centuries openly espoused racist views, some of whom later became active in the eugenics movement. Indeed, even calls for controlling the global population explosion as voiced by Paul Ehrlich in his 1968 book *The Population Bomb*, along with others, had distinct racist overtones (Purdy, 2015). It is thus not surprising that proponents of environmentalism in the early 1970s constructed a movement that defined sustainability goals in terms that failed to acknowledge the specific consequences policy decisions had upon marginalized populations. Instead, by defining sustainability as a universally inclusive goal, to which all groups should be equally committed, 1970s US environmentalism appealed to Anglo, middle-class elites, whose own culpability in perpetuating climate injustice remained unaddressed. This was true not only in the United States but became part of international development discourse as well. Later efforts in the early 1990s to incorporate principles of environmental justice into the sustainability discourse were thus reflective of a larger trend that influenced not only the higher education sector but the environmental movement more broadly (Agyeman and Evans, 2004).

How human beings view themselves in relation to the natural environment is the essential question that has framed the study and teaching of environmental studies and in this area, the insights of historian and theorist Dipesh Charkrabarty are quite enlightening, as he has argued that the current climate change crisis has compelled us to reassess that relationship. First, he concludes that the traditional distinction between human history and natural history as defined by nineteenth and early twentieth century historians is no longer defensible. That distinction was initially based upon the assumption that human beings unlike entities in the natural world were able to exercise purposeful agency through engaging in conscious thought. To the extent that natural science was a human creation, the natural world should be viewed as a human construct, whose function and purpose was defined by human thought. In and of itself, the natural world was considered to be static and unchanging in contrast to the dynamic flows of human activity. Fernand Braudel's classic work *The Mediterranean and the Mediterranean World in the Age of Philip II*, published originally in 1949, was one of the first twentieth-century attempts to challenge some of these assumptions, chronicling the ways in which natural environmental forces shaped human behavior and decision-making over time. But even in Braudel's estimation, natural forces were repetitive and slow changing (Braudel, 1996). Acknowledging the human role in the climate crisis has meant revising perceptions that the natural world is one of permanence and stasis. It has also meant reconceptualizing what it means to be human. Chakrabarty thus argues that we should no longer define ourselves simply as biological agents, in contrast to and distinct from other species. Instead, it is incumbent upon us to recognize our role as geological agents who with other living and nonliving entities are experiencing the dramatically changing state of the planet (Chakrabarty, 2009, 2021).

He goes on to argue that the notion of Anthropocene, the idea that we are living in a distinct geological age where it is human behavior that has shaped the climate and environment, has repercussions for ways in which we frame globalization and global capitalism. Of central importance to the concept of Anthropocene is the assumption that like other geological eras, it is bounded in time. Regardless of the destructive elements of climate change that we have unleashed and are currently experiencing, the eventual ending of the current geological era and the ultimate future of the planet ultimately lies outside of our control. Thus, the notion of Anthropocene includes ramifications that extend beyond analyses that focus upon the workings and deleterious effects of globalization and global capitalism per se upon human beings. More than subjecting fellow human beings to the social injustice that results from capitalist exploitation on a global level, our actions are threatening to the future of *all* living things on the planet. And, because the future of the planet involves all of its species of which we are only one, the current climate change crisis demands that the scale of analysis be extended to the planetary level beyond that of the global (Chakrabarty, 2009, 2021).

Formal educational institutional responses to issues of climate change at the primary, middle school, and secondary levels have been disappointing. In a UNESCO survey of the policy documents and curricular plans of forty-six countries, only 47 percent mentioned climate change and only 19 percent mentioned biodiversity. One-third of the respondents reported no coverage of content related to environmental issues of any type in their countries' teacher education programs, and while coverage of environmental topics was centered within biology, geography, and science areas, systematic inclusion across the curriculum was lacking. Gardening and "nature related" activities were prevalent in the early grades; more focused attention regarding environmental issues occurred at the middle and secondary levels (UNESCO, 2021).

Aside from the sins of curricular omission and marginalization, child-centered pedagogies that emphasize the importance of individualized learning, where the independent child is considered to be the center of all meaningful classroom activity, have also been criticized. Conceiving of childhood learning in such a way, it is argued, gives further support for mindsets that privilege the human over other species. It perpetuates an anthropocentric myopia that is evident in our failure to acknowledge the reality of species interdependency and shared custodial responsibility for planetary survival (Komatsu, Rappleye, and Silova, 2021).

One response has been to turn to the principles of critical pedagogy, in demanding that educators play a more active role in combatting the worst practices contributing to climate change with the term "eco-pedagogy" employed to characterize many of these views. It has been noted, for example, that Paolo Freire, in one of his last works, embraced the idea of applying Freirean principles to climate justice issues.

> It is urgent that we assume the duty of fighting for the fundamental ethical principles, like respect for the life of human beings, the life of other animals, the life of birds, the life of rivers and forests. I do not believe in love between men and women, between human beings, if we are not able to love the world. Ecology takes on fundamental importance at the end of the century. It has to be present in any radical, critical or liberationist educational practice. For this reason, it seems to me a lamentable contradiction to engage in progressive, revolutionary discourse and have a practice which negates life. A practice which pollutes the sea, the water, the fields, devastates the forests, destroys the trees, threatens the birds and animals, does violence to the mountains, the cities, to our cultural and historical memories. (Freire, 2004, 46–7 as cited in Kahn, 2010, 20)

Still, to the extent that Freire's humanistic perspective continues to conceive of human activity as being separate and independent from the natural world, it fails to fully address Chakrabarty's critique. To be clear, eco-pedagogy advocates additionally point to the writings of Ivan Illich and Herbert Marcuse in making the case for an educational approach to the climate crisis that involves literacy, consciousness-raising, and activism (Kahn, 2010). But in her book *Vibrant Matters*, Jane Bennett builds directly upon Chakrabarty's insights to argue that all matter, living and nonliving, contribute to the formation of events, and that it is thus incumbent upon us to think of agency in more expansive terms, as an assemblage of human and nonhuman interactions that directly influence one another (Bennett, 2010).

The issues raised within the environmental movement and within environmental studies discourse are complex and remain largely unresolved. Because the climate change crisis has existential repercussions for the future of the planet, it has forced us to reconsider what it means to be human, the degree of autonomy and agency we exercise over life events, and what our relationship to other living and nonliving entities is and should be. Given the enormity of these questions, it is not surprising that formal educational responses have often been partial and incomplete. The three international films that have been selected for review are also illustrative of the importance of these issues along with the inadequacy of our collective responses to them.

Anthropocene: The Human Epoch

Anthropocene: The Human Epoch was a 2018 award-winning Canadian documentary created through the collaborative efforts of director Jennifer Baichwal, cinematographer Nicholas de Pencier, and photographer Edward Burtynsky. It is the third film in a trilogy that took four years to complete, following the research of a team of scientists, the Anthropocene Working Group, who have been dedicated to chronicling the ways human activity is reshaping the planet. Relying upon the use of drone photography, *Anthropocene: The Human Epoch* was filmed across twenty-two countries and six continents. Visually stunning, it was recognized as the best Canadian film of 2018 by the Toronto Film Critics Association (The Anthropocene Project, n.d.).

Throughout the film, our disrespect for and myopia toward the natural world is highlighted. For example, a significant portion of the film focuses upon the mining and extraction of natural resources in the service of human consumption. The audience is shown a heavy metal smelting complex in the closed city of Norilsk, Novosibirsk, Siberia, where nickel ore processing takes place. They also see the removal of marble from the enormous Carrara quarries in Italy and witness lithium extraction in the Chilean Atacama Desert as well as logging in British Columbia. Land desecration affects daily human activity and such results are evident in a visual depiction of workers in the Barazuki Potash mine in Russia being compelled to drink their tea in total darkness while working and living underground. More dramatically, we also see the impact of the physical destruction of the German city Immerath as a result of energy company RWE's pursuit of open cast coal mining.

The consequences of human population growth and its effects are highlighted through depictions of the Dandora dump site, Nairobi's largest landfill, and Lagos' Redeemed Christian Church, a massive structure that has been built to hold up to one million worshippers. Another example of an enormous engineering project designed to accommodate large numbers of people is the Gotthard Base Tunnel in Switzerland, the largest of its type in the world, where it takes twenty minutes for railway passengers to ride through it. In all of these cases, filmmakers make it clear that human desire for food, travel, and assemblage is placated to the detriment of the natural environment. Indeed, when a UK air raid shelter is converted into an artificially controlled environment used to grow plant life, the absurdity of doing so while these other examples of environmental pillage are occurring simultaneously is made clear to the viewer. One important consequence of such human behavior in the Anthropocene is the expansion of species extinction, and the film faithfully chronicles that eventuality through noting the extinction of the Sumatra tiger while offering examples of ivory poaching and elephant tusk burning in Kenya.

But what are human reactions to these regular occurrences? Here, the filmmakers chronicle the celebration of Metallurgy Day in the Novosibirsk region and record participants joyously attending a festive air show created for the opening of the Gotthard Base Tunnel. We see sculptures referencing Michelangelo's celebration of the human form, with opera music playing in the background as the end product of Italian marble quarry extraction, and witness the ornate and intricate carvings of ivory products, transformed into craft products for wealthy consumers. And, of course, well-publicized long-term climate change effects, including the continued assault upon the Great Barrier Reef in Australia and the Batu Bulong Reef in Indonesia, are prominently pictured.

Anthropocene: The Human Epoch succeeds on a number of levels. Through its use of long camera and tracking shots and its employment of drone photography, it effectively communicates the enormous scale of environmental devastation the planet is currently experiencing. It dramatically juxtaposes images of the massive industrial machinery and technology that have been used to collect and secure natural resources with shots depicting the physical beauty of the different environments that have become the sites of ensuing damage. And, by framing the film into thematic segments—extraction, terraforming, climate change, and extinction—with each thematic title appearing on a slide with a black background that is in contrast with the vibrant subsequent imagery, the power of the theme and corresponding image is enhanced. Interestingly, the film contains a modest degree of dialogue with a few subjects interviewed to offer specific accounts and recollections. More generally, voice-over narration is employed. As a result, the camera's omniscient presence is continually affirmed.

That presence allows filmmakers to powerfully communicate four basic messages to their audience. First, the principal cause of the climate crisis involves human activity as opposed to random, natural occurrence. Second, there is abundant scientific evidence for this assertion. Third, the climate crisis is global in character and is getting progressively worse. And, finally, the human and natural worlds are in inexorable conflict with one another, However, as powerful as these messages may be, some are subject to further scrutiny. Given the history of climate change denial, encouraged and funded by fossil fuel corporations and affiliated interests, the importance of making a case for the existence of the climate crisis that has been induced by human activity, based upon existing scientific verification, to be presented in as emphatic a way as possible, is certainly understandable. However, as there has been an increased tendency to question the value of scientific authority in a post-COVID age, the communication of science-based information in and of itself may not be convincing to some. In this vein, the film can be viewed as mirroring those traditional environmental studies curricular spaces that privilege scientific investigation at the expense of buttressing complementary social science and humanities perspectives.

While we thus see the effects of human activity upon the environment, specific environmental justice concerns are not directly addressed in the film. Human behavior is depicted in universalist terms, and little attention is paid to how specific groups have been compelled to bear the brunt of climate crisis effects, subject to exploitation by those who are more powerful and privileged. In short, we fail to learn *why* humans act in the ways that they do and why they demonstrate little respect for the natural world or for one another. Instead, what is depicted is the modernist dichotomy of human beings living, exploiting, and reacting toward the natural world in ways that assert their inherent autonomy, independence, and conscious desire to separate themselves from that world. Such a vision is at odds with Chakrabarty and Bennett's analyses, which offer a more systematic postmodernist critique of those Western humanistic assumptions that view such an acceptance of human exceptionalism as misconceived in the twenty-first century.

My Octopus Teacher

My Octopus Teacher, released in 2020 and distributed by the Netflix streaming service, won the 2021 Academy Award for best documentary. Directed by Pippa Ehrlich and James Reed, the film focuses upon the activities of Craig Foster, himself a documentarian and naturalist, who engages in free diving, or diving into water for a significant period of time without the assistance of a breathing apparatus. In this case, the film chronicles Foster's diving in a South African cold underwater forest for the period of a year, where he observes and then interacts with an octopus. Because one can only stay under water for a relatively short period of time when committed to unassisted breathing in such a manner, the camera follows Foster when he is both under and above water.

My Octopus Teacher is as much about Craig Foster as it is about the octopus and sea life he observes. Admittedly depressed after completing a documentary film about the Kalahari Desert, Foster turns to free diving as a way of conquering his depression. In so doing, he begins to focus his observations of marine life on a specific female octopus whose trust he believes he can earn. The film thus chronicles the nature of this evolving relationship, at least in Foster's eyes. Grateful for allowing him to observe her world, the relationship becomes more and more intimate as Foster learns about the octopus' regular behavior. Indeed, at certain heteroerotic points, the camera records the octopus sitting on Foster's bare chest or touching his finger. It is thus noteworthy that with the exception of the octopus, females play a minor role in the film. The act of free diving is framed as a masculine pursuit, for at one point, Foster helps his young son pursue the activity, depicted almost as a rite of passage taught from father to son. It feels as if free diving becomes more than an excuse for Foster's exploration of the underwater forest but in addition becomes a testament to his parenting skills, helping him to cement the father/son relationship.

But why is the octopus so attractive to Foster and the film directors? On the one hand, Foster expresses gratitude for the willingness of the octopus to let him enter her world, allowing him to appreciate its beauty and wonder. But even more significantly, there are a number of attributes that Foster finds endearing. First, the octopus is praised for her intelligence and adaptability which are essential characteristics that allow her to succeed when competing against other creatures for her survival. We see the octopus use camouflage to hide among sea shells for protection from predators. At another point, she bores a hole and injects poison into a shell in order to get food, and in a separate instance, she lies on the back of a pyjama shark as a means of defending against a possible attack. When severely maimed after an attack, she is able to regenerate an arm, successfully coping with serious infirmity. Finally, she makes the ultimate sacrifice of motherhood, birthing so many baby octopi that after one year, she will be weakened to the point of suffering an inevitable mortality.

Of course, these events are colored by Foster's severe anthropomorphism, which not only allows him to project himself onto the other but aids in his construction of the other as a validation of self. The qualities Foster sees in the octopus that he most admires, its presumed sentience and adaptability, are essential to the Western, modernist construction of the human. But it is not simply the case that these are qualities worthy of admiration; in Foster's eyes, the octopus story is a morality tale. She is a source of good struggling to survive against the pyjama shark or other evil predators. Never mind that she preys on other unsuspecting creatures as well. And, in offering herself as an ultimate sacrifice after giving birth to her offspring, she affirms a view of motherhood that is decidedly patriarchal.

The audience is put in the position of voyeur, looking in from the outside, as the relationship between Foster and the female octopus develops. We form an association with Foster as we see the octopus through his male gaze, but we are also distant from him. It thus becomes paradoxical when we view the free diving technique, with its lack of apparatus and machinery attached to the diver, at the same time that we become continually aware of the presence of underwater cameras and crew who are concurrently filming Foster's movements and his interactions with the octopus. But because the relationship between diver and octopus is defined in large part by an artificial projection of its intimacy, we depend upon the camera as the independent authority to serve as our eyes and ears in making sense of the relationship. If Foster perceives the octopus as an object of fascination, the camera's presence allows the audience to objectify the totality of that relationship.

The calendar becomes an essential part of *My Octopus Teacher*, as the audience is repeatedly reminded in visual fashion of Foster's daily experiences. Specific days of the year are marked in chronological fashion from the beginning of the year and are repeatedly noted at the top of the screen. Time more generically becomes a prime character in the film, given Foster's physical ability to hold his breath under water for two or more minutes before being forced to come up for air. And, of course, the chronicling of time is of essential importance to the survival of the octopus herself, given her predestined mortality after the one-year period. Conceiving of time as encompassing the discrete and separate categories of past, present, and future affirms a modernist sensibility with regard to the way in which we frame our own lives. In *My Octopus Teacher*, its presence reinforces Foster's own perceptions of his relationship with the octopus, ensuring that the film focus stays on him.

Given such a focus, what then is the film saying about pedagogical issues involving the teacher/student relationship? By casting the octopus as Craig Foster's teacher, the film not only portrays the octopus as a sentient, adaptable creature, sacrificing her life for the benefit of her offspring, but views the octopus as an entity that is willing to trust Foster and share her environment with him. It is as a result of that trust that Foster is able to learn more about that environment and appreciate her skills in negotiating the challenges it presents. Thus, the "teaching" that is occurring is not simply a kind of information sharing but is in addition a type of behavioral modeling. Foster recognizes that he has entered a world for which he is largely ignorant and unable to negotiate. In so doing, his growing respect for that world and the abilities of the species that inhabits it are markedly different from the anthropocentrism displayed in *Anthropocene: The Human Epoch*, where the focus is largely restricted to human activity. Such awareness may even be considered to be a type of predicate for the consciousness raising that ecopedagogy proponents argue is essential, if we are to work effectively to preserve our natural world. But the perspective articulated in *My Octopus Teacher* is still pedagogically problematic for it asserts a speciesism that privileges the diver over the octopus. Those power dynamics are reinforced when Foster continually gives the octopus attributes that he as a human most values. To assert that the octopus is the teacher, and Foster, her student, implies that those customary power dynamics involving teacher and student are fluid and can be negotiated. Indeed, teachers often speak of how much they have "learned" from their students. But in the same way that Foster as a free diver is compelled to experience the octopus' environment on his own terms, teachers rarely if ever are willing or indeed are able to create a relationship where they share equal authority with their students. "Learning" from one's students of course regularly occurs and is indeed essential to good teaching and teaching improvement. But it occurs within an authoritative relationship that at its core is unchallenged. The speciesism that colors Foster's relationship with the octopus similarly preserves an anthropocentric view of the natural world that has contributed to the climate crisis.

My Octopus Teacher uses the components of affect we have previously described effectively in conveying its messaging. As has been noted, the camera photographs Foster's and the octopus' encounters with an intensity that suggests intimacy. The audience becomes emotionally attached to the welfare of the octopus as a result. But in its primary focus upon Foster, that relationship includes periods of assemblage and dis-assemblage, for every time that Foster surfaces from the sea, the assemblage is interrupted or broken, to be reestablished during the next dive. Whatever the limits of the film's anthropomorphism, we do see Foster as trying to engage in meaning-making as he learns about the octopus' world; his efforts offer evidence of his sincerity in an attempt to be respectful of an environment with which he is unfamiliar. And, of course, contingency colors much of the film through our awareness that his explorations, the life of the octopus, and indeed, the nature of their relationship are time dependent and of limited duration. The film's success is thus due in part to its use of affect in all of these domains in support of its messaging.

Heart of Sky, Heart of Earth

Heart of Sky, Heart of Earth is a 2011 documentary directed by Frauke Sandig and Eric Black, which chronicles the lives of members of Mayan communities in the Chiapas region of Mexico and Guatemala in their efforts to preserve their cultural identity while combatting environmental injustice. Widely acclaimed, the film is regularly shown at human rights and other film festivals located in Central and South America and was awarded first prize at the Planet in Focus International Environmental Film Festival in Toronto in 2012. Beautifully photographed, the film pays deference to key Mayan cosmological and spiritual perspectives, as enunciated in the *Popol Vuh*, the sacred narrative text for those who have resided in the Guatemalan highlands. It also chronicles the contemporary stories and experiences of select individuals who have endured poverty, addiction, political violence, and the destruction of their local environment.

The powerful themes derived from the *Popol Vuh*, which frame much of the content of the film, involve the interconnectedness of all aspects of nature, life's cyclical qualities, and the ethical responsibilities we have toward preserving our ancestor's spiritual presence in the natural world. At the very beginning of the film, it is noted with the camera focusing upon cloud formations in the sky that according to Mayan teachings, the sky existed before the earth was formed. After the earth was formed and was connected to the sky, plants, vegetation, and animals were created prior to the creation of humans (Gomez, 2015). Later in the film, reference is then made to Mayan creation stories where the first attempts to create humans out of mud failed when the mud washed away. After a second effort to create humans out of wood was also unsuccessful, the Gods were eventually able to create humans from the sacred plant, corn. The ties that connect personhood to a natural world of spiritual origins are thus conveyed in ways that are consistently intense and vivid. In addition, the importance of the Mayan calendar is highlighted, where life is depicted as a series of repeated events, ultimately dependent upon the will of the Gods. As the narration in the introduction to the film notes,

> Humans are just one part of everything in nature. Our dreams of the end of the Mayan calendar tell us the rivers will change their color. The Gods will finish off their people. And the next world will arise.
>
> Humans have forgotten how to live. They've forgotten how to be in harmony with nature. The Maya have the belief the world has already begun to purify itself. That's why there are so many floods and disasters. And it won't stop until the purification is complete. (Sandig and Black, 2012)

The importance of ancestor connection is emphasized in the personal narratives of many of the film's subjects. Josefa Chepita Hernandez Perez (Chepita) overcame a difficult family environment with an abusive father and felt compelled to leave home at the age of fifteen after feeling unwelcomed. Later, upon moving to the city of San Cristobal, she witnessed overt public discrimination directed toward Indigenous People living in the area, due to their appearance, lack of knowledge of Spanish, and economic position. However, she credits her Mayan spirituality and her respect for her elders who performed ritual ceremonies for the corn, for spring, and for water, as having motivated her to study and become a literacy teacher of Spanish, where she now instructs Indigenous adults non-conversant in the colonial language.

Carlos Chan K'in Chinuk (Chan K'in) wishes to become a shaman because he hopes to be able to cure people, having been guided by his father's prediction that when he reaches his father's age, he will have indeed assisted many people. He informs the audience that he lives with the trees because they are his life and we see him pointing out the importance of the Ceiba tree, the holy tree of the Mayans, whose roots contain the underground and whose branches hold up the stars. He notes that when a Ceiba tree falls in the forest, a star falls from the sky.

Alonzo Mendez is an art historian/archaeologist who takes the audience on a tour of the ruins of the ancient Chiapas city, Palenque. He sees parallels in the fall of Palenque and more generally, the decline of Mayan civilization and the current climate crisis, for in both cases, humans separated themselves from nature, with rulers being content to live in the comfort of palaces, raising themselves above the common man. The cyclical nature of accommodation to and then exploitation of the natural world is thus reaffirmed when examining the Palenque ruins. We are then taken to Tortuguero, an important archaeological site that held tablets referring to the Long Count, the ending of the Mayan calendar. The site has been desecrated as a result of modern development; what is left is a hole in the ground.

The lack of respect afforded Mayan peoples that continues to show its presence in contemporary times is a recurring theme in the film, most poignantly expressed in the words of Floridalma Pèrez Gonzalez (Flori). Flori recounts her family history, of having been forced to emigrate to Mexico from Guatemala in the aftermath of the genocidal massacres conducted by the Guatemalan government against the Maya people in the 1980s. After Flori's aunt was kidnapped, raped, and had her mouth cut open, the family walked by foot to Mexico, with Flori returning years later, reuniting her daughter with her cousins. Over 250,000 deaths occurred as a result of government action against its own people, with many others having disappeared. A majority of the victims were Maya. When interviewed in the film, Flori has become an activist, fighting for the rights of her people against political and corporate corruption. Other activists profiled in the film include Kajkan Felipe Mejia Sepet (Felipe), who in overcoming drug addiction precipitated by the massacres becomes a spiritual guide, assisting other survivors of the genocide; Jerónimo, a farmer who has become a member of the Zapatistas; and Gregoria Crisanta Pèrez (Crisanta), who along with Flori, attempts to organize a local community against the Marlin mine, owned by the Canadian corporation Goldcorp. They particularly lobby against the mine's use of cyanide, used for gold processing, and its deleterious effects on local children. At another point, the negative consequences of the North American Free Trade Association treaty (NAFTA) are discussed with regard to the Monsanto Corporation's flooding of the area with cheaper, genetically modified corn. Local farmers, unable to compete, have lost their livelihood, leading to increased immigration to the United States as well as greater family dislocation with children staying behind as their parents are forced to travel in their search for work. Not only is the corn, with its sacred meaning desecrated, but its role in contributing to the economic survival of the Indigenous population is compromised.

Analysis

Unlike *Anthropocene: The Human Epoch* or *My Octopus Teacher, Heart of Sky, Heart of Earth* presents a perspective that holistically integrates a treatment of environmental justice with sustainability concerns. Its producers are able to make the connection between oppression and environmental degradation in a compelling way that is reminiscent of Patricio Guzman's treatment of the enduring legacy of colonialism in *The Pearl Button*, discussed in Chapter 6. While its emphasis upon Mayan cosmology and spiritualism holds the film together, it is noteworthy that its subjects approach the issues of environmental justice and sustainability in different ways, with varying degrees of efficacy. Chan K'in, for example, in his quest to become a shaman, expresses some doubt as to whether he will ever achieve his goal of curing large numbers of individuals. He questions whether he will find enough community support for his efforts, and along with Alfonso acknowledges that the historical record indicates Mayan rulers allowed the destruction of their communities to occur because of their own greed and inability to take care of the earth. In that case, broad adherence to Mayan cosmological and spiritual teachings did not prevent environmental, political, and social catastrophe from occurring. Chepita, in her embrace of Mayan spirituality, is compelled to reconcile her recognition of the importance of her cultural identity with the exigencies of contemporary life that continually marginalize that identity. In teaching Indigenous adults Spanish, the language of her people's conquerors, she is assisting in their empowerment but only in recognition of their need to survive in a hostile setting. Flori, as a victim of government-sponsored mass atrocity, and Jerónimo, as a Zapatista leader, engage in community activism, but do so cognizant of the extreme power imbalances that continue to privilege multinationals, supported by authoritarian governments. They find meaning in their work, but do so recognizing that over the past decades, little has been done to reverse historical power imbalances. Suffice it to note that none of these approaches in and of themselves offer complete solutions to the existential issues that arise from the climate crisis and environmental injustice.

This being said, education is recognized as being important among all of the subjects in *Heart of Sky, Heart of Earth*. Whether it involves training to become a shaman or a language teacher, investigating the meaning of ancient scripts and archaeological carvings, exposing the deleterious effects of cyanide on Indigenous children, organizing political protest, or conducting communal rituals affirming the sacred importance of corn, the subjects in the film use, rely upon, and understand how important education is to their identity and their survival. The fact that its presence is visible within these different contexts is testimony to how the Mayan peoples have recognized its ubiquity as they affirm their belief in the interconnectedness of the human with the natural.

It is interesting that much of the power of this film lies in the forceful recounting of Mayan cosmological and spiritual teaching within the narration, spoken in both Spanish and Mayan languages, which is juxtaposed with the striking imagery of cloud formations in the sky along with photographs of the rain forest and its various elements. The stories told by the interviewees are also compelling, and it is clear that the elements of affect we have noted throughout this volume, including intensity of encounter, meaning-making, assemblage, and contingency, are vividly depicted within the film. As a conventional documentary, made specifically by and for a Global North audience, however, one wonders if the structure of the film creates a distance between the audience and its subjects that legitimizes audience complacency with regard to its responsibility in addressing the climate crisis and environmental justice concerns. To the extent that the spiritual practices and rituals chronicled in the film are displayed in ways that allow themselves to become exoticized, and to the degree that the struggle for environmental justice articulated by the courageous inhabitants of the Chiapas and Guatemala regions is framed as their struggle, as opposed to one for which there is universal responsibility, the film falls short. Suffice it to note all three of the documentaries discussed in this chapter while enhancing our understanding of the natural world to some extent are deficient in fully addressing the climate crisis in its complexity. Their failure to do so says as much about our own inadequacies in addressing the greatest challenge of our lifetime as it does about the films themselves.

Conclusion

We began this chapter with the admonition that the current global climate crisis has created existential questions regarding the prospects for planetary survival, the nature of environmental justice, and the imperative to reconsider our species-centered orientations toward the living and nonliving entities that surround us. As was noted in the introduction to this volume, theories of affect have played an important role in framing the discourse involving these issues. The Deleuzean emphasis upon intensities highlights the importance of appreciating the significance of our encounters with nonliving as well as living things. A recognition of the dynamic ways in which our collective responses to the climate crisis are repeatedly assembled and then dis-assembled underscores our inability to coalesce around a unified set of beliefs, actions, and commitments that might address current and future challenges. What we are becoming increasingly aware of, though, is that the distinctions between culture and nature which have served as traditional benchmarks framing the contours of social thought have to be reconsidered given human responsibility for those destructive practices that are endangering planetary survival. The search to find meaning amid the surrounding precarity that colors our present and future is another aspect of affect theory that has become particularly salient. It is for this reason that Chakrabarty's call for the development of a new planetary consciousness that not only recognizes human fallibility in contributing to planetary destruction but also reaffirms the conclusion that the fate of the planet cannot be controlled by human beings alone is a useful suggestion. To do so demands that we reconceive of what it means to be human to include the nonhuman and nonliving material entities with whom we share planetary space, recognizing their impact upon our own actions and emotions, acknowledging our dependence upon them. While theories of affect support such a perspective, its adoption would require a systematic rejection of the speciesism that has colored conventional humanistic beliefs that have been reproduced with schools as well as the academy. The three films discussed in this chapter both reiterate such speciesism to varying degrees and illustrate its limitations.

Anthropocene: A Human Epoch is historically important because it documented the global effects of human behavior that have contributed to the climate crisis at a time when climate change denial was quite strong, particularly within conservative Global North constituencies. Conceived of, produced, and disseminated in the pre-COVID years, its faith in scientific investigation to definitively chronicle climate change and document its ramifications offered a robust refutation of those who manipulated scientific evidence for their own political and economic interests. However, its emphasis upon human activity alone has limited its lasting effectiveness. The entire concept of the Anthropocene not only emphasizes the fact that human beings have dominated a specific geological epoch and have directly contributed to planetary destruction, but it like other epochs is time-bound and will end, to be replaced in the future with a nonhuman dominated era. It is the inevitability of such a future that demands a reconsideration of the way in which humans conceive of themselves in relationship to the planet, a reconsideration that is missing in the film's vision.

Similarly, although *My Octopus Teacher* does make an effort to emphasize the importance of human and nonhuman relations, the anthropomorphism and speciesism that it promotes excludes the possibility of moving toward a more inclusive and expansive view of planetary consciousness. Not only is the octopus valued for its supposed sentience and adaptability, qualities we associate with human behavior, but it is depicted as willfully engaging in a trustful, if subservient, relationship with free diver Craig Foster. Insofar as the film's focus becomes centered around Foster himself, as the octopus and her natural world become props for his self-actualization, the film legitimizes attitudes that exclude a broader commitment toward engaging in planetary consciousness. Both *Anthropocene: The Human Epoch* and *My Octopus Teacher* thus reiterate the limitations of the ways in which formal curricula and conventional pedagogies within schools and the academy address climate change and our relationship to planetary entities.

Of the three films reviewed, only *Heart of Sky, Heart of Earth* directly presents environmental justice concerns in a systematic way. In addition, with its emphasis upon Mayan cosmology, it offers a perspective that allows us to envision what a perspective embracing planetary consciousness might include. But in its inability to reconcile its subjects' varying commitments to these different emphasis areas, it also reflects a paralysis evident within the environmental movement. Does a commitment to pursue environmental justice reinforce speciesism through its emphasis upon human-to-human behavior? Can one even begin to conceive of what it means to embrace planetary consciousness without addressing the existing environmental injustice that is oppressive to much of the world's population? Such are the questions that remain unanswered as we confront the immediate and long-term implications of living within the Anthropocene. That these films ultimately fail to expand our understanding of these issues is unfortunate but it demonstrates our own failure to address them in creative and imaginative ways. It should also be noted that the conventional documentary form to which these three films adhere circumvents a radical reframing of the issues. And, overshadowing each of these efforts is the Global North audience to whom the films are directly addressed, an audience whose complacency with regard to the climate crisis is buttressed by its comparative economic privilege.

Concluding Remarks

One of the factors that has been a driving force in my personal and professional life has been a search for connections with people and with ideas, and I have come to believe that comparative and international education can be an academic field that offers one the opportunity to explore those possibilities. CIE, when done well, embraces the search for new ideas to be found in environments distinct from those for which one is most comfortable. The fact that it focuses upon the associative experiences related to teaching and learning, a most quintessential example of interconnection, reiterates its embrace of the process of connection as a central force in the shaping of human experience. I have also seen in the study of film new possibilities for sharing insights, discovering compelling ideas, and challenging conventional wisdom. At the same time, it has been noted that in the realms of both practice and theory, education and film have reflected darker aspects of human experience, amplifying racist, colonialist, classist, and anthropocentric perspectives that exemplify the negative traits of modernism and Western humanism.

This project has been one of seeking to uncover similarities within and among the two fields, often where such similarities are not immediately apparent. From a personal perspective, it has been deeply satisfying to explore how ideas are expressed in different forms and contexts. But I judge the ultimate success of this venture not simply in the accurate chronicling of existing ideas while noting their broader resonances but in its service as a forum for critiquing those ideas and exploring new and different alternatives.

In this vein, I have been struck by the work of Dacher Keltner and his colleagues, who have investigated the nature of awe from a social-psychological perspective. Keltner defines awe as "the feeling of being in the presence of something vast that transcends your current understanding of the world" (Keltner, 2023, 7). He goes on to list eight themes or variations that characterize how we express awe and characterizes them as wonders of life. They include moral beauty or "exceptional virtue, character, and ability . . . marked by a purity of goodness and intention" (Keltner, 2023, 11); collective effervescence, where "we feel like we are buzzing and crackling with some life force that merges people into a collective self, a tribe, an oceanic 'we'" (Keltner, 2023, 13); nature or the appreciation of the natural world; music, visual design, spiritual and religious awe; stories of life and death (Keltner, 2023, 13–17); and epiphanies or "philosophical insights, scientific discoveries, metaphysical ideas, personal realizations, mathematical equations, and sudden disclosures ... that transform life in an instant" (Keltner, 2023, 18).

For me, many of the films and the accompanying literature that I discuss in this volume relate to the forms of awe Keltner describes. Whether it be those Indigenous Peoples who continue to endure the effects of the sexual, physical, and emotional violence to which they were subjected in the religious schools they were forced to attend during their childhood in Canada, as depicted in the film *We Were Children*, or the leaders of the Windrush generation, who fought to protect their educational and human rights while combatting virulent racism in the UK, as represented in *Small Axe*, their cinematic representations heighten our appreciation of their moral beauty. The same can be said for the fictional character Cora in *The Underground Railroad* miniseries or Han Sanming, the real-life coal miner whose stoicism in the face of neoliberal modernization is portrayed in *Still Life*. When we see the enormity of planetary destruction through human activity in *Anthropocene: The Human Epoch*, our understanding of our collective responsibility for the consequences of the climate crisis is one example of the collective effervescence which Keltner describes. At the same time, our appreciation of the natural world is clearly triggered through the imagery displayed not only in *Anthropocene: The Human Epoch* but in *The Pearl Button* and *Heart of Sky, Heart of Earth* as well. As film is a visual medium, it is not surprising that the filmmaking process evokes the kind of awe Keltner describes as visual design. The best films are more than visual postcards, however, as they trigger many of our senses in their efforts to construct an enduring artistic product. The sense of alienation we feel in watching *Still Life*, and the sense of entrapment we experience while watching *Parasite*, as well as the suffocating enclosure we observe while watching *A Separation*, all offer their own sense of awe, due to the enormity of the emotions they evoke.

For me, exposure to Mayan cosmology in *Heart of Sky, Heart of Earth*, and reflecting upon Patricio Guzman's beautiful poetic narrative in *The Pearl Button*, creates a sense of awe for the spiritual dimension of meaning-making that is an essential component of human experience. In both of these instances, and certainly in *The Underground Railroad*, *Parasite*, and *The Octopus Teacher* as well, the precarity of life and death is expressed in powerful ways. Keltner's final thematic variation of awe involves epiphanies that arise from the sharing of ideas, discoveries, and disclosures, and in this area, both the academic literature and specific films offer such insight. One can only marvel at the writings of Walter Benjamin, Susan Sontag, and Zygmunt Bauman, in their discussions of art, photography, and the nature of consumerism and commodification. The insights of Dipesh Chakrabarty, with regard to the necessity of reconsidering the human/natural world dichotomy in a planetary age, provided a real intellectual epiphany for yours truly. And above all, Gilles Deleuze's efforts to apply philosophical principles involving the nature of movement and time to the study of film were similarly revelatory. But so did Bong Joon-ho's exquisite depiction of the violence embedded within modern constructions of social class and meritocracy, as did Ashgar Farhadi's insights involving the ways in which family, gender, religious observance, and moral suasion impact modernist constructions of social class and the state in Iran.

It is not surprising that Keltner's academic research involving awe draws from the work of Paul Ekman, one of the pioneers in the cross-cultural study of emotion, and a student of Silvan Tompkins, whose research on affect theory was particularly influential in its development. We have emphasized the relevance of principles of affect theory in this volume as they encapsulate the ways in which we navigate a range of experiences in both ordinary and extraordinary ways. It is easy to see the relevance of both emphasis areas to the study of CIE and film. But in so doing, it is worth noting that the investigation of both fields can lead to more than a fostering of emotional connection or intellectual curiosity. I would argue that the issues raised in both the academic literature involving CIE and film studies and the specific films we have discussed pose serious philosophical questions that deserve to be repeatedly revisited.

In his insightful book *Film Thought: Cinema as Reflective Form*, Robert Pippin refers to Hegel's notion of art as a form of self-knowledge that leads to self-realization. As he states,

> In his terms in the *Lectures*, human beings must "double themselves" (*sich verdoppeln*) not only to understand themselves, but to be themselves, given their distinct modes of being, as self-realizing beings. That is, the mode of self-knowledge distinctive for such beings is self-constituting as well as self-reflective, as human beings struggle to become who they take themselves to be. Art is understood as a distinct modality of such self-understanding, "externalization," and self-realizing. It is for Hegel an affective and sensible mode of self-understanding and is counted as just as indispensable as representational modes (religion) and conceptual modes (philosophy). (Pippin, 2020, 10–11)

Recognizing that the Hegelian notion of "self" can be viewed as problematic as is his labeling of self-knowledge and self-realization as distinct categories, it still can be employed as a useful heuristic in summarizing what we have learned from the films surveyed in the volume. What, then, are the forms of self-realization that the films discussed in this volume offer us, and what types of self-realization do they make possible? First, many of the films make it clear that an overemphasis upon education within formal institutional contexts can be misplaced. If we are to truly embrace the complexities that mark our daily experiences, then we need to admit that schooling in its modernist formations is not always relevant to how we navigate those experiences and when its presence is relevant, it can perform destructive as well as constructive functions. Its destructive potential was most graphically expressed in *The Underground Railroad*, *We Were Children*, *Rabbit Proof Fence*, and *The Pearl Button*. *The Small Axe* series was the only one of the films analyzed that saw schooling as being intrinsically valuable, offering faith in the possibility of educational reform. In *Parasite*, *Still Life*, *A Separation*, and *Tsotsi*, the role of education in addressing issues of social class and race was muted or barely present. At the very least, these films should compel us to give pause to the contention that schooling in its institutional form is an inherent public good that will consistently guarantee positive outcomes if supported and if constructed in equitable ways. In so doing, they reiterate the skepticism expressed by affect theorists and postmodernist thinkers who stress the power of contingency in shaping our experiences in ways that are unknowable, unpredictable, and uncontrollable.

More generally, the films we have discussed raise important questions involving larger issues concerned with causality, determinism, and agency. In many of these films, it is the random event that precipitates a positive or negative consequence, an event that is not necessarily predicted or repeated. In *The Underground Railroad*, for example, Cora's survival is repeatedly due to circumstance as much as it is due to her own resiliency. In the film *Tsotsi*, the main character's life is forever changed by a carjacking with an unobserved infant sitting in the backseat. In *A Separation*, when an elderly father wanders unaccompanied outside of his apartment, the lives of the main characters are forever changed. Causality does not simply involve predictability or the lack thereof. In searching for identifiable causes and measurable effects, we too often assume the inherent existence of a relationship between the two that is questionable. Can a single cause be attributable to any one event? Are causal effects always knowable? The films we have reviewed compel us to ask such questions, reminding us that causation need not occur linearly and may be multifaceted rather than unilateral. The embrace of ambiguity, which is frequently evident in many of the reviewed films, contrasts dramatically with the academic educational literature, with its emphasis upon closure in its assertion of certainty.

Many of the films subject to review affirm the presence of determinism in chronicling the day-to-day experiences of their characters. The Afro-pessimism expressed in *The Underground Railroad* is one example of such an outlook; Patricio Guzman's ability to tie together colonial with contemporary atrocity in *The Pearl Button* is another example. The evocation of a determinist perspective is not limited to historical rendering, however. The material fate of the residents of Fengjie, in *Still Life*, is predetermined when the film begins. The neoliberal forces of globalization and modernization that force their removal through the construction of the Three Gorges Dam are too powerful for inhabitants of the ancient Chinese city to resist. Nonetheless, the characters and subjects in these films operate with varying degrees of agency. In *The Underground Railroad*, *Still Life*, *A Separation*, and *Parasite*, for example, the circumscribed nature of the characters' agency makes their efforts to confront racial oppression, alienation, poverty, ethical ambiguity, and disrespect for one's class identity particularly sympathetic, even if their efforts bring about uncertain or at best mixed results. In *Rabbit Proof Fence*, *Small Axe*, and *Tsotsi*, the main characters are more successful and their agency is less circumscribed, although there are questions as to whether the structural violence to which the characters are exposed is given enough emphasis.

As Gilles Deleuze argued, the construction of time is an essential component of modern filmmaking, and its importance is highlighted in different ways in the films we have reviewed. Films such as *Small Axe*, *The Pearl Button*, and *Heart of Sky, Heart of Earth* present time conventionally. In each of these films, the past is depicted as very much influencing present circumstance, the lingering consequences of racism, settler colonialism, and capitalism being graphically documented. In *My Octopus Teacher*, the mapping of chronological time structures the entire film, be it through the few minutes Craig Foster is able to stay underwater as a free diver, to the daily reflections of what has been learned during particular dives, to the year's end, when the subject of the film will die after giving birth to numerous octopi. Time is of course a major component of *Anthropocene: The Human Epoch*, as well. As the title of the film indicates, the ascension of human beings to masters and potential destroyers of the planet represents a specific, time-bound geological age, with current behavior leading to potentially cataclysmic consequences in the future.

Yet in other instances, time is portrayed unconventionally. The magic realism employed in *The Underground Railroad* is a device that conveys the timelessness of the violence and oppression to which Cora and African-Americans more generally are subjected. Its usage reiterates the perspective that there is no end point to the perpetuation of racial oppression, at least in the US context. Magic realism is also used in *Still Life*, as a means of blurring the real with the imaginary, but also as a way of expressing a way for its characters to escape the alienation they feel in the present. In its ending, *Parasite* demonstrates that as the entrapment the Kim family experiences, due to their class position, continues in perpetuity, there is little difference for them and for other members of Korean society between past, present, and future. Indeed, the ambiguous ending in *A Separation* also raises questions not only regarding the limitations of modernist and religious perspectives in contemporary Iran but also whether their resolution can ever occur.

In short, the films that have been discussed trigger self-realization through asking us to reconsider conventional assumptions we entertain regarding the efficacy of the modern school, and more generally, assumptions governing our understandings of causation, determinism, agency, and the nature of time. But do they also induce self-actualization, at least as envisioned by Pippin through his channeling of Hegel? I believe that they do or at least have the potential to do so.

First, they compel us to think of the academic research we conduct in more expansive and creative ways. The fields of comparative and international education and film study both attempt to tackle issues involving representation. How do we know that what we are portraying, with regard to educational interchange or human experience more generally, is real? In addressing that question, we need to commit to deconstructing the conventions that shape our perceptions and admit to their self-serving nature. This is particularly true with regard to the treatment of research and film subjects, and the nature of the audience to whom researchers and filmmakers are addressing. We have previously noted that neoliberal values heavily influence both educational research and filmmaking domains. Those values, which include a belief in the importance of competition, a faith in meritocracy, and a general willingness to promote global capitalism, impact what kind of research is valued and is deemed worthy of investigation. They influence what subjects of commercial and documentary film are judged to be deserving of attention. And, the structures that have been put in place to ensure that ideas generated from these domains receive global recognition are themselves skewed to promote Global

North sensibilities. Being cognizant of such realities compels us to work harder to expand access for those who wish to study educational practice and/or promote meaningful aesthetic products such as filmmaking but have heretofore been ignored. The mandate to create greater inclusivity demands that our audiences be broadened to reach those not privileged by residing in Global North countries. It demands that the voices of those who are written about or are filmed are not appropriated by privileged outsiders. And, it requires that audiences be expanded to include those who remain isolated from receiving or participating in the global exchange of ideas.

There is some evidence that such initiatives are not only possible but are occurring. Indigenous filmmakers are increasingly finding the space to create their art and are receiving increased global recognition (Mayer, 2018). The Ecoversities Alliance, the Global Tapestry of Alternatives, and the Wellbeing Economic Alliance, mentioned in Chapter 1, represent grassroots efforts to create global educational networks that offer new educational possibilities missing within conventional institutions. It should further be noted that film series, such as *The Underground Railroad* and *Small Axe*, echoed popular social change sentiments expressed on a larger scale within the Black Lives Matter Movement. Using educational research or film to promote meaningful social justice alternatives is not only possible, but it is occurring, if on a scale smaller than one might have hoped for.

However, more will be needed to occur if the fruits of the self-actualization process to which Pippen refers are to bloom. Of greater consequence than any series of specific acts is an entire rethinking of the ways in which the academic study of education, or for our purposes, comparative and international education, can be opened up to new possibilities. In pursuit of such a goal, the lessons learned from film and film studies are instructive. Can we as educators and educational scholars become more comfortable acknowledging the ambiguity and precarity that colors educational efforts and processes? To do so would mean confessing that educational processes and outcomes can be as destructive or ineffectual as they are affirming, depending upon setting, circumstance, and context. Can we find ways of limiting the destructive tendencies of categorization and classification, and minimize the negative consequences of "othering?" To do so would require reevaluating our anthropocentrism while questioning the autonomy attributed to conceptions of self, consciousness, and will. It would demand that we do a better job of fostering interconnection with living and nonliving entities, and that we reevaluate what it really means to be human. The principles of affect, to which we subscribe, along with other postmodernist perspectives, embrace such an outlook. The examples we have offered through the study of film offer evidence that such an intellectual journey is both possible and can be quite satisfying. One can only hope that in our efforts to further understand the mysteries and the beauty of educational interaction, we take note.

References

Introduction

Ahmed, S. (2015), *The Cultural Politics of Emotion*, 2nd edition, New York: Routledge.

Albrecht-Crane, C. and Slack, J.D. (2003), "Toward a Pedagogy of Affect," in J.D. Slack (ed.), *Animations [of Deleuze and Guattari]*, 191–216. New York: Peter Lang.

Ball, A. (2018), "Manuel DeLanda, Assemblage Theory," *Parhesia*, 29, 241–7.

Barrett, L. (2018), *How Emotions Are Made*, Boston, MA: Mariner Books.

Bennett, J. (2009), *Vibrant Matter: A Political Ecology of Things*, Durham, NC: Duke University Press.

Berland, L. and Stewart, K. (2019), *The Hundreds*, Durham, NC: Duke University Press.

Butler, J. (2018), *Notes on a Performative Theory of Assembly*, Cambridge, MA: Harvard University Press.

Carney, S. and Madsen, U. (2021), *Education in Radical Uncertainty: Transgression in Theory and Method*, London: Bloomsbury Academic.

Chakrabarty, D. (2021), *The Climate of History in a Planetary Age*, Chicago, IL: University of Chicago Press.

Colmenares, E. (2018), "Affecting the Theory-Practice Gap in Social Justice Teacher Education: Exploring Student Teachers' Stuck Moments," Unpublished PhD Dissertation, New York: Teachers College, Columbia University.

DeLanda, M. (2016), *Assemblage Theory*, Edinburgh: Edinburgh University Press.

Deleuze, G. (1986a, 2017), *Cinema I: The Movement Image*, Minnesota: University of Minnesota Press.

Deleuze, G. (1986b, 2017), *Cinema II: The Time Image*, Minnesota: University of Minnesota Press.

Deleuze, G. and Guattari, F. (1987), *A Thousand Plateaus: Capitalism and Schizophrenia*, translated by B. Massumi, Minneapolis: University of Minnesota Press.

Epstein, I. (1986a), "Children's Rights and Juvenile Correctional Institutions in the People's Republic of China," *Comparative Education Review*, 30(3), 359–72.

Epstein, I. (1986b), "Reformatory Education in Chinese Society," *International Journal of Offender Therapy and Comparative Criminology*, 30(2), 87–100.

Epstein, I. (2015), "Introduction," in I. Epstein (ed.), *The Whole World Is Texting: Youth Protest in the Information Age*, 1–24, Rotterdam: Pittsburgh Studies in Comparative and International Education, Sense Publishers.

Epstein, I. (2019), *Affect Theory and Comparative Education Discourse: Essays on Fear and Loathing in Response to Global Educational Policy and Practice*, London; Bloomsbury Academic.

Haraway, D. (2008), *When Species Meet*, Minnesota: University of Minnesota Press.

Karkov, N. (2016), "Why Pluralism = Pluralism ≠ Monism: A Decolonial Feminist Critique of Deleuze and Guattari's Concept of Becoming," *Deleuze Studies*, 10(3), 379–94.

Latour, B. (2007), *Reassembling the Social: An Introduction to Actor Network Theory*, Oxford: Oxford University Press.

Lesko, N. and Talburt, S. (eds.) (2012), *Keywords in Youth Studies: Tracing Affects, Movements, Knowledges*, New York: Routledge.

Massumi, B. (1995), "The Autonomy of Affect," *Cultural Critique*, 31(Autumn), 83–109. Available online at: https://doi.org/10.2307/1354446. https://www.jstor.org/stable/1354446. Accessed on August 9, 2023.

Massumi, B. (2015), *The Power and End of the Economy*, Durham, NC: Duke University Press.

Nail, T. (2017), "What Is an Assemblage?" *SubStance*, 46(1), 21–37. Available online at: doi:10.3368/ss.46.1.21. Accessed on August 18, 2023.

Protevi, J. (2006), "Deleuze, Guattari, and Emergence," *Paragraph*, 29(2), 19–39. Available online at: https://www.jstor.org/stable/i40123172. Accessed on August 18, 2023.

Salajan, F.D. and jules, t.d. (2023), "Introduction," in F.D. Salajan and T.D. jules (eds.), *Comparative and International Education (Re)assembled*, London: Bloomsbury.

Savage, G.C. (2019), "What Is Policy Assemblage?" *Territory, Politics, Governance*, 8(3), 319. Available online at: doi:10.1080/21622671.2018.1559760. Accessed on August 18, 2023.

Smith, D., Protevi, J., and Voss, D. (2022), "Gilles Deleuze," *Stanford Encyclopedia of Philosophy*. Available online at: https://plato.stanford.edu/entries/deleuze/. Accessed on August 12, 2023.

Stewart, K. (2007), *Ordinary Affects*, Durham, NC: Duke University Press.

Vavrus, F. (2021), *Schooling as Uncertainty: An Ethnographic Memoir in Comparative Education*, London: Bloomsbury Academic.

Wetherell, M. (2012), *Affect and Emotion: A New Social Science Understanding*, Beverly Hills: Sage Publishing.

Whittle, A. and Spicer, A. (2008), "Is Actor Network Theory Critique?," *Organizational Studies*, 29(4), 611–29. Available online at: https://doi.org/10.1177/0170840607082223. Accessed on August 19, 2023.

Zembylas, M. (2015), *Emotion and Traumatic Conflict: Reclaiming Healing in Education*, Oxford: Oxford University Press.

Chapter 1

Bhabha, H. (1984), "On Mimicry and Man: The Ambivalence of Colonial Discourse," 102(28), 125–33. Available online at: https://doi.org/10.2307/778467; https://www.jstor.org/stable/778467. Accessed on February 19, 2022.

Bourdieu, P. and Passeron, J.C. (1977), *Reproduction in Education and Society*, Beverley Hills: Sage.

Chandler, D. (2013), "'Human-Centered' Development: Rethinking 'Freedom and Agency' in Discourses of International Development," *Millennium: Journal of International Studies*, 42(1), 3–23.

Danzinger, K. (1994), *Constructing the Subject: Historical Origins of Psychological Research*, Cambridge: Cambridge University Press.

Ecoversities.org (n.d.), "Our Story," *Ecoversities*. Available online at: https://ecoversities.org/about/. Accessed on February 20, 2022.

Epstein, E.H. (2008), "Setting the Normative Boundaries: Crucial Epistemological Benchmarks in Comparative Education," *Comparative Education*, 44 (4), 373–86.

Epstein, E.H. (2017), "The Nazi Seizure of the International Education Review: A Dark Episode in the Early Professional Development of Comparative Education," *Comparative Education*, 54(1), 49–61. doi:10.1080/03050068.2017.1396092.

Foucault, M. (1994), *Order of Things: An Archaeology of the Human Sciences*, New York: Vintage.

Gerasimov Institute of Cinematography (n.d.), "About," *Gerasimov Institute of Cinematography*. Available online at: https://www.topuniversities.com/universities/gerasimov-institute-cinematography. Accessed on February 18, 2022.

Global Tapestry of Alternatives (n.d.). "Weavers," *Global Tapestry of Alternatives*. Available online at: https://unitierraoax.org/english/. Accessed on February 20, 2022.

Goldin, C. and Katz, L. (1999), "The Shaping of Higher Education: The Formative Years in the United States, 1890–1940," *Journal of Economic Perspectives*, 11(1), 37–62.

Graeber, D. and Wengrow, D. (2021), *The Dawn of Everything: A New History of Humanity*, New York: Farrar, Straus, and Giroux.

Grieveson, L. and Wasson, H. (2008), "Introduction," in L. Grieveson and H. Wasson (eds.), *Inventing Film Studies*, xv, Durham, NC: Duke University Press.

Gross, R. (2012), *Psychology: The Science of Mind and Behavior*, 6th edition, Didcot: Hodder Education.

Hill, K. (n.d.), "August Lumiere and Louis Lumiere," *International Photography Hall of Fame and Museum*. Available online at: https://iphf.org/inductees/auguste-louis-lumiere/#:~:text=Auguste%20and%20Louis%20Lumi%C3%A8re%20%2C%20two,made%20the%20first%20motion%20picture. Accessed on February 18, 2022.

Hoodfar, H. (2020), "Building a Transnational Movement for Academic Freedom," in Jakob Lothe (ed.), *Research and Human Rights*, Oslo: Novus Press.

International Commission on the Futures of Education (2021), *Reimagining Our Futures Together: A New Social Contract for Education*, Paris: UNESCO. Available online at: https://unesdoc.unesco.org/ark:/48223/pf0000379707. Accessed on February 20, 2022.

James, P. (2018), "Creating Capacities for Human Flourishing: An Alternative Approach to Human Development," in P. Spinozzi and M. Mazanti (eds.), *Cultures of Sustainability and Wellbeing: Theories, Histories, and Policies*, 23–45. Abingdon: Routledge.

Lee, T.H.C. (1999), *Education in Traditional China: A History*, Leiden: Brill Publishers.

Leonard, T.C. (2005), "Mistaking Eugenics for Social Darwinism: Why Eugenics Is Missing from the History of American Economics," 37(Supp.1), 200–33. Available online at: https://doi.org/10.1215/00182702-37-Suppl_1-200. Accessed on February 19, 2022.

Prodger, P. (2003), *Time Stands Still: Muybridge and the Instantaneous Photography Movement*, Oxford: Oxford University Press.

Russell, D. (1995), "A Chronology of Cinema, 1889–1896," *Film History*, 7(2), 115–232.

Said, E. (1978), *Orientalism*, New York: Pantheon Books.

Santos, B. (2014), *Epistemologies of the South: Justice Against Epistemicide*, Boulder, CO: Paradigm Publishing.

Terman, L. (1916), *The Measurement of Intelligence: An Explanation of and a Complete Guide for the Use of the Stanford Revision and Extension of the Binet-SimonIntelligence Scale*, Boston, MA: Houghton-Mifflin, 91–2. Available online at: https://www.gutenberg.org/files/20662/20662-h/20662-h.htm#CHAPTER_VI. Accessed on February 19, 2022.

Universidad De La Tierra Oaxaca (n.d.), "Our History," *Universidad De La Tierra Oaxaca*. Available online at: https://unitierraoax.org/english/. Accessed on February 20, 2022.

USC Cinematic Arts (n.d.), "History," *USC Cinematic Arts*. Available online at: https://cinema.usc.edu/about/history/index.cfm. Accessed on February 18, 2022.

Wellbeing Economy Alliance (n.d.), "About," *Wellbeing Economy Alliance*. Available online at: https://weall.org/about. Accessed on February 20, 2022.

Chapter 2

Adick, C. (2018), "Bereday and Hilker: Origins of the 'Four Steps of Comparison' Model," *Comparative Education*, 54(1), 35–48. doi:10.1080/03050068.2017.1396088.

Altbach, P. (1977), "Servitude of the Mind? Education, Dependency, and Neo-colonialism," *Teachers College Record*, (79)2, 187–204.

Anderson, N. (2014), *Shadow Philosophy: Plato's Cave and Cinema*, London: Routledge.

Andreotti, V. (2011), "(Towards) Decoloniality and Diversity in Global Citizenship Education," *Globalization, Societies, and Education*, 9(3–4), 381–97.

Andrew, D. (2016), "Time Zones and Jetlag: The Flows and Phases of World Cinema," in L. Braudy and M. Cohen (eds.), *Film Theory and Criticism*, 813–39, New York: Oxford University Press.

Appadarai, A. (1996), *Modernity at Large*, Minneapolis: University of Minnesota Press.

Arnove R.F. (1980), "Comparative Education and World Systems Analysis," *Comparative Education Review*, 24(1), 48–62.

Bartlett, L. and Ghaffar-Kucher, A. (2013), *Refugees, Immigrants and Education in the Global South: Lives in Motion*, New York: Routledge.

Bartlett, L., Oliveira, G., and Ungemah, I. (2018), "Cruel Optimism: Migration and Schooling for Dominican Newcomer Immigrant Youth," *Anthropology and Education Quarterly*, 49(4), 444–61.

Bartlett, L. and Vavrus, F. (2017), *Rethinking Case Study Research: A Comparative Approach*, New York: Routledge.

Baudry, J.L. (2016), "Ideological Effects of the Basic Cinematographic Apparatus," in L. Braudy and M. Cohen (eds.), *Film Theory and Criticism*, 217–27, New York: Oxford University Press.

Bauman, Z. (2012), *Liquid Modernity*, Cambridge: Polity Press.

Bazin, A. (2016), "The Evolution of the Language of Cinema," in L. Braudy and M. Cohen (eds.), *Film Theory and Criticism*, 41–53, New York: Oxford University Press.

Beck, U. (1992), *The Risk Society*, Beverly Hills: Sage Publications.

Benjamin, W. (1935, 2005), *The Work of Art in the Age of Mechanical Reproduction*, Transcribed and edited by A. Blunden, Los Angeles: UCLA School of Film, Theatre and Television. Available online at: https://www.marxists.org/reference/subject/philosophy/works/ge/benjamin.htm. Accessed on June 12, 2022.

Bernstein, B. (1977), *Class, Codes, and Control*, Vol. 3, London: Routledge and Kegan Paul.

Bourdieu, P. and Passeron J.C. (1971), *Reproduction in Education and Society*, Beverly Hills: Sage Publications.

Bowles, S. and Gintis, H. (1976), *Schooling in Capitalist America*, New York: Basic Books.

Butler, J. (2018), *Notes on a Performative Theory of Assembly*, Cambridge, MA: Harvard University Press.

Chow, R. (2016), "Film and Cultural Identity," in L. Braudy and M. Cohen (eds.), *Film Theory and Criticism*, 885–92, New York: Oxford University Press.

DeJaeghere, J. and Walker, M. (2021), "The Capabilities Approach in Comparative and International Education: A Justice-Enhancing Framework," in T. jules, R. Shields, and M.A.M. Thomas (eds.), *The Bloomsbury Handbook of Theory in Comparative and International Education*, 461–74, London: Bloomsbury Academic.

Deleuze, G. (1986, 2017), *Cinema I: The Movement Image*, Minnesota: University of Minnesota Press.

Deleuze, G. (1989, 2013), *Cinema II: The Time Image*, Minnesota: University of Minnesota Press.

Dore, R., (1976), *The Diploma Disease: Education, Qualifications, and Development*, Berkeley: University of California Press.

Dyer, R. (2016), "Lighting for Whiteness," in L. Braudy and M. Cohen (eds.), *Film Theory and Criticism*, 660–71, New York: Oxford University Press.

Eisenstein, S. (2016), "The Dramaturgy of Film Form [The Dialectical Approach of Film Form]," in L. Braudy and M. Cohen (eds.), *Film Theory and Criticism*, 23–40, New York: Oxford University Press.

Emery, J., Powell, R., and Crookes, L. (2023), "Class, Affects, Margins," *The Sociological Review*, 71(2), 283–95. Available online at: https://doi.org/10.1177 /00380261221150076. Accessed on September 11, 2023.

Epstein, I. (2019), *Affect Theory and Comparative Education Discourse: Essays on Fear and Loathing in Response to Global Educational Policy and Practice*, London: Bloomsbury Academic.

Frank, A.G. (1966), "The Development of Underdevelopment," *Monthly Review*, 18(7), 17–31.

Freire, P. (1970), *Pedagogy of the Oppressed*, New York: Continuum.

Giddens, A. (1991), *Modernity and Self-identity in the Late Modern Age*, Palo Alto: Stanford University Press.

Gorur, R. (2011), "ANT on the PISA Trail: Following the Statistical Pursuit of Certainty," *Educational Philosophy and Theory*, 43(S1), 76–93. doi:10.1111/j.1469-5812.2009.00612.x

Holmes, B. (1977), "The Positivist Debate in Comparative Education— An Anglo-Saxon Perspective," *Comparative Education*, 13(2), 115–32, doi:10.1080/0305006770130108a.

Jencks, C., (1972), *Inequality*, New York: Basic Books.

jules, T. (2021), "Introduction," in T. jules, R. Shields, and M.A.M. Thomas (eds.), *The Bloomsbury Handbook of Theory in Comparative and International Education*, 1–17, London: Bloomsbury Academic.

Karabel, J. and Halsey, A.H. (1977), "Introduction," in J. Karabel and A.H. Halsey (eds.), *Power and Ideology in Education*, 1–86, New York: Oxford University Press.

Kelly, G.P. and Altbach, P.G. (1984), "Introduction, The Four Faces of Colonialism," in G.P. Kelly and P.G. Altbach (eds.), *Education and the Colonial Experience*, 1–5, New Brunswick: Transaction.

Kirylo, J.D. (2011), *Paolo Freire: The Man from Recife*, New York: Peter Lang.

Klees, S. Samoff, J., and Stromquist, N. (eds.) (2012), *World Bank and Education: Critiques and Alternatives*, Rotterdam: Sense.

Kracauer, S. (2016), "Basic Concepts," in L. Braudy and M. Cohen (eds.), *Film Theory and Criticism*, 113–25, New York: Oxford University Press.

Makel, M.C. and Pluker, J.A. (2014), "Facts Are More Important Than Novelty: Replication in the Educational Sciences," *Educational Researcher*, 43(6), 304–16.

Marks, L. (2000), *The Skin of the Film: Intercultural Cinema, Embodiment and the Senses*, Durham, NC: Duke University Press.

Marquis, M. (2021), "Structural Functionalism in Comparative and International Education," in T. jules, R. Shields, and M.A.M. Thomas (eds.), *The Bloomsbury Handbook of Theory in Comparative and International Education*, 23–36, London: Bloomsbury Academic.

Metz, C. (2016), "Some Points in the Semiotics of the Cinema," in L. Braudy and M. Cohen (eds.), *Film Theory and Criticism*, 54–60, New York: Oxford University Press.

Morgan, D. (2021), *The Lure of the Image*, Berkeley: University of California Press.

Mulvey, L. (2016), "Visual Pleasure and Narrative Cinema," in L. Braudy and M. Cohen (eds.), *Film Theory and Criticism*, 621–31, New York: Oxford University Press.

Noah, H. and Eckstein, M. (1969), *Toward a Science of Comparative Education*, New York: Macmillan.

Oliveira, G. (2018), *Motherhood Across Borders*, New York: New York University Press.

Parreira Do Amaral, M.P. and Erfurth, M. "Differentiation Theory and Externalization in Comparative and International Education," in T. jules, R. Shields, and M.A.M. Thomas (eds.), *The Bloomsbury Handbook of Theory in Comparative and International Education*, 313–25, London: Bloomsbury Academic.

Rice, T. (2019), *Films for the Colonies: Cinema and the Preservation of the British Empire*, Berkeley: University of California Press.

Salajan, F.D. and jules, t.d. (2023), "(Re)Assembling Comparative and International Education: New Frontiers and Directions in an Interdisciplinary Field," in F.D. Salajan and T.D. jules (eds.), *Comparative and International Education (Re) Assembled*, 3–20, London: Bloomsbury Academic.

Sarris, A. (2016), "Notes on the Auteur Theory in 1962," in L. Braudy and M. Cohen (eds.), *Film Theory and Criticism*, 400–3, New York: Oxford University Press.

Solanas, F. and Getino, O. (1969, 1983), "Towards a Third Cinema: Notes and Experiences for the Development of a Cinema of Liberation in the Third World," in J. Burton (ed.), *Twenty Five Years of the New Latin America Cinema*, 17–27, London: BFI.

Sontag, S. (1973), *On Photography*, New York: Picador.

Steiner-Khamsi, G. (ed.) (2004), *The Global Politics of Educational Borrowing and Lending*, New York: Teachers College Press.

Sum, N.-L. and Jessop, B. (2013), "Competitiveness, the Knowledge-Based Economy and Higher Education," *Journal of the Knowledge Economy*, 4(1), 24–44.

Tonini, D.C. (2021), "Human Capital Theory in Comparative and International Education," in T. jules, R. Shields, and M.A.M. Thomas (eds.), *The Bloomsbury Handbook of Theory in Comparative and International Education*, 69–86, London: Bloomsbury Academic.

Totaro, D. (2001), "Time, Bergson, and the Cinematographical Mechanism: Henri Bergson on the Philosophical Properties of Cinema," *Offscreen*, 5(1), January. Available online at: https://offscreen.com/view/bergson1. Accessed on June 11, 2022.

Trethewey, A.R. (1976), *Introducing Comparative Education*, Oxford: Pergamon Press.

Vavrus, F. and Bartlett, L. (eds.) (2022), *Doing Comparative Case Studies: New Designs and Directions*, New York: Routledge.

Wallerstein, I. (1989), *The Modern World System III: The Second Era of Great Expansion of the Capitalist World-Economy, 1730–1840s*. San Diego, CA: Academic Press, Inc.

Wells, P, (1999), "The Documentary Form: Personal and Social Realities," in Jill Neimes (ed.), *An Introduction to Film Studies*, 2nd edition, 211–35, London: Routledge.

Willis, P. (1977), *Learning to Labor*, New York: Columbia University Press.

Wiseman, A. (2021), "Framing Comparative and International Education Through a Neo-Institutional Lens," in T. jules, R. Shields, and M.A.M. Thomas (Eds.), *The Bloomsbury Handbook of Theory in Comparative and International Education*, 217–32, London: Bloomsbury Academic.

Chapter 3

Acland, C.R. (2008), "Classrooms, Clubs, and Community Circuits: Cultural Authority and the Film Council Movement, 1946–1957," in L. Grieveson and H. Wasson (eds.), *Inventing Film Studies*, 149–81, Durham, NC and London: Duke University Press.

Altbach, P.G. (1991), "Trends in Comparative Education," *Comparative Education Review*, 35(3), 491–507.

Anderson, M.L. (2008), "Taking Liberties: The Payne Fund Studies and the Creation of the Media Expert," in L. Grieveson and H. Wasson (eds.), *Inventing Film Studies*, 18–65, Durham, NC and London: Duke University Press.

Andrew, D. (2009), "The Core and Flow of Film Studies," *Critical Inquiry*, 35(4), 879–915.

Andrew, D. (2016), "Time Zones and Jetlag: The Flows and Phases of World Cinema," in L. Braudy and M. Cohen (eds.), *Film Theory and Criticism*, 813–39, New York: Oxford University Press.

Bakker, G. (2008), "The Economic History of the International Film Industry," in R. Whaples (ed.), *EH. Net Encyclopedia*, February 10. Available online at: https://eh.net/encyclopedia/the-economic-history-of-the-international-film-industry/.

Bauman, Z. (2012), *Liquid Modernity*, Cambridge: Polity Press.

Bo, L. (2020), "Paul Munroe," in E. Epstein (ed.), *North American Scholars of Comparative Education*, 23–36, New York: Routledge.

Brickman, W. (1977), "C.I.E.S.: An Historical Analysis," *Comparative Education Review*, 21(2/3), 398–404.

Druick, Z. (2007), "The International Educational Cinematograph Institute, Reactionary Modernism, and the Formation of Film Studies," *Canadian Journal of Film Studies*, 16(1), 80–97. Available online at: https://www.jstor.org/stable/24408070. Accessed on September 6, 2022.

Druick, Z. (2008), "'Reaching the Multimillions': Liberal Internationalism and the Establishment of Documentary Film," in L. Grieveson and H. Wasson (eds.), *Inventing Film Studies*, 66–92, Durham, NC and London: Duke University Press.

Film Reference (n.d.), "History of Film Festivals." Available online at: https://www.filmreference.com/encyclopedia/Criticism-Ideology/Festivals-HISTORY-OF-FILM-FESTIVALS.html. Accessed on September 6, 2022.

Friedrich, D. and Brandt, N.K. (2021), "The Dissertation and the Archive: Governing a Field through the Production of an Archive," *Comparative Education Review*, 65(2), 227–47.

Greenaway, D. and Haynes, M. (2003), "Funding Higher Education in the UK: The Role of Fees and Loans," *The Economic Journal*, 113(485), F150–F165.

Groening, S. (2008), "Timeline for a History of Anglophone Film Culture and Film Studies," in L. Grieveson and H. Wasson (eds.), *Inventing Film Studies*, 399–418, Durham, NC and London: Duke University Press.

Hans, N. (1964), *Comparative Education: A Study of Educational Factors and Traditions*, London: Routledge and Kegan Paul.

Kandel, I. (1933), *Comparative Education*, New York: Houghton Mifflin.

Lee, K. (2008), "'The Little State Department': Hollywood and the MPAA's Influence on US Trade Relations," *Northwestern Journal of International Law and Business*, 28(2), 371–97. Available online at: https://scholarlycommons.law.northwestern.edu/cgi/viewcontent.cgi?article=1671&context=njilb. Accessed on September 6, 2022.

Leverty, S. (n.d.), "NGOs, the UN, and the APA," *American Psychological Association Office of International Affairs*. Available online at: https://www.apa.org/international/united-nations/publications#:~:text=Statistics%20about%20the%20number%20of,in%20the%20hundreds%20of%20thousands. Accessed on September 7, 2022.

Mallinson, V. (1952), "Comparative Education Studies in Great Britain," *British Journal of Educational Studies*, 1(1), 60–3. Available online at: https://www.jstor.org/stable/3119437. Accessed on September 6, 2022.

Manzon, M. and Bray, M. (2006), "The Comparative and International Education Society (CIES) and the World Council of Comparative Education Societies (WCCES): Leadership, Ambiguities and Synergies," *Current Issues in Comparative Education*, 8(2), 69–83.

Null, W. (2020), "Isaac Kandel," in E. Epstein (ed.), *North American Scholars of Comparative Education*, 37–49, New York: Routledge.

Osborne, K. (2016), "The League of Nations Attempts to Reform History Teaching," *History of Education Quarterly*, 56(2), 215–40.

Rice, T. (2019), *Films for the Colonies: Cinema and the Preservation of the British Empire*, Berkeley: University of California Press.

Sedgwick, E.K. and Frank, A. (2003), "Shame in the Cybernetic Fold: Reading Silvan Tompkins," in E.K. Sedwick (ed.), *Touching Feeling: Affect, Pedagogy, Performativity*, 93–122, Durham, N.C.: Duke University Press.

Scott, A.J. (2002), "Hollywood in the Era of Globalization," *YaleGlobe Online*, November 29. Available online at: https://archive-yaleglobal.yale.edu/content/hollywood-era-globalization. Accessed on September 7, 2022.

Sutherland, M., Watson, K., and Crossley, M. (2008), "The British Association for International and Comparative Education (BAICE)," in V. Maseman, M. Bray, and M. Manzon (eds.), *Common Interests: Uncommon Goals: CERC Studies in Comparative Education*, Vol. 21, 155–69, Dordrecht and Hong Kong: Springer and the University of Hong Kong Research Center.

Takayama, K. (2018), "Beyond Comforting Histories: The Colonial/Imperial Entanglements of the International Institute, Paul Munroe, and Isaac Kandel at Teachers College, Colombia University," *Comparative Education Review*, 62(4), 459–81.

Wilson, D.N. (2003), "The Future of Comparative and International Education in a Globalized World," *International Review of Education*, 49(1–2), 15–33.

Chapter 4

Althusser, L. (2014), *On the Reproduction of Capitalism: Ideology and Ideological State Apparatuses*, London: Verso.

Apple, M. and Jungck, S. (1990), "You Don't Have to be a Teacher to Teach This Unit: 'Teaching, Technology, and Gender in the Classroom," *American Educational Research Journal*, 27(2), 227–51. Available online at: https://www.jstor.org/stable/1163008. Accessed on October 24, 2022.

Aviv, R. (2022), "Did the Oscar Winning Director Asgar Farhadi Steal Ideas?," *New Yorker*, November 7. Available online at: https://www.newyorker.com/magazine/2022/11/07/did-the-oscar-winning-director-asghar-farhadi-steal-ideas?utm_source=nl&utm_brand=tny&utm_mailing=TNY_Magazine_103122&utm_campaign=aud-dev&utm_medium=email&bxid=5bf82a5f24c17c5aa31980df&cndid=55486834&hasha=e3580c4fae9d9e2d2dbc41e19eaa607d&hashb=7f3f0db3d1f8341126521af403e9528ee7e63877&hashc=02f7e7d6def2356dc5d6f149d564fa6f864761d4896e541b1558fbc4a50ad609&esrc=Subs_2018&utm_term=TNY_Magazine. Accessed on November 1, 2022.

Bedard, M. (2021), "Parasite Screenplay Download: Plot, Characters, and Ending," *Studiobinder*, April 11. Available online at: https://www.studiobinder.com/blog/parasite-screenplay-script-pdf-download/. Accessed on October 26, 2022.

Bernstein, B. (1971), *Class, Codes, and Control*, Vols 1 and 3, London: Routledge and Kegan Paul.

Berry, M. (2022), *Jia Zhangke on Jia Zhangke*. Durham, NC and London: Duke University Press.

Bourdieu, P. and Passeron J.C. (1971), *Reproduction in Education and Society*, Beverly Hills: Sage Publications.

Bowles, S. and Gintis, H. (1976), *Schooling in Capitalist America*, New York: Basic Books.

Cea, M. (2019), "Parasite's Wild Ending, Broken Down," *GQ*, November 4. Available online at: https://www.gq.com/story/bong-joon-ho-breaks-down-parasites-wild-ending. Accessed on October 25, 2022.

Clark, P. (1989), "Reinventing China: The Fifth Generation Filmmakers," *Modern Chinese Literature*, 5(1), 121–36. Available online at: JSTOR, http://www.jstor.org/stable/41490655. Accessed on October 27, 2022.

Collins, R. (1979), *The Credential Society*. New York: Academic Press.

Cross, C. (2019), "Iranian Cinema Then and Now: An Interview with Blake Atwood and Pedram Parrtovi," *Michigan Quarterly Review*, 4, February 15–17. Available online at: https://sites.lsa.umich.edu/mqr/2019/04/iranian-cinema-then-and-now-an-interview-with-blake-atwood-and-pedram-partovi/. Accessed on October 26, 2022.

Desowitz, B. (2019), "'Parasite': Shooting Bong Joon Ho's Social Thriller Through the Lens of Class Divide," *Indiwire*, November 15. Available online at: https://www.indiewire.com/2019/11/parasite-cinematographer-hong-kyung-pyo-1202189824/. Accessed on October 25, 2022.

Dore, R. (1976), *The Diploma Disease*. Berkeley and Los Angeles: University of California Press.

Giroux, H. (1981), *Ideology, Culture, and the Process of Schooling*. Philadelphia and London: Temple University Press and Falmer Press.

Heath, S.B. (1983), *Ways with Words: Language, Life and Work in Communities and Classrooms*. Cambridge: Cambridge University Press.

Jessop, B. (1990), *State Theory: Putting Capitalist States in Their Place*. State College: Penn State University Press.

Kochai, J. (2017), "Ashgar Farhadi, A Separation," *Milestones*, April 18. Available online at: https://www.milestonesjournal.net/reviews/2017/4/18/asghar-farhadi-a-separation. Accessed on October 26, 2022.

Koehler, R. (2019), "Parasite (Preview)," *Cineaste*, XLV(2). Available online at: https://www.cineaste.com/spring2020/parasite. Accessed on October 25, 2022.

Linder, B. (2011), "Sixth Generation (Film Directors)," *Encyclopedia of Contemporary Chinese Culture*. Available online at: https://contemporary_chinese_culture.en-academic.com/710/Sixth_Generation_%28film_directors%29. Accessed on October 27, 2022.

Moaveni, A. (2022), "'It's Like a War Over There: Iranian Women Haven't Been This Angry in a Generation," *New York Times*, October 7. Available online at: https://www.nytimes.com/2022/10/07/opinion/iran-women-protests.html. Accessed on October 26, 2022.

Noh, M. (2020), "Parasite as Parable: Bong Joon-Ho's Cinematic Capitalism," *Crosscurrents*, 70(3), 248–62. Available online at: https://www.jstor.org/stable/26975087. Accessed on October 25, 2022.

OECD (2019), "Country Note: Korea: Programme for International Student Assessment (PISA) Results from PISA 2018," *OECD*. Available online at: https://www.oecd.org/pisa/publications/PISA2018_CN_KOR.pdf. Accessed on October 26, 2022.

Poulantzas, N. (2014), *State, Power, Socialism*, London: Verso.

Sennett, R. and Cobb, J. (1972), *The Hidden Injuries of Class*, New York: Alfred A. Knopf.

Shin, J.C. (2012), "Higher Education Development in Korea: Western University Ideas, Confucian Tradition, and Economic Development," *Higher Education*, 64(1), 59–72. Available online at: *JSTOR*, http://www.jstor.org/stable/41477919. Accessed on October 26, 2022.

Springwood, C.F. and King, C.R. (2001), "'Playing Indian': Why Native American Mascots Must End," *Chronicle of Higher Education*, November 9. Available online at: https://www.chronicle.com/article/playing-indian-why-native-american-mascots-must-end/. Accessed on October 25, 2022.

Vashchuk, A. (2021), "Symbols in the Oscar-winning Movie Parasite," *Kate Korea Club*, May 31. Available online at: https://www.katekorea.club/en/symbols-in-the-oscar-winning-movie-parasite/. Accessed on October 25, 2022.

Wikipedia, (2022), "Parasite (2019 Film)," *Wikipedia*. Available online at: https://en.wikipedia.org/wiki/Parasite_(2019_film). Accessed on October 25, 2022.

Willis, P. (1977), *Learning to Labor*, New York: Columbia University Press.

Wright, E.O. (1985), *Classes*, London: Verso.

Yonhap, (2019), "7 in 10 Korean Students Use Private Education: Data," *The Korean Herald*, February 27. Available online at: http://www.koreaherald.com/view.php?ud=20190227000843. Accessed on October 26, 2022.

Ypi, L. (2022), "Rosa Luxembourg," in E.N. Zalta (ed.), *The Stanford Encyclopedia of Philosophy*, Summer. Available online at: https://plato.stanford.edu/archives/sum2022/entries/luxemburg/. Accessed on October 24, 2022.

Chapter 5

Ally, N., Beere, R., and Moult, K. (2021), "Disciplinary Practices and 'School to Prison' Pathways in South Africa," *South African Crime Quarterly*, 70. Available online at: https://journals.assaf.org.za/index.php/sacq/article/view/11092. Accessed on November 19, 2022.

Anderson, C. (2016), *White Rage: The Unspoken Truth of Our Racial Divide*, New York: Bloomsbury.

BBC News (2020), "Shirley Oaks: 'Hundreds of Children Racially and Sexually Abused,'" *BBC News*, June 29. Available online at: https://www.bbc.com/news/uk-england-london-53221981. Accessed on December 14, 2022.

Blitzman, J. (2021), "Shutting Down the School to Prison Pipeline," *Human Rights Magazine*, 47(1). Available online at: https://www.americanbar.org/groups/crsj/publications/human_rights_magazine_home/empowering-youth-at-risk/. Accessed on November 19, 2022.

Brissett, N.O.M. and Bailey, C.Y. (2021), "Small Axe, Episode, 5, 'Education,'" *Comparative Education Review*, 65(2), 380–2.

Calabrese, R. (1990), "The Public School: A Source of Alienation for Minority Parents," *Journal of Negro Education*, 59(2), 148–54.

Chisolm, L. (2019), *Teacher Preparation in South Africa: History, Policy, and Future Directions*, Bingley: Emerald Publishing Limited.

Clair, M. and Denis, J.S. (2015), "Sociology of Racism," in J.D. Wright (ed.), *The International Encyclopedia of Social and Behavioral Sciences*, 19, 857–63. Available online at: https://scholar.harvard.edu/files/matthewclair/files/sociology_of_racism_clairandenis_2015.pdf. Accessed on November 2, 2022.

Coard, B. (1971), *How the West Indian Child Is Made Educationally Sub-Normal in the British School System*, London: New Beacon Press.

Cornelius, J. (1983), "'We Slipped and Learned to Read': Slave Accounts of the Literacy Process, 1830–1865," *Phylon*, 44(3), 171–86. Available online at: https://login.proxy.iwu.edu/login?url=https://www.jstor.org/stable/274930j. Accessed on December 5, 2022.

Cunningham, V. (2020), "The Argument of 'Afropessimism,'" *The New Yorker*, July 13. Available online at: https://www.newyorker.com/magazine/2020/07/20/the-argument-of-afropessimism. Accessed on November 6, 2022.

Delgado, R. and Stefancic, J. (2017), *Critical Race Theory*, 3rd edition, New York: New York University Press.

Dovey, L. (2007), "Redeeming Features: From 'Tsotsi' (1980) to 'Tsotsi' (2006)," *Journal of African Cultural Studies*, 19(2), 143–64. Available online at: https://www.jstor.org/stable/25473386. Accessed on December 22, 2022.

Drescher, S. (1990), "The Ending of the Slave Trade and the Evolution of European Scientific Racism," *Social Science History*, 14(3), 415–50. Available online at: https://www-jstor-org.proxy.iwu.edu/stable/1171358?seq=2#metadata_info_tab_contents. Accessed on November 5, 2022.

Fiske, S.T. (2010), "Interpersonal Stratification: Status, Power, and Subordination," in S.T. Fiske, D.T. Gilbert, and D. Lindzey (eds.), *Handbook of Social Psychology*, 5th edition, 941–82, New York: Wiley.

Foner, E. (2015), *Gateway to Freedom: The Hidden History of the Underground Railroad*, New York: Norton.

Fraser, N. (2010), *Social Justice: Reimagining Political Space in a Globalizing World*, New York: Columbia University Press.

George Padmore Institute (n.d), "The Black Education Movement (Early Period), 1965–1988," *George Padmore Institute*. Available online at: https://catalogue.georgepadmoreinstitute.org/records/BEM. Accessed on December 16, 2022.

Gillborn, D. (1997), "Ethnicity and Educational Performance in the United Kingdom: Racism, Ethnicity, and Variability in Achievement," *Anthropology and Education Quarterly*, 28(3), 375–93.

Gilroy, P. (1994), "Diaspora," *Paragraph*, 17(3), 207–12. Available online at: http://www.jstor.org/stable/43263438. Accessed on November 17, 2022.

Graham, M. and Robinson, G. (2004), "'The Silent Catastrophe': Institutional Racism in the British Educational System and the Underachievement of Black Boys," *Journal* of *Black Studies* 34(5), 653–71. Available online at: https://www.jstor.org/stable/3180922. Accessed on November 19, 2022.

Hall, S. (1995), "The Whites of Their Eyes: Racist Ideologies and the Media," in G. Hines and J.M. Humez (eds.), *Gender, Race, and Class in Media*, 18–22, Thousand Oaks, London, and New Delhi: Sage. Available online at: https://blog.richmond.edu/watchingthewire/files/2015/08/The-Whites-of-Their-Eyes.pdf. Accessed on November 4, 2022.

Haynes, S. (2020a), "The True Story Behind *Red, White, and Blue* from Steve McQueen's *Small Axe* Anthology," *Time*, December 4. Available online at: https://time.com/5917883/small-axe-red-white-and-blue-true-story/. Accessed on December 13, 2022.

Haynes, S. (2020b), "Alex Wheatle on the Life Story That Inspired Steve McQueen's Latest Small Axe Film," *Time*, December 11. Available online at: https://time.com/5919375/small-axe-alex-wheatle-true-story/. Accessed on December 14, 2022.

IMBd (n.d.), "Tsotsi (2005): Plot," *IMBd*. Available online at: https://www.imdb.com/title/tt0468565/plotsummary. Accessed on December 21, 2022.

Kozol, J. (1991), *Savage Inequalities*, New York: Crown.

LaFrance, A. and Newkirk III, V.R. (2017), "The Lost History of an American Coup d'Etat," *The Atlantic*, August 12. Available online at: https://www.theatlantic.com/politics/archive/2017/08/wilmington-massacre/536457/. Accessed on December 2, 2022.

Library of Congress (n.d.), "The Beginnings of American Railroads and Mapping," *Library of Congress*. Available online at: https://www.loc.gov/collections/railroad-maps-1828-to-1900/articles-and-essays/history-of-railroads-and-maps/the-beginnings-of-american-railroads-and-mapping/. Accessed on November 30, 2022.

Little, D. (2011), "Possessive Individualism," *Understanding Society*, August 17. Available online at: https://understandingsociety.blogspot.com/2011/08/possessive-individualism.html. Accessed on November 7, 2022.

MacPherson, C.B. (1962), *The Political Theory of Possessive Individualism: Hobbes to Locke*, Toronto: Oxford University Press.

Morris, R.C. (2010), "Style, Tsotwsi-style, and Tsotsitaal: The Histories, Aesthetics, and Politics of a South African Figure," *Social Text*, 28(2), 85–112. Available online at: https://doi.org/10.1215/01642472-2009-068. Accessed on December 19, 2022.

National Archives, (n.d.), "Mangrove 9 Protest: What Does This Reveal About Police Brutality and Racism in '70s Britain?" *National Archives*. Accessed online at: https://www.nationalarchives.gov.uk/education/resources/mangrove-nine-protest/. Accessed on December 12, 2022.

Nix, E. (2020), "Tuskegee Experiment: The Infamous Syphilis Study," *History*, December 15. Available online at: https://www.history.com/news/the-infamous-40-year-tuskegee-study. Accessed on December 2, 2022.

Nokes, G. (2022), "Black Exclusion Laws in Oregon," *Oregon Encyclopedia*, September 8. Available online at: https://www.oregonencyclopedia.org/articles/exclusion_laws/#.Y4kDAuzMKIY. Accessed on December 1, 2022.

Page, J., Whitting, G., and Mclean, C. (2007), "Engaging Effectively with Black and Minority Parents in Children's and Parental Services," *Research Report No. DCSF-RR013, Department for Children, Schools and Families*. Available online at: https://dera.ioe.ac.uk/6735/2/DCSF-RR013.pdf. Accessed on November 19, 2022.

Pahwa, N. (2020), "What's Fact and What's Fiction in Steve McQueen's Mangrove," *Slate*, November 20. Available online at: https://slate.com/culture/2020/11/mangrove-nine-steve-mcqueen-accuracy-small-axe.html. Accessed on December 12, 2022.

Parsons, C. (2021), "White Supremacy in Retreat? Past Histories and Contemporary Racisms in the Public Pedagogies of Britain and America," *Whiteness and Education*, 7(1), 93–110. Available online at: doi:10.1080/23793406.2021.1920047. Accessed online on November 20, 2022.

Patterson, O. (1982), *Slavery and Social Death*, Cambridge, MA: Harvard University Press.

Phillips, A. (2004), "Defending Equality of Outcome," *Journal of Political Philosophy*, 12(1), 1–19. Available online at: http://eprints.lse.ac.uk/533/1/equality_of_outcome.pdf. Accessed online on November 21, 2022.

Pierre, J. (2013), *The Predicament of Blackness: Postcolonial Ghana and the Politics of Race*, Chicago, IL: University of Chicago Press.

Rist, R. (1977), "On Understanding the Process of Schooling: Contributions of Labeling Theory," in J. Karabel and A.H. Halsey (eds.), *Power and Ideology in Education*, 292–305, New York: Oxford University Press.

Roberts, J. (2021), "Power in Pedagogy: Legacies of Apartheid in a South African School," *Whiteness and Education*, 6(2), 130–46. Available online at: https://doi.org/10.1080/23793406.2021.1917305. Accessed on November 20, 2022.

Robinson, C. (1983), *Black Marxism: The Making of the Black Radical Tradition*, Chapel Hill: University of North Carolina Press.

Schweiger, B.B. (2013), "The Literate South: Reading Before Emancipation," *Journal of the Civil War Era*, 3(3), 331–59. Available online at: https://www.jstor.org/stable/26062071?seq=1. Accessed online on December 5, 2022.

Tereshchenko, A., Mills, M., and Bradbury, A. (2020), "Making Progress? Employment and Retention of BAME Teachers in England," *Institute of London*. Available online at: https://discovery.ucl.ac.uk/id/eprint/10117331/1/IOE_Report_BAME_Teachers.pdf. Accessed on November 19, 2022.

Tulsa Historical Society and Museum (n.d.), "1921 Tulsa Race Massacre," *Tulsa Historical Society and Museum*. Available online at: https://www.tulsahistory.org/exhibit/1921-tulsa-race-massacre/. Accessed on December 2, 2022.

UN News (2022), "2030 Development Agenda 'Fails' on Racial Equality and Non-discrimination," *UN News*, July 5. Available online at: https://news.un.org/en/story/2022/07/1121942. Accessed on November 21, 2022.

Wardle, H. and Obermuller, L. (2019), "'Windrush Generation' and 'Hostile Environment,'" *Migration and Society*, 2(1), 81–9. Available online at: file:///Users/i

rvepstein_1/Downloads/Windrush_Generation_and_Hostile_Environ%20(1).pdf. Accessed on December 9, 2022.

Weheliye, A. (2014), *Habeas Viscus*, Durham, NC: Duke University Press.

Whitehead, C. (2016), *The Underground Railroad*, New York: Anchor Books.

Wilderson, F. (2020), *Afropessimism*, New York: W.W. Norton and Company.

Chapter 6

Amnesty International (n.d.), "Indigenous Peoples," *Amnesty International*. Available online at: https://www.amnesty.org/en/what-we-do/indigenous-peoples/. Accessed on January 22, 2023.

Anderson, B. (1983), *Imagined Communities*, London: Verso.

Austen, I. (2021), "Canada's Grim Legacy of Cultural Erasure, in Poignant School Photos," *New York Times*, October 27. Available online at: https://www.nytimes.com/2021/07/05/world/canada/Indigenous-residential-schools-photos.html. Accessed on March 20, 2023.

Austen, I. (2023), "Canada Settles 2 $ Billion Suit Over "Cultural Genocide" at Residential Schools," *New York Times*, January 21. Available online at: https://www.nytimes.com/2023/01/21/canada-indigenous-settlement.html. Accessed on March 20, 2023.

Baird, I. (2020), "Thinking About Indigeneity with Respect to Time and Space: Reflections from Southeast Asia," *Espace Populations Sociétés*. Available online at: http://journals.openedition.org/eps/9628; https://doi.org/10.4000/eps.9628. Accessed on January 22, 2023.

Carney, S. and Madsen, U.A. (2021), *Education in Radical Uncertainty: Transgressions in Theory and Method*, London: Bloomsbury Academic.

Healing Foundation (n.d.), "Who Are the Stolen Generations?" *Healing Foundation*. Available online at: https://healingfoundation.org.au/resources/who-are-the-stolen-generations/. Accessed on March 20, 2023.

Huaman, E. (2022), "How Indigenous Scholarship Changes the Field: Pluriversal Appreciation, Decolonial Aspirations, and Comparative Indigenous Education," *Comparative Education Review*, 66(3), 391–416.

IMBd (n.d.), "We Were Children: Plot," *IMBd*. Available online at: https://www.imdb.com/title/tt1934472/plotsummary/?ref_=tt_ov_pl. Accessed on March 20, 2023.

Olsen, C. (2004), "For Molly the Fence Was a Lifeline," *Sydney Morning Herald*, January 20. Available online at: https://www.latimes.com/local/obituaries/la-me-doris-pilkington-garimara-20140420-story.html. Accessed on March 20, 2023.

Quijano, A. (2007), "Coloniality and Modernity/Rationality," *Cultural Studies* 21(2), 168–78. Available online at: doi:10.1080/09502380601164353 http://dx.doi.org/10.1080/09502380601164353. Accessed on January 29, 2023.

Shajahan, R.A., Estera, A.L., Sura, K.L, and Edwards, K.T. (2022), "'Decolonizing' Curriculum and Pedagogy: A Comparative Review Across Disciplines and Global Higher Education Contexts," *Review of Educational Research*, 92(1), 73–113. Available online at: https://doi.org/10.3102/00346543211042423. Accessed on February 7, 2021.

Slaven, M. (2022), "The Windrush Scandal and the Individualization of Postcolonial Immigration Control in Britain," *Ethnic and Racial Studies*, 45(16), 49–71. Available online at: https://doi.org/10.1080/01419870.2021.2001555. Accessed on December 13, 2023.

Spriprakash, A., Rudolph S., and Gerrard, J. (2022), *Learning Whiteness: Education and the Settler Colonial State*, London: Pluto Press.

Truth and Reconciliation Commission of Canada, (2015), "Honoring the Truth, Reconciling the Future: Summary of the Final Report of the Truth and Reconciliation Commission of Canada," *Truth and Reconciliation Commission of Canada*. Available online at: https://ehprnh2mwo3.exactdn.com/wp-content/uploads/2021/01/Executive_Summary_English_Web.pdf. Accessed on March 20, 2023.

United Nations, (n.d.), "Indigenous Peoples at the United Nations," *Department of Economic and Social Affairs, United Nations*. Available online at: https://www.un.org/development/desa/indigenouspeoples/about-us.html. Accessed on January 22, 2023.

Wikipedia (n.d.). "Stolen Generations," *Wikipedia*. Available online at: https://en.wikipedia.org/wiki/Stolen_Generations. Accessed on March 20, 2023.

Williams, W. (2020), "Windrush: Lessons Learned Review: Independent Review by Wendy Williams, House of Commons," March. Available online at: https://assets.publishing.service.gov.uk/government/uploads/system/uploads/attachment_data/file/876336/6.5577_HO_Windrush_Lessons_Learned_Review_LoResFinal.pdf .Accessed on December 13, 2023.

Woo, E. (2014), "Doris Pilkington Garimara Dies; Wrote of Australia's 'Stolen Generations,'" *Los Angeles Times*, April 19. Available online at: https://www.latimes.com/local/obituaries/la-me-doris-pilkington-garimara-20140420-story.html. Accessed on March 20, 2023.

Wynter, S. (2003), "Unsettling the Coloniality of Being/Power/Truth/Freedom: Towards the Human, After Man, Its Overrepresentation—An Argument," *The New Centennial Review*, 3(3), 257–337. Project MUSE, doi:10.1353/ncr.2004.0015. Accessed on March 20, 2023.

Chapter 7

Agyeman, J. and Evans, B. (2004), "'Just Sustainability': The Emerging Discourse of Environmental Justice in Britain?," *The Geographical Journal*, 170(2), 155–64. Available online at: https://www.jstor.org/stable/3451592. Accessed on April 16, 2023.

Bennett, J. (2010), *Vibrant Matters*, Durham, NC: Duke University Press.

Braudel, F. (1996), *The Mediterranean and the Mediterranean World in the Age of Philip II*, Vol. I, Berkeley: University of California Press.

Chakrabarty, D. (2009), "The Climate of History: Four Theses," *Critical Inquiry*, 35(2), 197–222. Available online at: https://www.jstor.org/stable/10.1086/596640. Accessed on April 16, 2023.

Chakrabarty, D. (2021), *The Climate of History in a Planetary Age*, Chicago, IL: University of Chicago Press.

EPA (n.d.), "Environmental Justice," *United States Environmental Protection Agency*. Available online at: https://www.epa.gov/environmentaljustice. Accessed on April 16, 2023.

Gomez, M.C. (2015), "Maya Religion: Definition," *World History Encyclopedia*, July 29. Available online at: https://www.worldhistory.org/Maya_Religion/. Accessed on April 23, 2023.

Kahn, R. (2010), *Critical Pedagogy, Eco-literacy, & Planetary Crisis: The Ecopedagogy Movement*, New York and Berlin: Peter Lang.

Komatsu, H., Rappleye, and Silova, I. (2021), "Student-Centered Learning and Sustainability: Solution or Problem?," *Comparative Education Review*, 65(1), 6–28.

National Resources Defense Council (2015), "The Story of Silent Spring," *NRDC*, August 13. Available online at: https://www.nrdc.org/stories/story-silent-spring. Accessed on April 16, 2023.

Prendiville, B. (2014), "British Environmentalism: A Party in Movement?" *Revue Lisa*, XII(8). Available online at: https://doi.org/10.4000/lisa.7119. Accessed on April 16, 2023.

Purdy, J. (2015), "Environmentalism's Racist History," *New Yorker*, August 13. Available online at: https://www.newyorker.com/news/news-desk/environmentalisms-racist-history. Accessed on April 16, 2023.

Sandig, F. and Black, E. (2012), *Heart of Sky, Heart of Earth*, Umbrella Films.

Stock, P. and Burton, R.J.F. (2011), "Defining Terms for Integrated (Multi-Inter-Trans-Disciplinary) Sustainability Research," *Sustainability*, 3(8), 1090–113. Available online at: https://doi.org/10.3390/su3081090. Accessed on April 16, 2023.

The Anthropocene Project (n.d.), "Anthropocene: The Human Epoch." Available online at: https://theanthropocene.org/film/. Accessed on April 18, 2023.

UNESCO (2021), "Learn from Our Planet," *UNESCO*. Available online at: https://unesdoc.unesco.org/ark:/48223/pf0000377362/PDF/377362eng.pdf.multi. Accessed on April 16, 2023.

UNESCO (n.d.), "50th Anniversary of UNESCO's Man & the Biosphere Programme," *UNESCO*. Available online at: https://en.unesco.org/mab/50years. Accessed on April 16, 2023.

Concluding Remarks

Keltner, D. (2023), *Awe: The New Science of Everyday Wonder and How It Can Transform Your Life*, New York: Penguin Press.

Mayer, S. (2018), "Breaking Your Reservation: The Rise of Indigenous Cinema," *Sight and Sound*, April 10. Available online at: https://www2.bfi.org.uk/news-opinion/sight-sound-magazine/comment/festivals/breaking-your-reservation-rise-indigenous-cinema. Accessed on May 4, 2023.

Pippin, R.B. (2020), *Filmed Thought: Cinema as Reflective Form*, Chicago, IL: University of Chicago Press.

Index

Abbasid caliph Al Ma'mun   26
Aboriginal Protection Act   165
academic learning   100
academic study of film   69–76
Actor Network Theory   9, 12
affectionate discipline terminology   2
affect theory   14, 15, 34, 54–6, 59, 65–6, 91, 130, 135, 194, 198
  assemblage (*see* assemblage)
  contingency   5, 10–11, 25
  criticisms   11–13
  intensities of encounter   5–7, 23, 24
  meaning-making   5, 7–8, 24, 25, 54, 128, 153
  paradox of comparison   25–7
  proponents of   102, 112
  rejoinder   11–13
  self-reflection   24
Afro-pessimism   133, 138, 142, 152, 200
agencement   8
Ahmed, Sara   7
Althusser, Louis   47, 48, 50, 99
American filmmaker   51
Amnesty International statement   162
Anderson, Benedict   162
Anderson, Nathan   44
Andrew, Dudley   53, 76, 81, 82
Anthropocene: The Human Epoch (Baichwal)   17, 197, 200
  messages to audience   185
  mining and extraction of natural resources   183–4
  thematic segments   185
anthropocentric myopia   182, 183
anthropomorphism   187, 189, 194
anti-literacy laws   144
antitrust law   79
assemblage   5, 8–10, 19, 23–5, 37, 54, 56, 59, 63, 65–8, 91, 102, 112, 119, 126, 128, 135, 143, 153, 157, 175, 184, 189
  dynamism   24

  unpredictability   24
audience fragmentation   88
auteur theory   47

Baeumier, Alfred   33
Baird, Ian   161
Ball, Andrew   9
Bartlett, Lesley   64
The Battle of Chile and *Salvador Allende* (Guzman)   171
Bauman, Zygmunt   59, 90, 91, 198
Bayt-al Hikma/House of Wisdom   26
Bazin, Andre   46, 47
Beijing Film Academy   119, 120
Benet, Alfred   32
Benjamin, Walter   42–4, 50, 55, 90, 105, 198
Bennett, Jane   183, 185
Bereday, George   59
Bergson, Henri   6, 54, 55
Berlin Film Festival   80
Bernstein, Basil   62, 100, 101
Berry, Michael   123
Bhabha, Homi   35
biblical literacy   144
biracial children   166, 168
The Birth of a Nation (Griffith)   33
Black, Eric   189
Black diaspora   134, 135
Black Education Movement   151
Black exclusion laws   141
The Black Jacobins (James)   149
Black Lives Matter Movement   134, 151, 202
Black Supplementary Schools Movement   151
Bong Joon-Ho   102, 104, 106, 127
Bourdieu, Pierre   11, 62, 100, 101
Bowles, Samuel   99, 100
Brandt, Nancy Ku   78
Braudel, Fernand   181
Bretton Woods Conference   83

British Association of International and Comparative Education (BAICE)   85
British Black Panther Movement   147, 151
British Documentary Movement   74
British education   77
British Nationality Act   145
British Yearbook of Education   77
Brixton Rock (Wheatle)   149
Bullard, Robert   180
bureaucratic efficiencies, public school systems   28
bureaucratism   98
Burtynsky, Edward   183
Butler, Judith   12, 66

Cahiers du Cinema (Truffaut)   47
California Youth Authority   4
Canadian legal system   171
Cannes Film Festival   70, 78, 80, 102
   Grand Prix award   113
capitalism   48, 80, 98, 102, 104, 105
   consumer capitalism   105
   corporate capitalism   98, 110
   financial capitalism   98
   global capitalism   80, 87, 89, 134, 181, 201
   industrial capitalism   98
   Korean capitalism   103
   racial capitalism   132, 135, 138, 142, 157
   state capitalism   50
Carney, Stephen   164
Carson, Rachel   178
cave allegory   43, 44
Chakrabarty, Dipesh   180–3, 185, 194, 198
childhood learning   182
China's sixth-generation filmmakers   12
Chow, Rey   52, 53
Christian principles with Platonic concepts   164
CIE theory. *See* Comparative and International Education (CIE) theory
Cinema 1 (Deleuze)   13, 54
Cinema 2 (Deleuze)   13, 54, 55
cinematographical apparatus   54

Clair, Matthew   131
climate justice   15–17, 182
Close Up   73
Coard, Bernard   151
Cobb, Jonathan   107
coercive disciplinary policies   171
Cohen, Morris R.   58
Cohn-Séat, Gilbert   81
Colonial Film Unit   74
colonialism   35, 78, 130, 132, 163, 177, 192
   European colonialism   135
   settler colonialism   132, 134, 139, 161, 162, 175, 200
   Western colonialism   131
colonial modernism   167
colonial oppression   17, 164
commercial film   30, 69, 72, 112
commodification   44, 68, 87–91, 127, 198
Commonwealth Immigrants Act   146
community-based education   39
Comparative and International Education Society (CIES)   85
Comparative and International Education Society of Canada   85
Comparative and International Education (CIE) theory   65–6, 76–9, 201
   application   57
   causality   57–9
   conference formats   85
   emergence of   83–7
   identity   63–5
   periodic academic conference   85
   scholarship   12, 13, 15, 93
   social conflict   60–3
comparative dissertation   78
comparative education   28–30. *See also* Comparative and International Education (CIE) theory
   artifacts   30–1
   case study   31
Comparative Education (Kandel)   77
Comparative Education Society of Europe (CESE)   85
Conservation Movement   180
Conservation Society in 1966   178
consumer capitalism   105
contingency   5, 10–12, 15, 19, 23, 25, 54, 56, 59, 66–9, 91, 112, 175, 199

cooperative learning   38
The Cordillera of Dreams (*La cordillera de los sueños*) (Guzman)   172
corporal punishment   170
corporate capitalism   98, 110
Covid-19 pandemic   38
Creative Evolution   54
credentialism   59, 111
Crianza Mutua Colombia   37
Crianza Mutua Mexico   37
critical pedagogy   182
critical race theory (CRT)   134
critical scholarship   92
criticism   11–13, 15, 30, 45, 47, 50, 51, 54, 63, 89, 163
   of affect theory   130
   literary criticism   31
   of modern educational systems   111
   social criticism   74
cultural capital   62, 101, 110

decoloniality movement   163, 164, 176
degrees of similarity   10
DeLanda, Manuel   9
Deleuze, Gilles   5–13, 23, 54–6, 198, 200
Denis, Jeffrey S.   131
de Saussere, Fernando   47
deterritorialization process   9, 12
digital amputation   144
documentaries   15, 17, 51–2, 120, 160, 170, 172, 183, 186, 189, 193, 201
   filmmakers   171
   filmmaking   72, 74
   television documentary   178
Documentary News Letter   75
Doulton Report   150
Dumping in Dixie (Bullard)   180
Dyer, Richard   49, 132

The Ecologist   178
Ecoversities Alliance   36, 165, 202
Education   150, 152
educational actors   14, 63
educational exceptionalism   25
educational filmmaking   72, 75
educational institutions   16, 29, 34, 39, 61, 64, 99, 125, 128, 136, 176
educational psychology   28
educational racism   137, 150

Education in Radical Uncertainty (Carney and Madsen)   164
Ehrlich, Paul   180
Ehrlich, Pippa   186
Eisenstein, Sergei   30, 45, 46, 55
Ekman, Paul   7, 198
emotions   6, 7, 14, 108, 112, 154, 194, 197, 198
encyclopedic dissertation   78
Engels, Friedrich   97, 109
Enlightenment liberalism   133
Enlightenment thinking   5
environmental consciousness   17
   Anthropocene   181
   Anthropocene: The Human Epoch (Baichwal)   183–6
   climate change   181
   climate crisis, human role   181
   critical pedagogy   182
   environmental justice   179, 180, 192
   environmental science programs   179
   environmental studies   178, 179
   Heart of Sky, Heart of Earth (Sandig and Black)   189–93
   Man and the Biosphere Programme   178
   My Octopus Teacher (Ehrlich and Reed)   186–9
   "nature related" activities   182
   sustainability   180
environmental justice   179, 180, 192
Environmental Protection Agency   178
environmental studies   178–80, 183, 185
epistemicide   35
epistemological dualism   55
eugenics movement   33, 140, 143, 180
European colonialism   135
European film industries   69, 70, 81
Experimental Cinema   73

Fanon, Franz   35
Farhadi, Ashgar   113, 115–19, 127, 198
fear   3, 71, 168
feature-length films   15
Fees Must Fall protest   165
Film Art   73
film discourse   74
film expert   71, 73
film festivals   15, 53, 70, 71, 73, 80, 85. *See also* international film festival

Film Library 72, 73
filmmakers 16, 19, 25, 40, 46, 47, 51, 56, 81, 86, 88, 92, 113, 119, 128, 129, 184, 185
   American filmmaker 51
   China's sixth-generation filmmakers 12
   documentary filmmakers 171
   editing processes 31
   Indigenous filmmakers 202
   international filmmakers 14
   Nazi filmmakers 46
   role of 15, 24, 41
   Russian filmmaker 45, 51
   traditional educational models 18
filmmaking 25, 47, 79, 80, 91, 92, 117, 197, 200–202
   feminist critique of 48
   mastery 24
   movie lighting 49–50
   nonfiction filmmaking 74
   and psychoanalysis 48
   technical aspects 73
   technical proficiency 24
filmologie 82
Film Spectator 72
film study 86
   editing processes 31
   emergence of 81–3
   filmmakers (*see* filmmakers)
   literary criticism 31
   technological advances 31
film theory 13, 15, 30, 41–51, 67
   Andrew's analysis 76
   aura 42
   criticism 45
   documentaries 51–2
   editing process 45
   evolution of 54
   mise-en-scene 46
   montage 45, 46
   photograph *vs.* moving image 41–51
   structuralist principles 47
   technical (-optical) foundations 46
Film Thought: Cinema as Reflective Form (Pippin) 198
financial capitalism 98
Fitzroy, Robert 173
Flaherty, Robert 51, 52
Floyd, George 134

Focus International Environmental Film Festival 189
Follow the Rabbit Proof Fence (Garimara) 160, 166
formal learning 23
Foster, Craig 17
Foucault, Michel 11, 26
Fraser, Nancy 136, 151
Freire, Paolo 64, 182
Freirean principles, climate justice 182
French film 82
French filmmaking 69
French New Wave 55
Freudian notion of scopophilia 48
Friedrich, Daniel 78
Fugard, Athol 154
Fulbright Program 83

Garimara, Doris Pilkington 160, 166
German expressionist filmmakers 46
German filmmaking 69
Gerrard, Jessica 162
G.I. bill 84
Gilroy, Paul 134, 135
Gintis, Herbert 99, 100
global capitalism 80, 87, 89, 134, 181, 201
globalization 53, 59, 62, 68, 78, 81, 86, 87, 89–93, 107, 110, 112, 122, 123, 125–7, 160, 181, 200
global/local dichotomy 81
Global North assistance strategies 35
Global South international filmmaking 35
Global Tapestry of Alternatives 37
Graeber, David 26, 27, 91
Gramsci's notion of organic intellectual 74
Grand Lion Prize 120
Grand Prix award 113
Grierson, John 52, 74
Griffith, D.W. 33
ground radar technology 170
Guattari, Felix 5, 8–12, 23
Gulliver's Travels 144
Gunder-Frank, Andres 62
Gutierrez, Gustavo 65
Guzman, Patricio 171–5, 192, 197, 200

Haitian Revolution   149
Hall, Stuart   132
Hans, Nicholas   58
Heart of Earth   18
Heart of Sky, Heart of Earth (Sandig and Black)   189–93, 197, 200
Heath, Shirley Brice   100
The Hidden Injuries of Class (Sennett and Cobb)   107
Hilker, Franz   59
Hollywood production values and styles   81
Hollywood studios   30, 46, 53, 54, 69, 70, 72, 79, 87
Holmes, Brian   58
home movies   29, 72
Hood, Gavin   154
Horse in Motion   29–30
The Horse in Motion   45
How the West Indian Child Is Made Educationally Sub-Normal in the British School System (Coard)   151
Hughes, Howard   79
human capital theory   60
The Hundreds (Stewart)   8

ideological hegemony   99
Illich, Ivan   183
Indian Residential Schools Settlement Agreement   169
indigeneity
  Amnesty International   161
  colonial thinking   163
  cultural differences   161
  decoloniality movement   163–5
  definition   160
  identity construction   161
  imagined communities   162
  Indigenous identity   163, 168
  Indigenous knowledge   18, 163, 166–8, 175, 177
  individual autonomy   163
  native populations eradication   163
  The Pearl Button (*El botón de nácar*) (Guzman)   171–5
  possessive individualism   162
  Rabbit Proof Fence   165–8, 171
  relationship between humans and God   164
  rights-based language   162
  settler colonialism   161, 162, 175
  social protest   164
  theological implications   164
  Western humanism   164
  We Were Children   168–71
Indigenous filmmakers   202
industrial capitalism   98
institutional policies   34, 165
institutional racism   134, 136, 149, 152, 158, 165
institutional styles   1
instructional films   52
intensities of encounter   5–7, 23, 24
intergovernmental organizations   86
international audience   81, 87
International Commission on the Futures in Education   37
international development strategies   35, 60, 65
International Education Review (Schneider)   33, 79
international education scholars   14
International Exhibit of Cinematographic Art   70
international film festival
  Berlin Film Festival   80
  Brussels   70
  Cannes   70, 78, 80, 102
  Focus International Environmental Film Festival   189
  Sundance Film Festival   80
  Toronto Film Critics Association   183
  Toronto Film Festival   80
  Venice Film Festival   71, 78, 80, 120
international filmmakers   14
international films   14, 15, 34, 35, 51–4, 73, 76, 87, 92, 183
International Review of Educational Cinematography (IREC)   72
IQ test   32
Iranian Revolution   113
Italian neorealism   55

James, C.L.R.   149
Japan Comparative Education Society   85
The Jazz Singer   70
Jencks, Christopher   59
Jenkins, Barry   139, 152
Jia Zhangke   119

jules, tavis d.   12, 57, 66
Jullien de Paris, Marc-Antoine   76
juvenile delinquency theme   2

Kandel, Isaac   58, 77–9
Kantian imperative   6
Keltner, Dacher   196, 197
Kino-Pravda (film truth)   51
knowledge commons   38
knowledge discourse   5
Kodak, Eastman   72
Korean capitalism   103
Korean Comparative Education
    Society   85
Kracauer, Siegfried   46

Lacan, Jacques   48
La Revue internationale de filmologie   81
La Sortie des ouvriers de l'usine Lumière
    (*Workers Leaving the Lumière
    Factory*)   30
Latour, Bruno   9, 12
learning   2, 17, 25–8, 36–8, 124, 144, 196
    academic learning   100
    childhood learning   182
    formal learning   23
Learning to Labor (Willis)   62, 100
Learning Whiteness (Sriprakash, Rudolph
    and Gerrard)   162
LGBTQ+ civil rights movement   50
Li Bai   122
linguistic distinctiveness   53
liquid modernity   59, 91
literacy training   64
literary criticism   31
little theater movement   73
London Film Society   73
Lovers Rock   148, 152, 153
Luhmann, Niklas   61

Madsen, Ulla   164
mainstreamed educational research   28
The Making of Nazis (Kandel)   78, 79
Man and the Biosphere Programme   178
Mangrove   147
Man of Aran   51
Marcuse, Herbert   183
Marks, Laura   50–2, 108, 109, 142
Marx, Karl   97, 109
Marxist analysis of class conflict   98

Marxist theory   45, 47
Massumi, Brian   5–7, 23
May 1968 protests, France   82
Mayan calendar   190, 191
Mayan cosmology   192, 193
Mayan spirituality   192, 193
McPherson, C.B.   133
McQueen, Steve   150
meaning-making   5, 7–8, 24, 54, 128, 153
*The Mediterranean and the Mediterranean
    World in the Age of Philip II*
    (Braudel)   181
Mercado, Claudio   172
meritocracy   98, 111, 198, 201
Metz, Christian   47, 50
mind/body dualism   8
mise-en-scene   46
modernism   12, 18, 63, 116–19, 153, 160,
    167, 196
modernization theory   60
modern psychology   28
modern schooling   35, 98
montage   45, 46, 55
Morgan, Daniel   50, 51
Morris, Rosalind   153
Moscow film school   30, 72
Motion Picture Herald   73
Motion Pictures and Youth   71
al-Mulk, Nizam   27
Mulvey, Laura   48, 50
Munro, Paul   78
Museum of Modern Art   72
Mussolini, Benito   70
MV Windrush   146
My Octopus Teacher (Ehrlich and
    Reed)   17, 186–9

Nagel, Ernest   58
Nail, T.   9
Nanook of the North, followed by
    Moana   51
natal alienation   132, 133, 138
national cinemas   53, 54, 70, 80
National Defense and Education Act of
    1958   83
national educational systems   77, 89
national film industries   70–2, 80
The Nationalities Act   146
National Library   72
national paralysis   11

Nazi filmmakers 46
Nazi racist beliefs 33
neo-institutionalism 61
neoliberal educational policies 87
neoliberal hegemonic practices 68
neoliberalism 62, 68
neoliberal sensibilities 15
neuroscience 6
Neville, A.O. 167
"New Wave" period of Iranian cinema 113
Noh, Minjung 105
nomothetic principles 58
noncommercial films 72, 77, 79
nonfiction filmmaking 74
North American Free Trade Association treaty (NAFTA) 18, 191
North American slavery 139
Nostalgia for the Light (*Nostalgia de la luz*) (Guzman) 172
Nussbaum, Martha 65

Obermuller, L. 146
The Octopus Teacher 197
Okja (Bong) 102
online streaming services 15
Ordinary Affects (Stewart) 8
Organization for Economic Cooperation and Development (OECD) 86, 111
orientalism 35, 52

Palme d'Or award 102
Parasite (*Gisaenchung*) (Bong) 97, 101
   analysis 104–9
   class affiliation 109
   comedy and tragedy 112
   education 111–12
   humor and violence 112
   synopsis 102–4
Patterson, Orlando 132, 133
Payne Fund Studies 71, 73
Peace Corps 83
The Pearl Button (*El botón de nácar*) (Guzman) 17, 171–5, 192, 197, 200
   Silver Bear Award 172
Pedagogy of the Oppressed (Freire) 64
pedestrian forms of artistic expression 40

Pencier, Nicholas de 183
Percy, Eustice 77
Phillips, Anne 137
philosophical thinking 5
photograph *vs.* moving image 41–51
The Photoplay Composition Class 30
physics of emergence 6
Pierre, Jemima 135
Pippin, Robert 198
police racism 152
Popper, Karl 58
The Population Bomb (Ehrlich) 180
possessive individualism 133, 138, 142, 162, 175
post-humanism discourse 5
post-Second World War cinema 79–81
post-Second World War filmmakers 46
post-structuralism 11
Poulantzas, Nicos 99
The Power and End of Economy (Massumi) 5
principles of ruling ideology 49
professional responsibility 3
Program of International Student Assessment (PISA) 89
pro-Nazi German films 70–1
pro-Nazi propaganda journal 79
psychoanalytic theory 47, 48, 50
psychometric dissertation 78
Pudovkin, Vsevolod 30

Quijano, Aníbal 163, 164

Rabbit Proof Fence 165–8, 171
racial capitalism 132, 135, 138, 142, 157
racial differences 32
racial oppression 201
racism 33, 75, 162
   abolition of slavery 133
   anti-blackness 135
   anti-Black racism 132
   Black diaspora 134, 135
   Black Lives Matter Movement 134
   blackness 135
   and colonialism 130, 132
   continuous residency 146
   critical race theory (CRT) 134
   disaporic identity 152
   disparities 136
   Doulton Report 150

and education   136–8, 143–5, 150
Enlightenment liberalism   133
equality of opportunity   137
equality of outcome   137
European colonialism   135
Global North policies   138
institutional logics   153
institutional racism   134, 136, 149, 152, 165
juvenile justice and prison systems   137
labeling theory   137, 152
lack of recognition and/or respect   137
police racism   152
possessive individualism   133, 138
precarity   153
racial capitalism   132, 135, 138, 142, 157
racial differences   32
racial oppression   145, 201
self-identification   131
slavery   132, 144
Small Axe (McQueen)   135, 145–53
social death   133
social injustice   151
social justice   151
Tsotsi   153–7
UK racism   151
The Underground Railroad   138–45
whiteness   131, 132, 135
racist oppression   145, 201
Randall slave plantation   143
Red, White, and Blue   148
Reed, James   186
Reifenstahl, Leni   52
Reimagining Our Futures Together: A New Social Contract   37–40
Rhodes Must Fall Movement   164, 165
Rice, Tom   74
Riefensthal, Leni   33
right to education   38
right to information   38
RKO studios   79
Robbin Report   84
Robinson, Cedric   134
Rosa Luxemburg's Theory of Accumulation   99
Rudolph, Sophie   162
Russian filmmaker   45, 51

Sadler, Michael   76
Said, Edward   35
Salajan, Florin D.   12, 66
The Salesman (Farhadi)   113
Sandig, Frauke   189
Santos, Boaventura De Sousa   35
Sarris, Andrew   47
Schneider, Fredrick   33
Schooling in Capitalist America   99
Schreiwer, Jurgen   61
self-awareness   25
Sellers, William   74, 75
Sen, Amytra   65
Sennett, Richard   107
A Separation (Jodaeiye Nader az Simin)   199
    analysis   115–19
    synopsis   113–15
settler colonialism   132, 134, 139, 161, 162, 175, 200
shadow education   111
silent films   69, 70
Silent Spring (Carson)   178
skepticism   8, 19, 39, 55, 59, 150, 199
skewed analysis   50
Slavery and Social Death (Patterson)   132
Small Axe (McQueen)   135, 197, 202
    Alex Wheatle   149, 151
    analysis   151–3
    Education   150, 152
    Lovers Rock   148, 152, 153
    Mangrove   147–8
    Red, White, and Blue   148
    synopses   147–51
Snowpiercer (Bong)   102
social capital   12, 101, 110
social class   15, 16, 66
    class affiliation   117
    class conflict   101, 109, 117
    cultural capital   101
    and education   97–102
    formation and reproduction   100
    ideological hegemony   99
    middle-class parenting   100
    modern schooling   98
    Parasite (Gisaenchung)   102–12
    precarity   109, 112, 116, 128
    A Separation (Jodaeiye Nader az Simin)   113–19
    shadow education   111

South Korean educational system   111
Still Life (*San Xia Hao Ren*)   119–26
   working-class jobs   99, 100
social contract framework   39
social death   133
social exclusion practices   2
social protest   164
social reproduction theories   62
Sontag, Susan   42–4, 90, 198
South Korean educational system   111
Soviet Union   69
Spinoza, Benedict   6
Sriprakash, Arathi   162
state-based teacher-training institutions   84
state capitalism   50
Steiner-Khamsi, Gita   61
Stewart, Kathleen   8
Still Life (*San Xia Hao Ren*)   200, 201
   analysis   122–6
   synopsis   120–2
structural functionalism   60
structuralist principles   47
study of education   29, 130, 202
Sui Dynasty   26
Sundance Film Festival   80
symbolic violence   23, 34, 35
   categorization   35
   classification   35
   erasure   34
   self-projection   34, 35
   self-substitution   34, 35
systems theory   61

"talking" picture   70
Tang Dynasty   26, 122
Tarkovsky, Andre   30
Teach for All teacher-training projects   87
television   79, 80, 87, 88
   cable television   87
Terman, Lewis   32
Third Cinema movement   81
A Thousand Plateaus (Deleuze and Guattari)   5, 8, 12
Tompkins, Sylvan   7
Toronto Film Critics Association   183
Toronto Film Festival   80
Totaro, Donato   54

Travelers' tales   76
Trends in International Mathematics and Science Study (TIMSS) projects   89
Triumph of the Will (Riefensthal)   33, 52
Truffaut, Francois   47
Truth and Reconciliation Commission of Canada   168
Tsotsi   153–7, 168, 199
Tulsa Massacre of 1921   141
Tuskegee syphilis experiment study   140

The Underground Railroad   152, 197, 199–202
   attributes of affect   143
   dis-assemblage   143
   education   143–5
   synopsis   140–2
UNESCO   37–9, 53, 76, 83, 86, 178, 181
United Nations Declaration of the Rights of Indigenous Peoples   162
United Nations Sustainability Development Goals   138
Unitierra   37
US Agency for International Development (AID)   86
US-centric teacher training   2
US Civil Rights Movement   180
US Comparative Education Society   84
USC School of Cinematic Arts   30
US Environmental Protection Agency   179
US film industry   69
US higher education institutions   83
U.S. vs. Paramount   79

Vavrus, Fran   64
Venice Biennial Exhibition of Italian Art   70
Venice Film Festival   71, 78, 80
   Grand Lion Prize   120
Vertov, Dziga   51
Vibrant Matters (Bennett)   183
Vietnam War   82
Vikalp Sangam (Alternative Confluence, India)   37
visual arts   41
Visual Education and *Educational Screen*   72

visual perception   50
Visual Pleasure and the Narrative Cinema (Mulvey)   48
Visual Review   72
vocational training   39

Wallerstein, Immanuel   62
Wardle, H.   146
Weheliye, Alexander   134
Wellbeing Economic Alliance   37
Wengrow, David   26, 27, 91
Western academy   29
Western colonialism   131
Western educational practices   35
Western European educational systems   84
Western social science research   14
Wetherell, Margaret   8

We Were Children   17, 168–71, 197
Wheatle, Alex   149, 151
Whitehead, Colson   138–40, 152
whiteness theory   50
Wilderson, Frank   133
Williams, W.   147
Willis, Paul   62, 100
Wilmington Massacre of 1898   141
Windrush Generation   147
working-class culture   99, 100
World Bank and International Monetary Fund   83
World Congress of Comparative Education Societies   85
Wright, Erik Olin   101
Wynter, Sylvia   164

Zarita, Raul   172

www.ingramcontent.com/pod-product-compliance
Lightning Source LLC
Chambersburg PA
CBHW071829300426
44116CB00009B/1486